ETHICAL THEORIES IN ISLAM

ETHICAL THEORIES IN ISLAM

S M Hasan

MD PUBLICATIONS PVT LTD
NEW DELHI
www.mdppl.com

Published by :

MD Publications Pvt Ltd
"MD House", 11, Darya Ganj,
New Delhi - 110 002
Phone : +91-11-45355555
E-mail : contact@mdppl.com
Website: www.mdppl.com

ISBN: 978-81-7533-269-0

Published and Printed by Mr. Pranav Gupta on behalf of **MD Publications Pvt Ltd** at Mohit Enterprises, Delhi.

PREFACE

Islamic ethics (*akhlâq*), defined as "good character," historically took shape gradually from the 7th century and was finally established by the 11th century. It was eventually shaped as a successful amalgamation of the Qur'anic teachings, the teachings of the Sunnah of Muhammad, the precedents of Islamic jurists, the pre-Islamic Arabian tradition, and non-Arabic elements (including Persian and Greek ideas) embedded in or integrated with a generally Islamic structure.

The foundational source in the gradual codification of Islamic ethics was the Muslim understanding and interpretations of the Qur'an and practices of Muhammad. Its meaning has always been in context of active submission to God (Arabic: Allah), performed by the community in unison. The motive force in Islamic ethics is the notion that every human being is called to "command the good and forbid the evil" in all spheres of life. Muslims understand the role of Muhammad as attempting to facilitate this submission. Another key factor in the field of Islamic ethics is the belief that mankind has been granted the faculty to discern God's will and to abide by it.

The importance of Moral and Ethics in Islamic Shariah can be understood by the fact that there is so much text in Quran and Sunnah that if we were to collect all of it, it will create many voluminous books. Islam is a religion that came to guide the high standard of morality to human race. Muhammad repeatedly said that the best Muslim is the one who has the best Moral character.

Islam teaches that the only God is Allah, and that it is a sin (known as shirk) to make other things or people equal to

Allah by admiring them, worshipping them, or putting inappropriate effort and desire into obtaining them. Other actions that are strictly forbidden include murder, theft, adultery, lending money for profit, the practice of magic, cowardice in fulfilling Allah's wishes, saying bad things about other people, and using drugs or alcohol. The sacred book, the Koran, promotes faith in God, promoting justice for everyone, forgiving others, and being compassionate, merciful, generous, humble, and tolerant. Muslims are also expected to take responsibility for the well-being of all life, and to be courageous in following God's laws and in standing up to injustice and tyranny.

All the pillars in Islam teaches disciple, self-control, piousness, humility, humbleness, modesty, high morals, caring and love, and purify Muslims so much so that they attain moral perfection both inner and outward, while people see it and when no one is watching them, from their tongue and what they have in their heart. They complete eliminate hypocrisy and Riya (show off), and instill real character and noble qualities.

I am very grateful to Mr. Pranav Gupta, Director of MD Publications Pvt Ltd, New Delhi, for his kind cooperation and support for this book.

S M Hasan

CONTENTS

1

Introduction

Islamic Ethics

Islamic ethics (*akhlâq*), defined as "good character," historically took shape gradually from the 7th century and was finally established by the 11th century. It was eventually shaped as a successful amalgamation of the Qur'anic teachings, the teachings of the Sunnah of Muhammad, the precedents of Islamic jurists, the pre-Islamic Arabian tradition, and non-Arabic elements (including Persian and Greek ideas) embedded in or integrated with a generally Islamic structure. Although Muhammad's preaching produced a "radical change in moral values based on the sanctions of the new religion and the present religion, and fear of God and of the Last Judgment", the tribal practice of Arabs did not completely die out. Later Muslim scholars expanded the religious ethic of the Qur'an and Hadith in immense detail.

Foundational Motifs

The foundational source in the gradual codification of Islamic ethics was the Muslim understanding and interpretations of the Qur'an and practices of Muhammad. Its meaning has always been in context of active submission to God (Arabic: Allah), performed by the community in unison. The motive force in Islamic ethics is the notion that every human being is called to "command the good and forbid the evil" in all spheres of life. Muslims understand the role of Muhammad as attempting to facilitate this submission. Another key factor in the field of Islamic ethics is the belief that mankind has been granted the faculty to discern God's will and to abide by it. This faculty most crucially involves reflecting over the meaning of existence, which, as John Kelsay in the *Encyclopedia of Ethics* phrases, "ultimately points to the reality of God."

Therefore, regardless of their environment, humans are believed to have a moral responsibility to submit to God's will and to follow Islam. This natural inclination is, according to the Qur'an, subverted by mankind's focus on material success: such focus first presents itself as a need for basic survival or security, but then tends to manifest into a desire to become distinguished amongst one's peers. Ultimately, the focus on materialism, according to the Islamic texts, hampers with the innate reflection as described above, resulting in a state of *jahiliyya* or "heedlessness."

Muslims believe that Muhammad, like other prophets in Islam, was sent by God to remind human beings of their moral responsibility, and challenge those ideas in society which opposed submission to God. According to Kelsay, this challenge was directed against five main characteristics of pre-Islamic Arabia:

1. The division of Arabs into varying tribes (based upon blood and kinship). This categorization was confronted by the ideal of a unified community based upon Islamic piety, an "*ummah;*"
2. The acceptance of the worship of a multitude of deities besides Allah - a view challenged by strict Islamic monotheism, which dictates that Allah has no partner in worship nor any equal;
3. The trait of *muruwwa* (manliness), which Islam discouraged, instead emphasizing on the traits of humility and piety;

4. The focus on achieving fame or establishing a legacy, which was replaced by the concept that mankind would be called to account before God on the day of resurrection;
5. The reverence of and compliance with ancestral traditions, a practice challenged by Islam — which instead assigned primacy to submitting to God and following revelation.

These changes lay in the reorientation of society as regards to identity and life of the Muslim belief, world view, and the hierarchy of values. From the viewpoint of subsequent generations, this caused a great transformation in the society and moral order of life in the Arabian Peninsula. For Muhammad, although pre-Islamic Arabia exemplified "heedlessness," it was not entirely without merit. Muhammad approved and exhorted certain aspects of the Arab pre-Islamic tradition, such as the care for one's near kin, for widows, orphans, and others in need and for the establishment of justice. However, these values would be reordered in importance and placed in the context of strict monotheism.

Moral Commandments

The Qur'an defines and sets the standards of social and moral values for Muslims. S. A. Nigosian, Professor of religious studies at the University of Toronto, states that a lengthy passage in the Qur'an "represents the fullest statement of the code of behaviour every Muslim must follow". Nigosian and Ghamidi hold that these resemble the Ten Commandments in the Bible.

Early reforms under Islam

Many reforms in human rights took place under Islam between 610 and 661, including the period of Muhammad's mission and the rule of the four immediate successors who established the Rashidun Caliphate. Historians generally agree that Muhammad preached against what he saw as the social evils of his day, and that Islamic social reform in areas such as social security, family structure, slavery, and the rights of women and ethnic minorities improved on what was present in existing Arab society at the time. For example, according to Bernard Lewis, Islam "from the first denounced aristocratic privilege, rejected hierarchy, and adopted a formula of the career open to the talents." John Esposito sees Muhammad as a reformer who condemned practices of the pagan Arabs such as female infanticide, exploitation of the poor, usury, murder, false contracts, and theft. Bernard Lewis believes that the egalitarian nature of Islam "represented a very considerable advance on the practice of both the Greco-Roman and the ancient Persian world."

The Constitution of Medina, also known as the *Charter of Medina,* was drafted by Muhammad in 622. It constituted a formal agreement between Muhammad and all of the significant tribes and families of Yathrib (later known as Medina), including Muslims, Jews, and pagans. The document was drawn up with the explicit concern of bringing to an end the bitter inter tribal fighting between the clans of the Aws (Aus) and Khazraj within Medina. To this effect it instituted a number of rights and responsibilities for the Muslim, Jewish and pagan communities of Medina bringing them within the fold of one community-the Ummah. The Constitution established the security of the community, freedom of religion, the role of Medina as a haram or sacred place (barring all violence and weapons), the security of women, stable tribal relations within Medina, a tax system for supporting the community in time of conflict, parameters for exogenous political alliances, a system for granting protection of individuals, a judicial system for resolving disputes, and also regulated the paying of blood-white (the payment between families or tribes for the slaying of an individual in lieu of lex talionis).

Muhammad made it the responsibility of the Islamic government to provide food and clothing, on a reasonable basis, to captives, regardless of their religion. If the prisoners were in the custody of a person, then the responsibility was on the individual. Lewis states that Islam brought two major changes to ancient slavery which was to have far-reaching consequences. "One of these was the presumption of freedom; the other, the ban on the enslavement of free persons except in strictly defined circumstances," Lewis continues. The position of the Arabian slave was "enormously improved": the Arabian slave "was now no longer merely a chattel but was also a human being with a certain religious and hence a social status and with certain quasi-legal rights."

Esposito states that reforms in women's rights affected marriage, divorce, and inheritance. Women were not accorded with such legal status in other cultures, including the West, until centuries later. *The Oxford Dictionary of Islam* states that the general improvement of the status of Arab women included prohibition of female infanticide and recognizing women's full personhood. "The dowry, previously regarded as a bride-price paid to the father, became a nuptial gift retained by the wife as part of her personal property." Under Islamic law, marriage was no longer viewed as a "status" but rather as a "contract", in which the woman's consent was imperative. "Women were given inheritance rights in a patriarchal society that had previously restricted inheritance to male relatives."

Annemarie Schimmel states that "compared to the pre-Islamic position of women, Islamic legislation meant an enormous progress; the woman has the right, at least according to the letter of the law, to administer the wealth she has brought into the family or has earned by her own work." William Montgomery Watt states that Muhammad, in the historical context of his time, can be seen as a figure that testified on behalf of women's rights and improved things considerably. Watt explains: "At the time Islam began, the conditions of women were terrible - they had no right to own property, were supposed to be the property of the man, and if the man died everything went to his sons." Muhammad, however, by "instituting rights of property ownership, inheritance, education and divorce, gave women certain basic safeguards." Haddad and Esposito state that "Muhammad granted women rights and privileges in the sphere of family life, marriage, education, and economic endeavors, rights that help improve women's status in society."

Sociologist Robert Bellah (*Beyond belief*) argues that Islam in its seventh-century origins was, for its time and place, "remarkably modern...in the high degree of commitment, involvement, and participation expected from the rank-and-file members of the community." This because, he argues, that Islam emphasized on the equality of all Muslims, where leadership positions were open to all. Dale Eickelman writes that Bellah suggests "the early Islamic community placed a particular value on individuals, as opposed to collective or group responsibility."

Pillars of Islam and Development of Excellent Moral and Character

The importance of Moral and Ethics in Islamic Shariah can be understood by the fact that there is so much text in *Quran* and Sunnah that if we were to collect all of it, it will create many voluminous books. Islam is a religion that came to guide the high standard of morality to human race. Mohammad repeatedly said that the best Muslim is the one who has the best Moral character.

Usama bin Sharik reported: "We were sitting in the company of the Prophet (pbuh) so quietly as if the birds were sitting on our heads. None of us had the courage to speak. In the meantime some people came and asked Muhammad: "Who among His slaves is dearest to Allah?" He replied: "One who has the best moral character"

"Muhammad was asked: "Which Muslim has the perfect faith?" He answered: "One who has the best moral character."

Muhammad said: "On judgment day there will be no deed weightier in the scale of the believer than his noble character. Allah (swt) does not like an obscene and rude talker, and the person who has a good character achieves the status of a person who prays and fasts".

- Islam is the religion that heavily focuses on character building and doesn't grant the place in paradise by merely admitting into Islam. In fact, it teaches that sins can be washed not just by accepting commands of Allah but by physically doing these commands in Actions, and that bad deed can be washed away by doing good deeds. The people who acts on Allah's commands and perform good deed invariably attain good character.
- There is strong relationship between Strong Iman (faith) and good character. A person cannot attain full or perfect faith without attaining good character. In fact, a per-son with bad character is likely to find a place in hell then in paradise. Anas reported Muhammad as saying: "A person can reach a high status in the hereafter by his good conduct though he may be weak in matters of worship, and he can also go down to the lowest part of Hell by his wicked character".
- The person with good character elevates himself to the status of those who are pious in their prayers and worships. Aisha (ra) reported Muhammad saying: "A believer with his noble manners achieves the rank of one who prays late night and fast during the day".
- Similarly, Ibn Omar related that he heard Muhammad saying: "A Muslim who worships in moderation reaches by means of his good manners and noble nature the rank of a person who fasts and recites the holy *Quran* in the night prayers."

- Islam has five main pillars, namely belief in the oneness of God (tawheed), daily prayers (salah), charity (zakat), fasting (sawm), and pilgrimage to Mecca (hajj). These are various acts of worship and obedience to Allah. All of these pillars are attributes directly towards character building and bestowing high morals and ethics into Muslims. For instance:
    1. The oneness of God (tawheed) is to believe in Allah as one God with unmatched power and attributes, and admit to these unmatched powers of Allah by submitting to commands of Allah unconditionally. Tawheed teaches humbleness, human nature, humility, philanthropy, piousness, righteousness and doing the right thing and abstaining from all evil and sinful activities.
    2. Daily prayers (salah) are five prayers evenly distributed throughout the day. Allah said in *Quran* that prayer protect from sins and unlawful activities: "... and perform As-Salat (Verily, AsSalat (the prayer) prevents from Al-Fahsha (great sins of every kind, unlawful sexual intercourse, etc.) and Al-Munkar (disbelief, polytheism, and every kind of evil wicked deed, etc.) ..." [al-Ankaboot 29:45]
    3. Charity (zakat) is due on all Muslim (based on financial ability). Zakat not only serves the purpose of welfare of citizens, but it also establishes relationship of kindness and love amongst various classes of the society. It reduces the love of material wealth in heart and increases the sense of helping other people in need.
    4. Sawm (fasting) is compulsory for Muslim in month of Ramadan. Fasting brings piousness and tawqa to Muslims. It not only teaches self control and abstinence from worldly desires but it also

teaches the pain of others (who do not get enough food to eat).

5. The pilgrimage to Mecca (hajj) is a ritually obligatory on Muslims who can afford it (financially and physically). The hajj teaches attributes of self control, high morals, humility, modesty, brotherhood, kindness and caring.

All these pillars teaches disciple, self-control, piousness, humility, humbleness, modesty, high morals, caring and love, and purify Muslims so much so that they attain moral perfection both inner and outward, while people see it and when no one is watching them, from their tongue and what they have in their heart. They complete eliminate hypocrisy and Riya (show off), and instill real character and noble qualities.

Deen Islam and Foundation of Moral Code

Islamic Civilization created a huge impact on global scene. Some writers charge that Islamic Civilization is influenced with nations that lived prior to it, especially roman civilization. And that Arabs only added a mix to it. They try to link its root to Persians, Egyptians, Greeks, Romans, and Babylonians etc. This is a mistake on their part. Though nations do get influenced with customs and prior cultures but Islamic civilization is original in nature and it's build on principals that were not borrowed from any other civilizations. However, what can be added is that Arab customs and traditions became part of secondary dealings and became part of civilization.

Some people consider Civilization as intellectual state, ethics, morals, culture, customs, tradition, science, art, industry, governance, politics etc. The fact is that these are not the fundamental of a civilization but the results and gains of it. These are the produce of core fundamentals that is the soul of a civilization. Hence, it is important when one reviews a civilization it looks at the fundamental principles and its basis. For instance,

i. Believes and Thoughts:
   a. Concept of Creation and Human's status in relation to creation: What is the concept of creation of universe and relationship between us (human) and universe?
   b. Objective of Life and end result of our struggle: What is the purpose of our existence in this universe, and why are we doing this entire struggle? What is that objective and end game that we are running after?
   c. Believes and thoughts: What are the founding principles upon which Human character development shapes up? What kind of mindset this civilization is building? What is the relationship between the ultimate objective and this special type of character building?

ii. Human development, Moral Standards and Ethical Code: What kind of human being it is creating? What kind of ethical and moral standards its setting for this human to live and achieve that ultimate objective. And though that civilization is building of a nation, but the individual humans are those who collectively build a nation. And building strong characters, ethics, morals and values in individual humans is what builds a strong nation.

iii. Collective System (of governance, justice, protection and dealings): Lastly, what kind of relationship it builds between various members of the nation. What is relationship between family members, between neighbor, between friends and society, rulers and ruled, judge, politicians, industrialist, businessman, priest, and common man etc. what are their rights and boundaries?

Mawdudi states that Civilization is build upon these five essences and so as Islamic Civilization. Hence, it is important to understand how an Islamic civilization approaches character building in light of these fundamentals. We will briefly discuss some of these points, but mainly focus on our original topic in relating Five Pillars of Islam with Human Development and Character Building.

Environmentalism

Perhaps due to resource scarcity in most Islamic nations, there was an emphasis on limited (and some claim also sustainable) use of natural capital, i.e. producing land. Traditions of haram and hima and early urban planning were expressions of strong social obligations to stay within carrying capacity and to preserve the natural environment as an obligation of khalifa or "stewardship". Muhammad is considered a pioneer of environmentalism for his teachings on environmental preservation. His hadiths on agriculture and environmental philosophy were compiled in the *Book of Agriculture* of the Sahih Bukhari, which included the following saying:

"There is none amongst the believers who plants a tree, or sows a seed, and then a bird, or a person, or an animal eats thereof, but it is regarded as having given a charitable gift [for which there is great recompense]."

Several such statements concerning the environment are also found in the *Qur'an*, such as the following:

"And there is no animal in the earth or bird that flies with its two wings, but that they are communities like you."

The earliest known treatises dealing with environmentalism and environmental science, especially pollution, were Arabic medical treatises written by al-Kindi, Qusta ibn Luqa, al-Razi, Ibn Al-Jazzar, al-Tamimi, al-Masihi, Avicenna, Ali ibn Ridwan, Ibn Jumay, Isaac Israeli ben Solomon, Abd-el-latif, Ibn al-Quff, and Ibn al-Nafis. Their works covered a number of subjects related to pollution such as air pollution, water pollution, soil contamination, municipal solid waste mishandling, and environmental impact assessments of certain localities. Cordoba, Al-Andalus also had the first waste containers and waste disposal facilities for litter collection.

Humanism

Many medieval Muslim thinkers pursued humanistic, rational and scientific discourses in their search for knowledge, meaning and values. A wide range of Islamic writings on love poetry, history and philosophical theology show that medieval Islamic thought was open to the humanistic ideas of individualism, occasional secularism, skepticism and liberalism. Certain aspects of Renaissance humanism has its roots in the medieval Islamic world, including the "art of *dictation*, called in Latin, *ars dictaminis*," and "the humanist attitude toward classical language", in this case classical Arabic.

Democratic Participation

In the early Islamic Caliphate, the head of state, the Caliph, had a position based on the notion of a successor to Muhammad's political authority, who, according to Sunnis, were ideally elected by the people or their representatives. After the Rashidun Caliphs, later Caliphates during the Islamic Golden Age had a lesser degree of democratic participation, but since "no one was superior to anyone else except on the basis of piety and virtue" in Islam, and following the example of Muhammad, later Islamic rulers often held public consultations with the people in their affairs. Democratic religious pluralism also existed in classical Islamic law, as the religious laws and courts of other religions, including Christianity, Judaism and Hinduism, were usually accommodated within the Islamic legal framework, as seen in the early Caliphate, al-Andalus, Indian subcontinent, and the Ottoman Millet system.

Electing or Appointing a Caliph

Fred Donner, in his book *The Early Islamic Conquests* (1981), argues that the standard Arabian practice during the early Caliphates was for the prominent men of a kinship group, or tribe, to gather after a leader's death and elect a leader from amongst them, although there was no specified procedure for this shura, or consultative assembly.

Candidates were usually from the same lineage as the deceased leader, but they were not necessarily his sons. Capable men who would lead well were preferred over an ineffectual direct heir, as there was no basis in the majority Sunni view that the head of state or governor should be chosen based on lineage alone. Al-Mawardi has written that the caliph should be Qurayshi. Abu Bakr Al-Baqillani has said that the leader of the Muslims simply should be from the majority. Abu Hanifa an-Nu'man also wrote that the leader must come from the majority.

Majlis ash-Shura

Traditional Sunni Islamic lawyers agree that *shura* loosely translated as 'consultation of the people', is a function of the caliphate. The Majlis ash-Shura advises the caliph. The importance of this is premised by the following verses of the *Qur'an*:

"...those who answer the call of their Lord and establish the prayer, and who conduct their affairs by Shura. [are loved by God]"

"...consult them (the people) in their affairs. Then when you have taken a decision (from them), put your trust in Allah"

The majlis is also the means to elect a new caliph. Al-Mawardi has written that members of the majlis should satisfy three conditions: they must be just; they must have enough knowledge to distinguish a good caliph from a bad one, and must have sufficient wisdom and judgment to select the best caliph. Al-Mawardi also said in emergencies when there is no caliphate and no majlis, the people themselves should create a majlis, select a list of candidates for caliph, then the majlis should select from the list of candidates.

Some modern interpretations of the role of the Majlis ash-Shura include those by Islamist author Sayyid Qutb and by Taqiuddin al-Nabhani, the founder of a transnational political movement devoted to the revival of the Caliphate. In an analysis of the shura chapter of the *Qur'an,* Qutb argued Islam requires only that the ruler consult with at least some of the ruled (usually the elite), within the general context of God-made laws that the ruler must execute. Taqiuddin al-Nabhani, writes that Shura is important and part of the "the ruling structure" of the Islamic caliphate, "but not one of its pillars," and may be neglected without the Caliphate's rule becoming unIslamic. Non-Muslims may serve in the majlis, though they may not vote or serve as an official.

Freedom of Expression

Another reason the Islamic world flourished during the Middle Ages was an early emphasis on freedom of speech. This was first declared in the Rashidun Caliphate by the second Caliph, Umar, in the 7th century:

"Only decide on the basis of proof, be kind to the weak so that they can express themselves freely and without fear, deal on an equal footing with litigants by trying to reconcile them."

Another such example can be found in a letter written by the fourth Caliph, Ali ibn Abi Talib to his governor of Egypt, Malik al-Ashtar. The Caliph advices his governor on dealings with the poor masses thus;

"Out of your hours of work, fix a time for the complainants and for those who want to approach you with their grievances. During this time you should do no other work but hear them and pay attention to their complaints and grievances. For this purpose you must arrange public audience for them during this audience, for the sake of Allah, treat them with kindness, courtesy and respect. Do not let your army and police be in the audience hall at such times so that those who have grievances against your regime may speak to you freely, unreservedly and without fear."

Nahjul Balaagha Letter 53

Citizens of the Rashidun Caliphate were also free to criticize the Rashidun Caliphs, as the rule of law was binding on the head of state just as much as it was for the citizens. For example, there was an incident when Umar heard loud sounds from a drunkard inside a house. After knocking on the door and no one answered, Umar climbed over the roof and into the courtyard, where he saw the owner and criticized him for letting a drunkard into his house. In turn, the owner of the house criticized Umar for breaking the law by entering his house without permission. After Umar forgave him, the owner criticized him again, asking him who gave him the right to "forgive what God has condemned as a crime?"

There were also numerous other situations where citizens insulted Caliph Umar, but he tolerated the insults and simply provided them explanations. Similar situations also occurred during the time of Caliph Ali. For example, there was an occasion when he was giving a *Khutbah* speech and a Kharijite rudely interrupted him with insulting language. Ali's companions urged that the man be punished but Ali declined on the grounds that his "right to freedom of speech must not be imperilled."

During the Abbasid Caliphate, freedom of speech was also declared by al-Hashimi, a cousin of Caliph al-Ma'mun, in the following letter to a non-Muslim he was attempting to convert using reason:

"Bring forward all the arguments you wish and say whatever you please and speak your mind freely. Now that you are safe and free to say whatever you please appoint some arbitrator who will impartially judge between us and lean only towards the truth and be free from the empery of passion, and that arbitrator shall be Reason, whereby God makes us responsible for our own rewards and punishments. Herein I have dealt justly with you and have given you full security and am ready to accept whatever decision Reason may give for me or against me. For "There is no compulsion in religion" (Qur'an 2:256) and I have only invited you to accept our faith willingly and of your own accord and have pointed out the hideousness of your present belief. Peace be with you and the blessings of God!"

According to George Makdisi and Hugh Goddard, "the idea of academic freedom" in universities was "modelled on Islamic custom" as practiced in the medieval Madrasah system from the 9th century. Islamic influence was "certainly discernible in the foundation of the first delibratelyplanned university" in Europe, the University of Naples Federico II founded by Frederick II, Holy Roman Emperor in 1224.

Human Rights

In the field of human rights, early Islamic jurists introduced a number of advanced legal concepts which anticipated similar modern concepts in the field. These included the notions of the charitable trust and the trusteeship of property; the notion of brotherhood and social solidarity; the notions of human dignity and the dignity of labour; the notion of an ideal law; the condemnation of antisocial behaviour; the presumption of innocence; the notion of "bidding unto good" (assistance to those in distress); and the notions of sharing, caring, universalism, fair industrial relations, fair contract, commercial integrity, freedom from usury, women's rights, privacy, abuse of rights, juristic personality, individual freedom, equality before the law, legal representation, non-retroactivity, supremacy of the law, judicial independence, judicial impartiality, limited sovereignty, tolerance, and democratic participation.

Many of these concepts were adopted in medieval Europe through contacts with Islamic Spain and the Emirate of Sicily, and through the Crusades and the Latin translations of the 12th century. The concept of inalienable rights was found in early Islamic law and jurisprudence, which denied a ruler "the right to take away from his subjects certain rights which inhere in his or her person as a human being." Islamic rulers could not take away certain rights from their subjects on the basis that "they become rights by reason of the fact that they are given to a subject by a law and from a source which no ruler can question or alter."

There is evidence that John Locke's formulation of inalienable rights and conditional ruler ship, which were present in Islamic law centuries earlier, may have also been influenced by Islamic law, through his attendance of lectures given by Edward Pococke, a professor of Islamic studies. Early Islamic law recognized two sets of human rights. In addition to the category of civil rights and political rights (covered in the Universal Declaration of Human Rights), Islamic law also recognized an additional category: social, economic and cultural rights. This latter category was not recognized in the Western legal tradition until the Inter-national Covenant on Economic, Social and Cultural Rights in 1966.

The right of privacy, which was not recognized in Western legal traditions until modern times, was recognized in Islamic law since the beginning of Islam. In terms of women's rights, women generally had more legal rights under Islamic law than they did under Western legal systems until the 19th and 20th centuries. For example, "French married women, unlike their Muslim sisters, suffered from restrictions on their legal capacity which were removed only in 1965." Noah Feldman, a Harvard University law professor, notes:

As for sexism, the common law long denied married women any property rights or indeed legal personality apart from their husbands. When the British applied their law to Muslims in place of Shariah, as they did in some colonies, the result was to strip married women of the property that Islamic law had always granted them — hardly progress toward equality of the sexes.

In the *North Carolina Law Review* journal, Professor John Makdisi of the University Of North Carolina School Of Law writes in "The Islamic Origins of the Common Law" article:

The manner in which an act was qualified as morally good or bad in the spiritual domain of Islamic religion was quite different from the manner in which that same act was qualified as legally valid or invalid in the temporal domain of Islamic law. Islamic law was secular, not canonical... Thus, it was a system focused on ensuring that an individual received justice, not that one is a good person.

Count Leon Ostorog, a French jurist, wrote the following on classical Islamic law in 1927:

Those Eastern thinkers of the ninth century laid down, on the basis of their theology, the principle of the Rights of Man, in those very terms, comprehending the rights of individual liberty, and of inviolability of person and property; described the supreme power in Islam, or Califate, as based on a contract, implying conditions of capacity and performance, and subject to cancellation if the conditions under the contract were not fulfilled; elaborated a Law of War of which the humane, chivalrous prescriptions would have put to the blush certain belligerents in the Great War; expounded a doctrine of toleration of non-Moslem creeds so liberal that our West had to wait a thousand years before seeing equivalent principles adopted.

Some scholars have suggested that the idea of "a charter defining the duties of a sovereign toward his subjects, as well as subjects toward the sovereign", which led to the "genesis of European legal structures" and the development of the *Magna Carta*, may have been "brought back by Crusaders who were influenced by what they had learned in the Levant about the governing system" established by Saladin. It has also been suggested that "much of the West understands of liberalism in law, economics and society has roots in medieval Islam."

Another influence of Islamic law on European law was the presumption of innocence, which was introduced to Europe by King Louis IX of France soon after he returned from Palestine during the Crusades. Prior to this, European legal procedure consisted of either trial by combat or trial by ordeal. In contrast, Islamic law was based on the presumption of innocence from its beginning, as declared by the Caliph Umar in the 7th century. Other freedoms and rights recognized in the Islamic legal system based on the *Qur'an* since the 7th century, but not recognized in the Western world until much later, include "the rights to know, to choose belief and behaviour, to read and write, the right to power, and even the right to choose government."

Rule of Law

Islamic jurists anticipated the concept of the rule of law, the equal subjection of all classes to the ordinary law of the land, where no person is above the law and where officials and private citizens are under a duty to obey the same law. A Qadi (Islamic judge) was also not allowed to discriminate on the grounds of religion, race, colour, kinship or prejudice. There were also a number of cases where Caliphs had to appear before judges as they prepared to take their verdict. The following hadith established the principle of rule of law in relation to nepotism and accountability:

Narrated 'Aisha: The people of Quraish worried about the lady from Bani Makhzum who had committed theft.

They asked, "Who will intercede for her with Allah's Apostle?" Some said, "No one dares to do so except Usama bin Zaid the beloved one to Allah's Apostle." When Usama spoke about that to Allah's Apostle Allah's Apostle said: "Do you try to intercede for somebody in a case connected with Allah's Prescribed Punishments?" Then he got up and delivered a sermon saying, "What destroyed the nations preceding you, was that if a noble amongst them stole, they would forgive him, and if a poor person amongst them stole, they would inflict Allah's Legal punishment on him. By Allah, if Fatima, the daughter of Muhammad (my daughter) stole, I would cut off her hand."

Various Islamic lawyers do however place multiple conditions, and stipulations e.g. the poor cannot be penalised for stealing out of poverty, before executing such a law, making it very difficult to reach such a stage. It is well known during a time of drought in the Rashidun caliphate period, capital punishments were suspended until the effects of the drought passed.

According to Noah Feldman, a law professor at Harvard University, the legal scholars and jurists who once upheld the rule of law were replaced by a law governed by the state due to the codification of Sharia by the Ottoman Empire in the early 19th century:

How the scholars lost their exalted status as keepers of the law is a complex story, but it can be summed up in the adage that partial reforms are sometimes worse than none at all. In the early 19th century, the Ottoman Empire responded to military setbacks with an internal reform movement. The most important reform was the attempt to codify Shariah. This Westernizing process, foreign to the Islamic legal tradition sought to transform Shariah from a body of doctrines and principles to be discovered by the human efforts of the scholars into a set of rules that could be looked up in a book. Once the law existed in codified form, however, the law itself was able to replace the scholars as the source of authority. Codification took from the scholars their all-important claim to have the final say over the content of the law and transferred that power to the state.

Accountability of Rulers

Sunni Islamic lawyers have commented on when it is permissible to disobey, impeach or remove rulers in the Caliphate. This is usually when the rulers are not meeting public responsibilities obliged upon them under Islam. Al-Mawardi said that if the rulers meet their Islamic responsibilities to the public, the people must obey their laws, but if they become either unjust or severely ineffective then the Caliph or ruler must be impeached via the Majlis ash-Shura. Similarly Al-Baghdadi believed that if the rulers do not uphold justice, the ummah via the majlis should give warning to them, and if unheeded then the Caliph can be impeached. Al-Juwayni argued that Islam is the goal of the ummah, so any ruler that deviates from this goal must be impeached. Al-Ghazali believed that oppression by a caliph is enough for impeachment.

Rather than just relying on impeachment, Ibn Hajar al-Asqalani obliged rebellion upon the people if the caliph began to act with no regard for Islamic law. Ibn Hajar al-Asqalani said that to ignore such a situation is *haraam*, and those who cannot revolt inside the caliphate should launch a struggle from outside. Al-Asqalani used two ayahs from the Qur'an to justify this:

"...And they (the sinners on qiyama) will say, 'Our Lord! We obeyed our leaders and our chiefs, and they misled us from the right path. Our Lord! Give them (the leaders) double the punishment you give us and curse them with a very great curse'..."

Islamic lawyers commented that when the rulers refuse to step down via successful impeachment through the Majlis, becoming dictators through the support of a corrupt army, if the majority agrees they have the option to launch a revolution against them. Many noted that this option is only exercised after factoring in the potential cost of life.

Right of Revolution

According to scholar Bernard Lewis, the Qur'an and Sunnah have several points to make on governance regarding the right of revolution in Islam:

The Quran, for example, makes it clear that there is a duty of obedience: "Obey God, obey the Prophet, obey those who hold authority over you." And this is elaborated in a number of sayings attributed to Muhammad. But there are also sayings that put strict limits on the duty of obedience. Two dicta attributed to the Prophet and universally accepted as authentic are indicative. One says, "there is no obedience in sin"; in other words, if the ruler orders something contrary to the divine law, not only is there no duty of obedience, but there is a duty of disobedience. This is more than the right of revolution that appears in Western political thought. It is a duty of revolution, or at least of disobedience and opposition to authority. The other pronouncement, "do not obey a creature against his creator," again clearly limits the authority of the ruler, whatever form of ruler that may be.

Medical Ethics

The ethical standards of Muslim physicians was first laid down in the 9th century by Ishaq bin Ali Rahawi, who wrote the *Adab al-Tabib* (*Conduct of a Physician*), the first treatist dedicated to medical ethics. He regarded physicians as "guardians of souls and bodies", and wrote twenty chapters on various topics related to medical ethics, including:

- What the physician must avoid and beware of
- The manners of visitors
- The care of remedies by the physician

- The dignity of the medical profession
- The examination of physicians
- The removal of corruption among physicians

Drugs

The earliest known prohibition of illegal drugs occurred under Islamic law, which prohibited the use of Hashish, a preparation of cannabis, as a recreational drug. Classical jurists in medieval Islamic jurisprudence, however, accepted the use of the Hashish drug for medicinal and therapeutic purposes, and agreed that its "medical use, even if it leads to mental derangement, remains exempt" from punishment. In the 14th century, the Islamic scholar Az-Zarkashi spoke of "the permissibility of its use for medical purposes if it is established that it is beneficial."

According to Mary Lynn Mathre, with "this legal distinction between the intoxicant and the medical uses of cannabis, medieval Muslim theologians were far ahead of present-day American law."

Medical Peer Review

The earliest known lawsuits were described in the *Ethics of the Physician* by Ishaq bin Ali al-Rahwi (854–931) of al-Raha, Syria, who describes it as part of an early medical peer review process, where the notes of a practicing Islamic physician were reviewed by peers and he/she could face a lawsuit from a maltreated patient if the reviews were negative.

Neuroethics

Most ancient and medieval societies believed that mental illness was caused by either demonic possession or as punishment from a god, which led to a negative attitude towards mental illness in Judeo-Christian and Greco-Roman societies. On the other hand, Islamic neuroethics and neurotheology held a more sympathetic attitude towards the mentally ill, as exemplified in Sura 4:5 of the Qur'an:

"Do not give your property which God assigned you to manage to the insane: but feed and cloth the insane with this property and tell splendid words to him."

This Quranic verse summarized Islam's attitudes towards the mentally ill, who were considered unfit to manage property but must be treated humanely and be kept under care by a guardian, according to Islamic law. This positive neuroethical understanding of mental health consequently led to the establishment of the first psychiatric hospitals in the medieval Islamic world from the 8th century, and an early scientific understanding of neuroscience and psychology by medieval Muslim physicians and psychologists, who discovered that mental disorders are caused by dysfunctions in the brain.

Military Ethics

The early Islamic treatises on international law from the 9th century onwards covered the application of Islamic ethics, Islamic economic jurisprudence and Islamic military jurisprudence to international law, and were concerned with a number of modern international law topics, including the law of treaties; the treatment of diplomats, hostages, refugees and prisoners of war; the right of asylum; conduct on the battlefield; protection of women, children and non-combatant civilians; contracts across the lines of battle; the use of poisonous weapons; and devastation of enemy territory.

The Islamic legal principles of international law were mainly based on *Qur'an* and the Sunnah of Muhammad, who gave various injunctions to his forces and adopted practices toward the conduct of war. The most important of these were summarized by Muhammad's successor and close companion, Abu Bakr, in the form of ten rules for the Muslim army:

Stop, O people, that I may give you ten rules for your guidance in the battlefield. Do not commit treachery or deviate from the right path. You must not mutilate dead bodies. Neither kill a child, nor a woman, nor an aged man. Bring no harm to the trees, nor burn them with fire, especially those which are fruitful. Slay not any of the enemy's flock, save for your food. You are likely to pass by people who have devoted their lives to monastic services; leave them alone.

Prisoners of War

After Sultan al-Kamil defeated the Franks during the Crusades, Oliverus Scholasticus praised the Islamic laws of war, commenting on how al-Kamil supplied the defeated Frankish army with food:

"Who could doubt that such goodness, friendship and charity come from God? Men whose parents, sons and daughters, brothers and sisters, had died in agony at our hands, whose lands we took, whom we drove naked from their homes, revived us with their own food when we were dying of hunger and showered us with kindness even when we were in their power."

Peace and Justice

As in other Abrahamic religions, peace is a basic concept of Islam. The Arabic term "Islam" itself is usually translated as "submission"; submission of desires to the will of God. It comes from the term *aslama,* which means "to surrender" or "resign oneself". The Arabic word *salaam* ("peace") has the same root as the word *Islam*. One Islamic interpretation is that individual personal peace is attained by utterly submitting to Allah. The greeting "Salaam alaykum", favoured by Muslims, has the literal meaning "Peace be with you". Muhammad is reported to have said once, "Mankind are the dependents, or family of God, and the most beloved of them to God are those who are the most excellent to His dependents." "Not one of you believes until he loves for his brother what he loves for himself." Great Muslim scholars of prophetic tradition such as Ibn Hajar al-Asqalani and Sharafuddin al Nawawi have said that the words 'his brother' mean any person irrespective of faith.

Welfare

The concepts of welfare and pension were introduced in early Islamic law as forms of *Zakat* (charity), one of the Five Pillars of Islam, since the time of the Abbasid caliph Al-Mansur in the 8th century. The taxes (including *Zakat* and *Jizya*) collected in the treasury of an Islamic government was used to provide income for the needy, including the poor, elderly, orphans, widows, and the disabled. According to the Islamic jurist Al-Ghazali, the government was also expected to store up food supplies in every region in case a disaster or famine occurs. The Caliphate was thus one of the earliest welfare states. From the 9th century, funds from the treasury were also used towards the *Waqf* (charitable trusts), often for the purpose of building of Madrassahs and Bimaristan hospitals.

2

Ethical Theories and Morality

Morality (from the Latin *moralitas* "manner, character, proper behaviour") has three principal meanings. In its first, descriptive usage, morality means a code of conduct which is held to be authoritative in matters of right and wrong. Morals are created by and define society, philosophy, religion, or individual conscience. An example of the descriptive usage could be "common conceptions of morality have changed significantly over time." In its second, normative and universal sense, morality refers to an ideal code of conduct, one which would be espoused in preference to alternatives by all rational people, under specified conditions. In this "prescriptive" sense of morality as opposed to the above described "descriptive" sort of sense, moral value judgments such as "murder is immoral" are made. To deny 'morality' in this sense is a position known as moral skepticism, in which the existence of objective moral "truths" is rejected.

In its third usage, 'morality' is synonymous with ethics, the systematic philosophical study of the moral domain. Ethics seeks to address questions such as how a moral outcome can be achieved in a specific situation (applied ethics), how moral values should be determined (normative ethics), what morals people actually abide by (descriptive ethics), what the fundamental nature of ethics or morality is, including whether it has any objective justification (metaethics), and how moral capacity or moral agency develops and what its nature is (moral psychology). In applied ethics, for example, the prohibition against taking human life is controversial with respect to capital punishment, abortion and wars of invasion.

In normative ethics, a typical question might be whether a lie told for the sake of protecting someone from harm is justified. In meta-ethics, a key issue is the meaning of the terms "right" or "wrong". Moral realism would hold that there are true moral statements which report objective moral facts, whereas moral anti-realism would hold that morality is derived from any one of the norms prevalent in society (cultural relativism); the edicts of a god (divine command theory); is merely an expression of the speakers' sentiments (emotivism); an implied imperative (prescriptive); falsely presupposes that there are objective moral facts (error theory).

Some thinkers hold that there is no correct definition of right behaviour, that morality can only be judged with respect to particular situations, within the standards of particular belief systems and socio-historical contexts. This position, known as moral relativism, often cites empirical evidence from anthropology as evidence to support its claims. The opposite view, that there are universal, eternal moral truths is known as moral absolutism. Moral absolutists might concede that forces of social conformity significantly shape moral decisions, but deny that cultural norms and customs define morally right behaviour.

Philosophical Perspectives

Clarifying the Morality

The fact that there are at least three different usages of the term "morality" has led to much confusion when that word is used in discussions. Because of that confusion, many thinkers are forced to spend a certain amount of time dealing with that confusion before they even begin to use the term "morality" in their discussions. One example of that helpful clarification process is found in Walter Terence Stace's book, *The Concept of Morals*, in which he clarifies his own usage of the terms "ethics" and "morality," and their differences. There are many other examples.

Anthropological Perspectives

Tribal and Territorial Moralities

Celia Green has made a distinction between tribal and territorial morality. She characterizes the latter as predominantly negative and proscriptive: it defines a person's territory, including his or her property and dependents, which is not to be damaged or interfered with. Apart from these proscriptions, territorial morality is permissive, allowing the individual whatever behaviour does not inter-fere with the territory of another. By contrast, tribal morality is prescriptive, imposing the norms of the collective on the individual. These norms will be arbitrary, culturally dependent and 'flexible', whereas territorial morality aims at rules which are universal and absolute, such as Kant's 'categorical imperative'. Green relates the development of territorial morality to the rise of the concept of private property, and the ascendancy of contract over status.

In-group and Out-group

Some observers hold that individuals have distinct sets of moral rules that they apply to different groups of people. There is the "ingroup," which includes the individual and those they believe to be of the same culture or race, and there is the "outgroup," whose members are not entitled to be treated according to the same rules. Some biologists, anthropologists and evolutionary psychologists believe this ingroup/outgroup difference is an evolutionary mechanism, one which evolved due to its enhanced survival aspects.

Gary R. Johnson and V.S. Falger have argued that nationalism and patriotism are forms of this ingroup/outgroup boundary.

Comparing Cultures

Peterson and Seligman approach the anthropological view looking across cultures and across millennia. They conclude that certain virtues have prevailed in all cultures they examined. The major virtues they identified include *wisdom / knowledge; courage; humanity; justice; temperance; and transcendence*. Each of these includes several divisions. For instance *humanity* includes *love, kindness*, and *social intelligence*. Fons Trompenaars, author of *Did the Pedestrian Die* tested members of different cultures with various moral dilemmas. One of these was whether the driver of a car would have his friend, a passenger riding in the car, lie in order to protect the driver from the consequences of driving too fast and hitting a pedestrian. Trompenaars found that different cultures had quite different expectations (from none to almost certain).

Evolutionary Perspectives

Some evolutionary biologists, particularly socio-biologists, believe that morality is a product of evolutionary forces acting at an individual level and also at the group level through group selection (though whether "group selection" actually occurs is a controversial topic in evolutionary theory). Some sociobiologists contend that the set of behaviours that constitute morality evolved largely because they provided possible survival and/or reproductive benefits (i.e. increased evolutionary success). Humans consequently evolved "prosocial" emotions, such as feelings of empathy or guilt, in response to these moral behaviours.

In this respect, morality is not absolute, but relative and constitutes any set of behaviours that encourage human cooperation based on their ideology. Biologists contend that all social animals, from ants to elephants, have modified their behaviours, by restraining selfishness in order to make group living worthwhile. Human morality though sophisticated and complex relative to other animals, is essentially a natural phenomenon that evolved to restrict excessive individualism and foster human cooperation. On this view, moral codes are ultimately founded on emotional instincts and intuitions that were selected for in the past because they aided survival and reproduction (inclusive fitness). The strength of the maternal bond is one example. Another is the Westermarck effect, seen as underpinning taboos against incest, which decreases the likelihood of inbreeding depression.

The phenomenon of 'reciprocity' in nature is seen by evolutionary biologists as one way to begin to understand human morality. Its function is typically to ensure a reliable supply of essential resources, especially for animals living in a habitat where food quantity or quality fluctuates unpredictably. For example, on any given night for vampire bats, some individuals fail to feed on prey while others consume a surplus of blood. Bats that have successfully fed then regurgitate part of their blood meal to save a nonspecific from starvation. Since these animals live in close-knit groups over many years, an individual can count on other group members to return the favor on nights when it goes hungry.

It has been convincingly demonstrated that chimpanzees show empathy for each other in a wide variety of contexts. They also possess the ability to engage in deception, and a level of social 'politics' prototypical of our own tendencies for gossip and reputation management. Christopher Boehm (1982) has hypothesized that the incremental development of moral complexity throughout hominid evolution was due to the increasing need to avoid disputes and injuries in moving to open savanna and developing stone weapons. Other theories are that increasing complexity was simply a correlate of increasing group size and brain size, and in particular the development of theory of mind abilities. Richard Dawkins in *The God Delusion* suggested that our morality is a result of our biological evolutionary history and that the Moral Zeitgeist helps describe how morality evolves from biological and cultural origins and evolves with time within a culture.

Neuroscientific and Psychiatric Perspectives

Mirror-neurons

Research on *mirror neurons*, since their discovery in 1996, suggests that they may have a role to play not only in action understanding, but also in emotion sharing empathy. Cognitive neuro-scientist Jean Decety thinks that the ability to recognize and vicariously experience what another individual is undergoing was a key step forward in the evolution of social behaviour, and ultimately, morality. The inability to feel empathy is one of the defining characteristics of psychopathy, and this would appear to lend support to Decety's view.

Psychological Perspectives

In modern psychology, morality is considered to change through personal development. A number of psychologists have produced theories on the development of morals, usually going through stages of different morals. Lawrence Kohlberg, Jean Piaget, and Elliot Turiel have cognitive-developmental approaches to moral development; to these theorists' morality forms in a series of constructive stages or domains. Social psychologists such as Martin Hoffman and Jonathan Haidt emphasize social and emotional development based on biology, such as empathy. Moral identity theorists, such as William Damon and Mordechai Nisan, see moral commitment as arising from the development of a self-identity that is defined by moral purposes: this moral self-identity leads to a sense of responsibility to pursue such purposes. Of historical interest in psychology are the theories of psychoanalysts such as Sigmund Freud, who believe that moral development is the product of aspects of the super-ego as guilt-shame avoidance.

Morality in Judicial Systems

In most systems, the lack of morality of the individual can also be a sufficient cause for punishment, or can be an element for the grading of the punishment. Especially in the systems where modesty (i.e., with reference to sexual crimes) is legally protected or otherwise regulated, the definition of morality as a legal element and in order to determine the cases of infringement, is usually left to the vision and appreciation of the single judge and hardly ever precisely specified.

In such cases, it is common to verify an application of the prevalent common morality of the interested community that consequently becomes enforced by the law for further reference. The government of South Africa is attempting to create a Moral Regeneration movement. Part of this is a proposed Bill of Morals, which will bring a biblical-based "moral code" into the realm of law. This move by a nominally secular democracy has attracted relatively little criticism.

Morality and Politics

If morality is the answer to the question 'how ought we to live' at the individual level, politics can be seen as addressing the same question at the social level. It is therefore unsurprising that evidence has been found of a relationship between attitudes in morality and politics. Jonathan Haidt and Jesse Graham have studied the differences between liberals and conservatives, in this regard. According to their model, political conservatives make their moral choices using five moral variables (harm/care, fairness/reciprocity, in-group loyalty, authority/respect, purity/sanctity), whereas liberals use only two (harm/care and fairness/reciprocity). Haidt also hypothesizes that the origin of this division in the United States can be traced to geohistorical factors, with conservatism strongest in closely knit, ethnically homogenous communities, in contrast to port-cities, where the cultural mix is greater, thus requiring more liberalism.

Group morality develops from shared concepts and beliefs and is often codified to regulate behaviour within a culture or community. Various defined actions come to be called moral or immoral. Individuals who choose moral action are popularly held to possess "moral fiber", whereas those who indulge in immoral behaviour may be labeled as socially degenerate. The continued existence of a group may depend on widespread conformity to codes of morality; an inability to adjust moral codes in response to new challenges is sometimes credited with the demise of a community (a positive example would be the function of Cistercian reform in reviving monasticism; a negative example would be the role of the Dowager Empress in the subjugation of China to European interests). Within nationalist movements, there has been some tendency to feel that a nation will not survive or prosper without acknowledging one common morality, regardless of in what it consists. Political Morality is also relevant to the behaviour internationally of national governments, and to the support they receive from their host population. Noam Chomsky states that

"... if we adopt the principle of universality: if an action is right (or wrong) for others, it is right (or wrong) for us. Those who do not rise to the minimal moral level of applying to themselves the standards they apply to others – more stringent ones, in fact – plainly cannot be taken seriously when they speak of appropriateness of response; or of right and wrong, good and evil."

"In fact, one of the, maybe the most, elementary of moral principles is that of universality, that is, If something's right for me, it's right for you; if it's wrong for you, it's wrong for me. Any moral code that is even worth looking at has that at its core somehow. But that principle is overwhelmingly disregarded all the time. If you want to run through examples we can easily do it. Take, say, George W. Bush, since he happens to be president. If you apply the standards that we applied to Nazi war criminals at Nuremberg, he'd be hanged. Is it an even conceivable possibility? It's not even discussable. Because we don't apply to ourselves the principles we apply to others. There's a lot of talk about 'terror' and how awful it is. Whose terror? Our terror against them? I mean, is that considered reprehensible? No, it's considered highly moral; it's considered self-defense. Now, their terror against us, that's awful, and terrible. But, to try to rise to the level of becoming a minimal moral agent, and just entering into the domain of moral discourse is very difficult because that means accepting the principle of universality. And you can experiment for yourself and see how often that's accepted, either in personal or political life. Very rarely."

Moral Codes

Codified morality is generally distinguished from custom, another way for a community to define appropriate activity, by the former's derivation from natural or universal principles. In certain religious communities, the Divine is said to provide these principles through revelation, sometimes in great detail. Such codes may be called laws, as in the Law of Moses, or community morality may be defined through commentary on the texts of revelation, as in Islamic law. Such codes are distinguished from legal or judicial right, including civil rights, which are based on the accumulated traditions, decrees and legislation of a political authority, though these latter often invoke the authority of the moral law.

Morality can also be seen as the collection of beliefs as to what constitutes a good life. Since throughout most of human history, religions have provided both visions and regulations for an ideal life, morality is often confused with religious precepts. In secular communities, lifestyle choices, which represent an individual's conception of the good life, are often discussed in terms of "morality." Individuals sometimes feel that making an appropriate lifestyle choice invokes a true morality, and that accepted codes of conduct within their chosen community are fundamentally moral, even when such codes deviate from more general social principles.

Moral codes are often complex definitions of right and wrong that are based upon well-defined value systems. Although some people might think that a moral code is simple, rarely is there anything simple about one's values, ethics, etc. or, for that matter, the judgment of those of others. The difficulty lies in the fact that morals are often part of a religion and more often than not about culture codes. Sometimes, moral codes give way to legal codes, which couple penalties or corrective actions with particular practices. Note that while many legal codes are merely built on a foundation of religious and/or cultural moral codes, of times they are one and the same.

Examples of moral codes include the Golden Rule; the Noble Eightfold Path of Buddhism; the ancient Egyptian code of Ma'at; the ten commandments of Judaism, Christianity, and Islam; the yamas and niyama of the Hindu scriptures; the ten Indian commandments; and the principle of the Dessek. Another related concept is the moral core which is assumed to be innate in each individual, to those who accept that differences between individuals are more important than posited Creators or their rules. This, in some religious systems and beliefs (e.g. Taoism, Moralism and Gnosticism), is assumed to be the basis of all aesthetics and thus moral choice. Moral codes as such are therefore seen as coercive – part of human politics.

Moral Psychology

Religiosity and Morality

In the scientific literature, the degree of religiosity is generally found to be associated with higher ethical attitudes. Although a recent study by Gregory S. Paul published in the

Journal of Religion and Society argues for a positive correlation between the degree of *public religiosity* in a society and certain measures of dysfunction. An analysis published later in the same journal contends that a number of methodological problems undermine any findings or conclusions to be taken from the research. In another response, Gary Jensen builds on and refines Paul's study. His conclusion, after carrying out elaborate multivariate statistical studies, is that a complex relationship exists between religiosity and homicide with some dimensions of religiosity encouraging homicide and other dimensions discouraging it."

Meanwhile, other studies seem to show positive links in the relationship between religiosity and moral behaviour — for example, surveys suggesting a positive connection between faith and altruism. Modern research in criminology also acknowledges an *inverse* relationship between religion and crime; with many studies establishing this beneficial connection (though some claim it is a modest one). Indeed, a meta-analysis of 60 studies on religion and crime concluded, "religious behaviours and beliefs exert a moderate deterrent effect on individuals' criminal behaviour".

Religion as a Source of Moral Authority

Religious belief systems usually include the idea of divine will and divine judgment and usually correspond to a moral code of conduct, and many religions claim that religion and morality are intimately connected. For example, the Roman Catholic Church maintains that although morality can be derived from unaided reason as it is simply the "right ordering" of man's actions, ultimately it derives from God because God created man and nature and that the ultimate sanction for immorality is the loss of a relationship with God.

Views of Historians and Scholars

There are several different views on Islamic science among historians of science. The traditionalist view, as exemplified by Bertrand Russell, holds that Islamic science, while admirable in many technical ways, lacked the intellectual energy required for innovation and was chiefly important as a preserver of ancient knowledge and transmitter to medieval Europe. The revisionist view, as exemplified by Abdus Salam and George Saliba, holds that a Muslim scientific revolution occurred during the Middle Ages, an expression with which scholars such as Donald Routledge Hill and Ahmad Y Hassan express the view that Islam was the driving force behind the Muslim achievements, while Robert Briffault even sees Islamic science as the foundation of modern science.

The most prominent view in recent scholarship, however, as exemplified by Toby E. Huff, Will Durant, Fielding H. Garrison, Muhammad Iqbal Hossein Nasr and Bernard Lewis, holds that Muslim scientists did help in laying the foundations for an experimental science with their contributions to the scientific method and their empirical, experimental and quantitative approach to scientific inquiry, but that their work cannot be considered a Scientific Revolution, like that which occurred in early modern Europe and led to the emergence of modern science, with the exception of Ibn al-Haytham's *Book of Optics* which is widely considered a revolution in the fields of optics and visual perception.

Rise

During the early Muslim conquests, the Muslim Arab forces, led primarily by Khalid ibn al-Walid, conquered the Sassanid Persian Empire and more than half of the Byzantine Roman Empire, establishing the Arab Empire across the Middle East, Central Asia, and North Africa, followed by further expansions across Pakistan, southern Italy and the Iberian Peninsula. As a result, the Islamic governments inherited the knowledge and skills of the ancient Middle East, of Greece, of Persia and of India. The art of papermaking was obtained from two Chinese prisoners at the Battle of Talas (751), resulting in paper mills being built in Samarkand and Baghdad. The Arabs improved upon the Chinese techniques using linen rags instead of mulberry bark.

Most notable Arab scientists and Iranian scientists lived and practiced during the Islamic Golden Age, though not all scientists in Islamic civilization were Arab or Muslim. Some argue that the term "Arab-Islamic" does not appreciate the rich diversity of eastern scholars who have contributed to science in that era. During the Islamic Golden Age, Muslim scholars made significant advances in science, mathematics, medicine, astronomy, engineering, and many other fields. During this time, early Islamic philosophy developed and was often pivotal in scientific debates — key figures were usually scientists and philosophers. The number of important and original Arabic works written on the mathematical sciences is much larger than the combined total of Latin and Greek works on the mathematical sciences.

Scientific Institutions

A number of important institutions previously unknown in the ancient world have their origins in the medieval Islamic world, with the most notable examples being: the public hospital (which replaced healing temples and sleep temples) and psychiatric hospital, the public library and lending library, the academic degree-granting university, the astronomical observatory as a research institute (as opposed to a private observation post as was the case in ancient times), and the trust (Waqf). The first universities which issued diplomas were the Bimaristan medical university-hospitals of the medieval Islamic world, where medical diplomas were issued to students of Islamic medicine who were qualified to be practicing doctors of medicine from the 9th century.

Sir John Bagot Glubb wrote:

"By Mamun's time medical schools were extremely active in Baghdad. The first free public hospital was opened in Baghdad during the Caliphate of Haroon-ar-Rashid. As the system developed, physicians and surgeons were appointed who gave lectures to medical students and issued diplomas to those who were considered qualified to practice. The first hospital in Egypt was opened in 872 AD and thereafter public hospitals sprang up all over the empire from Spain and the Maghrib to Persia."

The Guinness Book of World Records recognizes the University of Al Karaouine in Fez, Morocco as the oldest university in the world with its founding in 859. Al-Azhar University, founded in Cairo, Egypt in the 10th century, offered a variety of academic degrees, including postgraduate degrees, and is often considered the first full-fledged university. A number of distinct features of the modern library were introduced in the Islamic world, where libraries not only served as a collection of manuscripts as was the case in ancient libraries, but also as a public library and lending library, a centre for the instruction and spread of sciences and ideas, a place for meetings and discussions, and sometimes as a lodging for scholars or boarding school for pupils.

The concept of the library catalog was also introduced in medieval Islamic libraries, where books were organized into specific genres and categories. Another common feature during the Islamic Golden Age was the large number of Muslim polymaths or "universal geniuses", scholars who contributed too many different fields of knowledge. Muslim polymaths were known as "Hakeems" and they had a wide breadth of knowledge in many different fields of religious and secular learning, comparable to the later "Renaissance Men", such as Leonardo da Vinci, of the European Renaissance period.

Polymath scholars were so common during the Islamic Golden Age that it was rare to find a scholar who specialized in any single field at the time. Notable Muslim polymaths included al-Biruni, al-Jahiz, al-Kindi, Abu Bakr Muhammad al-Razi, Ibn Sina, al-Idrisi, Ibn Bajja, Ibn Zuhr, Ibn Tufayl, Ibn Rushd, al-Suyuti Geber, al-Khwarizmi, the Banû Mûsâ, Abbas Ibn Firnas, al-Farabi, al-Masudi, al-Muqaddasi, Alhacen, Omar Khayyám, al-Ghazali, al-Khazini, Avempace, al-Jazari, Ibn al-Nafis, Nasîr al-Dîn al-Tûsî, Ibn al-Shatir, Ibn Khaldun, and Taqi al-Din, among many others.

Decline

Islamic science and the numbers of Islamic scientists were traditionally believed to have begun declining from the 12th or 13th centuries. It was believed that, though the Islamic civilization would still produce scientists that they became the exception, rather than the rule. Recent scholarship, however, has come to question this traditional picture of decline, pointing to continued astronomical activity as a sign of a continuing and creative scientific tradition through to the 16th century, of which the work of Ibn al-Shatir (1304–1375) in Damascus is considered the most noteworthy example.

This was also the case for other areas of Islamic science, such as medicine, exemplified by the works of Ibn al-Nafis and Þerafeddin Sabuncuoðlu, and the social sciences, exemplified by Ibn Khaldun's *Muqaddimah* (1370), which itself points out that science was declining in Iraq, Al-Andalus and Maghreb, but continuing to flourish in Persia, Syria and Egypt. One reason given for the scientific decline was when the orthodox Ash'ari school of theology challenged the more rational Mu'tazili school of theology, with al-Ghazali's *The Incoherence of the Philosophers* (*Tahafut al-falasifa*) being the most notable example.

This interpretation was introduced by the Hungarian Orientalist Ignaz Goldziher, who believed that there was an intrinsic antagonism between Islamic orthodoxy and the Greek-influenced traditions of science. Recent scholarship has questioned this traditional view, however, with a number of scholars pointing out that the Ash'ari school supported science but were only opposed to speculative philosophy and that some of the greatest Muslim scientists such as Alhazen, Biruni, Ibn al-Nafis and Ibn Khaldun were themselves followers of the Ash'ari school. Emilie Savage-Smith also pointed out that Al-Ghazali's positive views towards medicine, particularly anatomy, were a source of encouragement for the increased use of dissection by Muslim physicians (such as Avenzoar and Ibn al-Nafis) in the 12th and 13th centuries.

Other reasons for the decline of Islamic science include conflicts between the Sunni and Shia Muslims, and invasions by Crusaders and Mongols on Islamic lands between the 11th and 13th centuries, especially the Mongol invasions of the 13th century. The Mongols destroyed Muslim libraries, observatories, hospitals, and universities, culminating in the destruction of Baghdad, the Abbasid capital and intellectual centre, in 1258, which is traditionally believed to have marked an end to the Islamic Golden Age.

From the 13th century, some traditionalist Muslims believed that the Crusades and Mongol invasions may have been a divine punishment from God against Muslims deviating from the Sunnah, a view that was held even by the famous polymath Ibn al-Nafis. Such traditionalist views as well as numerous wars and conflicts at the time are believed to have created a climate which made Islamic science less successful than before. However, Y. Ziedan has pointed out that the sack of Baghdad in 1258 was followed by intense scientific activity across Damascus and Cairo, as many Muslim scholars wrote huge encyclopedias (including an 80-volume medical encyclopedia by Ibn al-Nafis) in an attempt to preserve the scientific heritage of the Islamic world and cope with the loss of Baghdad.

Another reason given for the decline of Islamic science is the disruption to the cycle of equity based on Ibn

Khaldun's famous model of Asabiyyah (the rise and fall of civilizations), which points to the decline being mainly due to political and economic factors rather than religious factors. With the fall of Islamic Spain in 1492, the scientific and technological initiative of the Islamic world was inherited by Europeans and laid the foundations for Europe's Renaissance and Scientific Revolution.

Influence on European Science

Contributing to the growth of European science was the major search by European scholars for new learning which they could only find among Muslims, especially in Islamic Spain and Sicily. These scholars translated new scientific and philosophical texts from Arabic into Latin. One of the most productive translators in Spain was Gerard of Cremona, who translated 87 books from Arabic to Latin, including Muhammad ibn Mûsâ al-Khwârizmî's *On Algebra and Almucabala,* Jabir ibn Aflah's *Elementa astronomica,* al-Kindi's *On Optics,* Ahmad ibn Muhammad ibn Kathîr al-Farghânî's *On Elements of Astronomy on the Celestial Motions,* al-Farabi's *On the Classification of the Sciences,* the chemical and medical works of Razi, the works of Thabit ibn Qurra and Hunayn ibn Ishaq, and the works of Arzachel, Jabir ibn Aflah, the Banû Mûsâ, Abû Kâmil Shujâ ibn Aslam, Abu al-Qasim, and Ibn al-Haytham (including the *Book of Optics*).

Other Arabic works translated into Latin during the 12th century include the works of Muhammad ibn Jâbir al-Harrânî al-Battânî and Muhammad ibn Mûsâ alKhwârizmî (including *The Compendious Book on Calculation by Completion and Balancing*), the works of Abu al-Qasim (including the *al-Tasrif*), Muhammad al-Fazari's *Great Sindhind* (based on the *Surya Siddhanta* and the works of Brahmagupta), the works of Razi and Avicenna (including *The Book of Healing* and *The Canon of Medicine*), the works of Averroes, the works of Thabit ibn Qurra, al-Farabi, Ahmad ibn Muhammad ibn Kathîr al-Farghânî,

Hunayn ibn Ishaq, and his nephew Hubaysh ibn al-Hasan, the works of al-Kindi, Abraham bar Hiyya's *Liber embadorum*, Ibn Sarabi's (Serapion Junior) *De Simplicibus*, the works of Qusta ibn Luqa, the works of Maslamah Ibn Ahmad al-Majriti, Ja'far ibn Muhammad Abu Ma'shar a-lBalkhi, and al-Ghazali, the works of Nur Ed-Din Al Betrugi, including *On the Motions of the Heavens*, Ali ibn Abbas al-Majusi's medical encyclopedia, *The Complete Book of the Medical Art*, Abu Mashar's *Introduction to Astrology*, the works of Maimonides, Ibn Zezla (Byngezla), Masawaiyh, Serapion, al-Qifti, and Albe'thar. Abû Kâmil Shujâ ibn Aslam's *Algebra*, the chemical works of Geber, and the *De Proprietatibus Elementorum*, an Arabic work on geology written by a pseudoAristotle. By the beginning of the 13th century, Mark of Toledo translated the *Qur'an* and various medical works.

Fibonacci presented the first complete European account of the Hindu-Arabic numeral system from Arabic sources in his *Liber Abaci* (1202). Al-Khazini's *Zij as-Sanjari* was translated into Greek by Gregory Choniades in the 13th century and was studied in the Byzantine Empire. The astronomical corrections to the Ptolemaic model made by al-Battani and Averroes and the non-Ptolemaic models produced by Mo'ayyeduddin Urdi (Urdi lemma), Nasîr al-Dîn al-Tûsî (Tusi-couple) and Ibn al-Shatir were later adapted into the Copernican heliocentric model. Al-Kindi's (Alkindus) law of terrestrial gravity influenced Robert Hooke's law of celestial gravity, which in turn inspired Newton's law of universal gravitation. Abû al-Rayhân alBîrûnî's *Ta'rikh al-Hind* and *Kitab al-qanun al-Mas'udi* were translated into Latin as *Indica* and *Canon Mas'udicus* respectively. Ibn al-Nafis' *Commentary on Compound Drugs* was translated into Latin by Andrea Alpago (died 1522), who may have also translated Ibn al-Nafis' *Commentary on Anatomy in the Canon of Avicenna*, which first described pulmonary circulation and coronary circulation, and which may have had an influence on Michael Servetus, Realdo Colombo and William Harvey. Translations of the algebraic and geometrical works of Ibn al-Haytham, Omar Khayyám and Nasîr al-Dîn al-Tûsî were later influential in the development of non-Euclidean geometry in Europe from the 17th century. Ibn Tufail's *Hayy ibn Yaqdhan* was translated into Latin by Edward Pococke in 1671 and into English by Simon Ockley in 1708 and became "one of the most important books that heralded the Scientific Revolution." Ibn al-Baitar's *Kitab al-Jami fi al-Adwiya al-Mufrada* also had an influence on European botany after it was translated into Latin in 1758.

Scientific Method

Muslim scientists placed a greater emphasis on experimentation than previous ancient civilizations (for example, Greek philosophy placed a greater emphasis on rationality rather than empiricism), which was due to the emphasis on empirical observation found in the *Qur'an* and Sunnah, and the rigorous historical methods established in the science of hadith. Muslim scientists thus combined precise observation, controlled experiment and careful records with a new approach to scientific inquiry which led to the development of the scientific method. In particular, the empirical observations and experiments of Ibn al-Haytham (Alhacen) in his *Book of Optics* (1021) is seen as the beginning of the modern scientific method, which he first introduced to optics and psychology. Rosanna Gorini writes:

"According to the majority of the historians al-Haytham was the pioneer of the modern scientific method. With his book he changed the meaning of the term optics and established experiments as the norm of proof in the field. His investigations are based not on abstract theories, but on experimental evidences and his experiments were systematic and repeatable."

Other early experimental methods were developed by Geber (for chemistry), Muhammad al-Bukhari (for history and the science of hadith), al-Kindi (for the Earth sciences), Avicenna (for medicine), Abû Rayhân al-Bîrûnî (for astronomy and mechanics), Ibn Zuhr (for surgery) and Ibn Khaldun (for the social sciences). The most important development of the scientific method, the use of experimentation and quantification to distinguish between competing scientific theories set within a generally empirical orientation, was introduced by Muslim scientists.

Ibn al-Haytham, a pioneer of modern optics, used the scientific method to obtain the results in his *Book of Optics*. In particular, he combined observations, experiments and rational arguments to show that his modern intromission theory of vision, where rays of light are emitted from objects rather than from the eyes, is scientifically correct, and that the ancient emission theory of vision supported by Ptolemy and Euclid (where the eyes emit rays of light), and the ancient intromission theory supported by Aristotle (where objects emit physical particles to the eyes), were both wrong. It is known that Roger Bacon was familiar with Ibn al-Haytham's work. Ibn al-Haytham is featured on the 10,000 Iraqi dinar note.

Ibn al-Haytham developed rigorous experimental methods of controlled scientific testing in order to verify theoretical hypotheses and substantiate inductive conjectures. Ibn al-Haytham's scientific method was similar to the modern scientific method in that it consisted of the following procedures:

1. Observation
2. Statement of problem
3. Formulation of hypothesis
4. Testing of hypothesis using experimentation
5. Analysis of experimental results
6. Interpretation of data and formulation of conclusion
7. Publication of findings

The development of the scientific method is considered to be fundamental to modern science and some — especially philosophers of science and practicing scientists

— consider earlier inquiries into nature to be *pre-scientific*. Some consider Ibn al-Haytham to be the "first scientist" for this reason. In *The Model of the Motions*, Ibn al-Haytham also describes an early version of Occam's razor, where he employs only minimal hypotheses regarding the properties that characterize astronomical motions, as he attempts to eliminate from his planetary model the cosmological hypotheses that cannot be observed from Earth.

"The debt of our science to that of the Arabs does not consist in startling discoveries or revolutionary theories; science owes a great deal more to Arab culture, it owes its existence. The ancient world was, as we saw, pre- scientific. The astronomy and mathematics of the Greeks were a foreign importation never thoroughly acclimatized in Greek culture. The Greeks systematized, generalized and theorized, but the patient ways of investigation, the accumulation of positive knowledge, the minute methods of science, detailed and prolonged observation, experi-mental inquiry, were altogether alien to the Greek temperament. [...] What we call science arose in Europe as a result of a new spirit of inquiry, of new methods of investigation, of the method of experiment, observation, measurement, of the development of mathematics in a form unknown to the Greeks. That spirit and those methods were introduced into the European world by the Arabs."

Science is the most momentous contribution of Arab civilization to the modern world, but its fruits were slow in ripening. Not until long after Moorish culture had sunk back into darkness did the giant to which it had given birth, rise in his might. It was not science only which brought Europe back to life. Other and manifold influences from the civilization of Islam communicated its first glow to European life."

George Sarton wrote in the *Introduction to the History of Science*:

"The main, as well as the least obvious, achievement of

the Middle Ages was the creation of the experimental spirit and this was primarily due to the Muslims down to the 12th century."

Oliver Joseph Lodge wrote in the *Pioneers of Science*:

"The only effective link between the old and the new science is afforded by the Arabs. The dark ages come as an utter gap in the scientific history of Europe, and for more than a thousand years there was not a scientific man of note except in Arabia."

Muhammad Iqbal wrote in *The Reconstruction of Religious Thought in Islam*:

"Thus the experimental method, reason and observation introduced by the Arabs were responsible for the rapid advancement of science during the medieval times."

The first documented description of a peer review process is found in the *Ethics of the Physician* written by Ishaq bin Ali al-Rahwi (854–931) of al-Raha, Syria, who describes the first medical peer review process. His work, as well as later Arabic medical manuals, state that a visiting physician must always make duplicate notes of a patient's condition on every visit. When the patient was cured or had died, the notes of the physician were examined by a local medical council of other physicians, who would review the practicing physician's notes to decide whether his/her performance have met the required standards of medical care. If their reviews were negative, the practicing physician could face a lawsuit from a maltreated patient.

Applied Sciences

"The Saracens themselves were the originators not only of algebra, chemistry, and geology, but of many of the socalled improvements or refinements of civilization, such as street lamps, window-panes, firework, stringed instruments, cultivated fruits, perfumes, spices, etc..."

In the applied sciences, a significant number of inventions and technologies were produced by medieval Muslim scientists and engineers such as Abbas Ibn Firnas, Taqi alDin, and particularly al-Jazari, who are considered a pioneer in modern engineering. Some of the inventions believed to have come from the medieval Islamic world include the programmable automaton, coffee, the soap bar, shampoo, pure distillation, liquefaction, crystallisation, purification, oxidisation, evaporation, filtration, distilled alcohol, uric acid, nitric acid, alembic, the crankshaft, the valve, the combination lock, quilting, the pointed arch, the scalpel, the bone saw, forceps, surgical catgut, the windmill, inoculation, the fountain pen, cryptanalysis, frequency analysis, the three-course meal, stained glass and quartz glass, Persian carpet, the celestial globe, explosive rockets and incendiary devices, and artificial pleasure gardens.

Agricultural Sciences

During the Muslim Agricultural Revolution, Muslim scientists made significant advances in botany and laid the foundations of agricultural science. Muslim botanists and agriculturists demonstrated advanced agronomical, agro technical and economic knowledge in areas such as meteorology, climatology, hydrology, soil occupation, and the economy and management of agricultural enterprises. They also demonstrated agricultural knowledge in areas such as pedology, agricultural ecology, irrigation, preparation of soil, planting, spreading of manure, killing herbs, sowing, cutting trees, grafting, pruning vine, prophylaxis, phytotherapy, the care and improvement of cultures and plants, and the harvest and storage of crops.

Al-Dinawari (828-896) is considered the founder of Arabic botany for his *Book of Plants*, in which he described at least 637 plants and discussed plant evolution from its birth to its death, describing the phases of plant growth and the production of flowers and fruit. In the 13th century, the Andalusian-Arabian biologist Abu al-Abbas al-Nabati developed an early scientific method for botany, introducing empirical and experimental techniques in the testing, description and identification of numerous materia medica, and separating unverified reports from those supported by actual tests and observations. His student Ibn al-Baitar published the *Kitab al-Jami fi al-Adwiya al-Mufrada,* which is considered one of the greatest botanical compilations in history, and was a botanical authority for centuries. It contains details on at least 1,400 different plants, foods, and drugs, 300 which were his own original discoveries. His work was also influential in Europe after it was translated into Latin Qur'an, Science and Ethics in 1758.

Medicine

Muslim physicians made many significant advances and contributions to medicine, including anatomy, ophthalmology, pathology, the pharmaceutical sciences (including pharmacy and pharmacology), physiology, and surgery. Muslim physicians set up some of the earliest dedicated hospitals, which later spread to Europe during the Crusades, inspired by the hospitals in the Middle East. Al-Kindi wrote *De Gradibus,* in which he first demonstrated the application of quantification and mathematics to medicine, particularly in the field of pharmacology.

This includes the development of a mathematical scale to quantify the strength of drugs, and a system that would allow a doctor to determine in advance the most critical days of a patient's illness. Razi (Rhazes) (865-925), a pioneer of pediatrics, recorded clinical cases of his own experience and provided very useful recordings of various diseases. His *Comprehensive Book of Medicine,* which introduced measles and smallpox, was very influential in Europe. In his *Doubts about Galen,* al-Razi was also the first to prove both Galen's theory of humorism and Aristotle's theory of classical elements false using experimentation. He also introduced urinalysis and stool tests.

Abu al-Qasim (Abulcasis), considered a pioneer of modern

surgery, wrote the *Al-Tasrif* (1000), a 30-volume medical encyclopedia which was taught at Muslim and European medical schools until the 17th century. He invented numerous surgical instruments, including the first instruments unique to women, as well as the surgical uses of catgut and forceps, the ligature, surgical needle, scalpel, curette, retractor, surgical spoon, sound, surgical hook, surgical rod, and specula, bone saw, and plaster. In 1021, Ibn al-Haytham (Alhacen) made important advances in eye surgery, as he studied and correctly explained the process of sight and visual perception for the first time in his *Book of Optics* (1021).

Avicenna, who was a pioneer of experimental medicine and was also an influential thinker and medical scholar, wrote *The Canon of Medicine* (1025) and *The Book of Healing* (1027), which remained standard textbooks in both Muslim and European universities until at least the 17th century. Avicenna's contributions include the introduction of systematic experimentation and quantification into the study of physiology, the discovery of the contagious nature of infectious diseases, the introduction of quarantine to limit the spread of contagious diseases, the introduction of experimental medicine, evidence-based medicine, clinical trials, randomized controlled trials, efficacy tests, and clinical pharmacology, the importance of dietetics and the influence of climate and environment on health, the distinction of mediastinitis from pleurisy, the contagious nature of phthisis and tuberculosis, the distribution of diseases by water and soil, and the first careful descriptions of skin troubles, sexually transmitted diseases, perversions, and nervous ailments, as well the use of ice to treat fevers, and the separation of medicine from pharmacology, which was important to the development of the pharmaceutical sciences.

Ibn Zuhr (Avenzoar) is considered a pioneer of experimental surgery, for introducing the experimental method into surgery in the 12th century, as he was the first to employ animal testing in order to experiment with surgical procedures before applying them to human patients. He also performed the first dissections and postmortem autopsies on both humans as well as animals.

In 1242, Ibn al-Nafis, considered a pioneer of circulatory physiology, was the first to describe pulmonary circulation and coronary circulation, which form the basis of the circulatory system, for which he is considered one of the greatest physiologists in history. He also described the earliest concept of metabolism, and developed new systems of physiology and psychology to replace the Avicennian and Galenic systems, while discrediting many of their erroneous theories on the four humours, pulsation, bones, muscles, intestines, sensory organs, bilious canals, esophagus, stomach, etc. Ibn al-Lubudi (1210-1267) rejected the theory of four humours supported by Galen and Hippocrates, discovered that the body and its preservation depend exclusively upon blood, rejected Galen's idea that women can produce sperm, and discovered that the movement of arteries are not dependent upon the movement of the heart, that the heart is the first organ to form in a fetus' body (rather than the brain as claimed by Hippocrates), and that the bones forming the skull can grow into tumors.

The *Tashrih al-badan* (*Anatomy of the body*) of Mansur ibn Ilyas (c. 1390) contained comprehensive diagrams of the body's structural, nervous and circulatory systems. During the Black Death bubonic plague in 14th century alAndalus, Ibn Khatima and Ibn al-Khatib hypothesized that infectious diseases are caused by "contagious entities" which enter the human body. Other medical innovations first introduced by Muslim physicians include the discovery of the immune system, the use of animal testing, and the combination of medicine with other sciences (including agriculture, botany, chemistry, and pharmacology), as well as the invention of the injection syringe by Ammar ibn Ali al-Mawsili in 9th century Iraq, the first drugstores in Baghdad (754), the distinction between medicine and pharmacy by the 12th century, and the discovery of at least 2,000 medicinal and chemical substances.

Formal Sciences

Logic

Early Islamic law placed importance on formulating standards of argument, which gave rise to a novel approach to logic in Kalam, but this approach was later influenced by ideas from Greek philosophy and Hellenistic philosophy with the rise of the Mu'tazili theologians, who highly valued Aristotle's *Organon*. The works of Hellenistic-influenced Islamic philosophers were crucial in the reception of Aristotelian logic in medieval Europe, along with the commentaries on the *Organon* by Averroes. The works of al-Farabi, Avicenna, al-Ghazali and other Muslim logicians who often criticized and corrected Aristotelian logic and introduced their own forms of logic, also played a central role in the subsequent development of medieval European logic.

Islamic logic not only included the study of formal patterns of inference and their validity but also elements of the philosophy of language and elements of epistemology and metaphysics. Due to disputes with Arabic grammarians, Islamic philosophers were very interested in working out the relationship between logic and language, and they devoted much discussion to the question of the subject matter and aims of logic in relation to reasoning and speech. In the area of formal logical analysis, they elaborated upon the theory of terms, propositions and syllogisms. They considered the syllogism to be the form to which all rational argumentation could be reduced, and they regarded syllogistic theory as the focal point of logic. Even poetics was considered as a syllogistic art in some fashion by many major Islamic logicians.

Important developments made by Muslim logicians included the development of "Avicennian logic" as a replacement of Aristotelian logic. Avicenna's system of logic was responsible for the introduction of hypothetical syllogism, temporal modal logic, and inductive logic. Other important developments in Islamic philosophy include the development of a strict science of citation, the isnad or "backing", and the development of a scientific method of open inquiry to disprove claims, the ijtihad, which could be generally applied to many types of questions. From the 12th century, despite the logical sophistication of al-Ghazali, the rise of the Asharite School in the late middle Ages slowly limited original work on logic in the Islamic world, though it did continue into the 15th century.

Mathematics

"Recent research paints a new picture of the debt that we owe to Islamic mathematics. Certainly many of the ideas which were previously thought to have been brilliant new conceptions due to European mathematicians of the sixteenth, seventeenth and eighteenth centuries are now known to have been developed by Arabic/Islamic mathematicians around four centuries earlier."

Al-Khwarizmi (780-850), from whose name the word algorithm derives, contributed significantly to algebra, which is named after his book, *Kitab al-Jabr*, the first book on elementary algebra. He also introduced what is now known as Arabic numerals, which originally came from India, though Muslim mathematicians did make several refinements to the number system, such as the introduction of decimal point notation. Al-Kindi (801-873) was a pioneer in cryptanalysis and cryptology. He gave the first known recorded explanations of cryptanalysis and frequency analysis in *A Manuscript on Deciphering Cryptographic Messages*.

The first known proof by mathematical induction appears in a book written by Al-Karaji around 1000 AD, who used it to prove the binomial theorem, Pascal's triangle, and the sum of integral cubes. The historian of mathematics, F. Woepcke, praised Al-Karaji for being "the first who introduced the theory of algebraic calculus." Ibn al-Haytham was the first mathematician to derive the formula for the sum of the fourth powers, and using the method of induction, he developed a method for determining the general formula for the sum of any integral powers, which was fundamental to the development of integral calculus. The 11th century poet-mathematician Omar Khayyám was the first to find general geometric solutions of cubic equations and laid the foundations for the development of analytic geometry, algebraic geometry and non-Euclidean geometry. Sharaf al-Din al-Tusi (1135-1213) found algebraic and num-erical solutions to cubic equations and was the first to discover the derivative of cubic polynomials, an important result in differential calculus.

Other achievements of Muslim mathematicians include the invention of spherical trigonometry, the discovery of all the trigonometric functions besides sine and cosine, early inquiry which aided the development of analytic geometry by Ibn al-Haytham, the first refutations of Euclidean geometry and the parallel postulate by Nasîr al-Dîn al-Tûsî, the first attempt at a non-Euclidean geometry by Sadr al-Din, the development of symbolic algebra by Abû al-Hasan ibn Alî al-Qalasâdî, and numerous other advances in algebra, arithmetic, calculus, cryptography, geometry, number theory and trigonometry.

Natural Sciences

Astrology

Islamic astrology, in Arabic *ilm al-nujum* is the study of the heavens by early Muslims. In early Arabic sources, *ilm al-nujum* was used to refer to both astronomy and astrology. In medieval sources, however, a clear distinction was made between *ilm al-nujum* (science of the stars) or *ilm al-falak* (science of the celestial orbs), referring to astrology, and *ilm al-haya* (science of the figure of the heavens), referring to astronomy. Both fields were rooted in Greek, Persian, and Indian traditions. Despite consistent critiques of astrology by scientists and religious scholars, astrological prognostications required a fair amount of exact scientific knowledge and thus gave partial incentive for the study and development of astronomy.

The first semantic distinction between astronomy and astrology was given by al-Biruni in the 11th century, though he himself refuted the study of astrology. The study of astrology was also refuted by other Muslim astronomers at the time, including al-Farabi, Ibn al-Haytham, Avicenna and Averroes. Their reasons for refuting astrology were both due to the methods used by astrologers being conjectural rather than empirical and also due to the views of astrologers conflicting with orthodox Islam.

Astronomy

In astronomy, the works of Egyptian/Greek astronomer Ptolemy, particularly the *Almagest*, and the Indian work of Brahmagupta, were significantly refined over the years by Muslim astronomers. The astronomical tables of Al-Khwarizmi and of Maslamah Ibn Ahmad al-Majriti served as important sources of information for Latinized European thinkers rediscovering the works of astronomy, where extensive interest in astrology was discouraged. In the 11th century, Muslim astronomers began questioning the Ptolemaic system, beginning with Ibn al-Haytham, and they were the first to conduct elaborate experiments related to astronomical phenomena, beginning with Abû al-Rayhân al-Bîrûnî's introduction of the experimental method into astronomy.

Many of them made changes and corrections to the Ptolemaic model and proposed alternative non- Ptolemaic models within a geocentric framework. In particular, the corrections and critiques of al-Battani, Ibn al-Haytham, and Averroes, and the non-Ptolemaic models of the Maragha astronomers, Nasir al-Din al-Tusi (Tusi-couple),

Mo'ayyeduddin Urdi (Urdi lemma), and Ibn al-Shatir, were later adapted into the heliocentric Copernican model, and that Copernicus' arguments for the Earth's rotation were similar to those of al-Tusi and Ali al-Qushji. Some have referred to the achievements of the Maragha School as a "Maragha Revolution", "Maragha School Revolution", or "Scientific Revolution before the Renaissance".

Other contributions from Muslim astronomers include Biruni speculating that the Milky Way galaxy is a collection of numerous nebulous stars, the development of a planetary model without any epicycles by Ibn Bajjah (Avempace), the development of universal astrolabes, the invention of numerous other astronomical instruments, continuation of inquiry into the motion of the planets, Ja'far Muhammad ibn Mûsâ ibn Shâkir's discovery that the heavenly bodies and celestial spheres are subject to the same physical laws as Earth, the first elaborate experiments related to astronomical phenomena and the first semantic distinction between astronomy and astrology by Abû al-Rayhân al-Bîrûnî, the use of exacting empirical observations and experimental techniques, the discovery that the celestial spheres are not solid and that the heavens are less dense than the air by Ibn al-Haytham, the separation of natural philosophy from astronomy by Ibn al-Haytham and al-Qushji, the rejection of the Ptolemaic model on empirical rather than philosophical grounds by Ibn al-Shatir, and the first empirical observational evidence of the Earth's rotation by al-Tusi and al-Qushji. Several Muslim astronomers also discussed the possibility of a heliocentric model with elliptical orbits, such as Ja'far ibn Muhammad Abu Ma'shar al-Balkhi, Ibn al-Haytham, Abû al-Rayhân al-Bîrûnî, al-Sijzi, 'Umar al-Katibi al-Qazwini, and Qutb al-Din al-Shirazi.

Chemistry

The 9th century chemist, Geber (Jabir ibn Hayyan), is considered a pioneer of chemistry, for introducing an early experimental method for chemistry, as well as the alembic, still, retort, pure distillation, liquefaction, crystallisation, purification, oxidisation, evaporation, and filtration. Al-Kindi was the first to refute the study of traditional alchemy and the theory of the transmutation of metals, followed by Abû Rayhân al-Bîrûnî, Avicenna, and Ibn Khaldun. Avicenna also invented steam distillation and produced the first essential oils, which led to the development of aromatherapy. Razi first distilled petroleum, invented kerosene and kerosene lamps, soap bars and modern recipes for soap, and antiseptics.

In his *Doubts about Galen,* al-Razi was also the first to prove both Aristotle's theory of classical elements and Galen's theory of humourism wrong using an experimental method. In the 13th century, Nasîr al-Dîn al-Tûsî stated an early version of the law of conservation of mass, noting that a body of matter is able to change, but is not able to disappear. "Chemistry as a science was almost created by the Moslems; for in this field, where the Greeks (so far as we know) were confined to industrial experience and vague hypothesis, the Saracens introduced precise observation, controlled experiment, and careful records. They invented and named the alembic (al-anbiq), chemically analyzed innumerable substances, composed lapidaries, distinguished alkalis and acids, investigated their affinities, studied and manufactured hundreds of drugs. Alchemy, which the Moslems inherited from Egypt, contributed to chemistry by a thousand incidental discoveries, and by its method, which was the most scientific of all medieval operations."

George Sarton wrote in the *Introduction to the History of Science*:

"We find in his (Jabir, Geber) writings remarkably sound views on methods of chemical research, a theory on the geologic formation of metals (the six metals differ essentially because of different proportions of sulphur and mercury in them); preparation of various substances (e.g., basic lead carbor..tic, arsenic and antimony from their sulphides)."

Earth sciences

Muslim scientists made a number of contributions to the Earth sciences. Alkindus was the first to introduce experimentation into the Earth sciences. Biruni is considered a pioneer of geodesy for his important contributions to the field, along with his significant contributions to geography and geology.

Among his writings on geology, Biruni wrote the following on the geology of India:

"But if you see the soil of India with your own eyes and meditate on its nature, if you consider the rounded stones found in earth however deeply you dig, stones that are huge near the mountains and where the rivers have a violent current: stones that are of smaller size at a greater distance from the mountains and where the streams flow more slowly: stones that appear pulverised in the shape of sand where the streams begin to stagnate near their mouths and near the sea - if you consider all this you can scarcely help thinking that India was once a sea, which by degrees has been filled up by the alluvium of the streams."

John J. O'Connor and Edmund F. Robertson write in the *MacTutor History of Mathematics archive*:

"Important contributions to geodesy and geography were also made by al-Biruni. He introduced techniques to measure the earth and distances on it using triangulation. He found the radius of the earth to be 6339.6 km, a value not obtained in the West until the 16th century. His *Masudic canon* contains a table giving the coordinates of six hundred places, almost all of which he had direct knowledge."

Fielding H. Garrison wrote in the *History of Medicine*:

"The Saracens themselves were the originators not only of algebra, chemistry, and geology, but of many of the socalled improvements or refinements of civilization..."

George Sarton wrote in the *Introduction to the History of Science*:

"We find in his (Jabir, Geber) writings remarkably sound views on methods of chemical research, a theory on the geologic formation of metals (the six metals differ essentially because of different proportions of sulphur and mercury in them)..."

In geology, Avicenna hypothesized on two causes of mountains in *The Book of Healing* (1027) and developed the law of superposition and concept of uniformitarianism. In cartography, the Piri Reis map drawn by the Ottoman cartographer Piri Reis in 1513 was one of the earliest world maps to include the Americas, and perhaps the first to include Antarctica. His map of the world was considered the most accurate in the 16th century.

The earliest known treatises dealing with environmentalism and environmental science, especially pollution, were Arabic treatises written by al-Kindi, al-Razi, Ibn Al-Jazzar, al-Tamimi, al-Masihi, Avicenna, Ali ibn Ridwan, Abd-el-latif, and Ibn al-Nafis. Their works covered a number of subjects related to pollution such as air pollution, water pollution, soil contamination, municipal solid waste mishandling, and environmental impact assessments of certain localities. Cordoba, al-Andalus also had the first waste containers and waste disposal facilities for litter collection.

Physics

In the optics field of physics, Ibn Sahl (c. 940-1000), a mathematician and physicist connected with the court of Baghdad, wrote a treatise *On Burning Mirrors and Lenses* in 984 in which he set out his understanding of how curved mirrors and lenses bend and focus light. Ibn Sahl is now credited with first discovering the law of refraction, usually called Snell's law. He used this law to work out the shapes of lenses that focus light with no geometric aberrations, known as anaclastic lenses.

Ibn al-Haytham (Alhazen) (965-1039), who is considered a pioneer of optics and the scientific method, developed a broad theory of light and optics in his *Book of Optics* which explained vision, using geometry and anatomy, and stated that each point on an illuminated area or object radiates light rays in every direction, but that only one ray from each point, which strikes the eye perpendicularly, can be seen. The other rays strike at different angles and are not seen. He used the example of the camera obscura and pinhole camera, which produces an inverted image, to support his argument. This contradicted Pto-lemy's theory of vision that objects are seen by rays of light emanating from the eyes.

Alhacen held light rays to be streams of minute particles that travelled at a finite speed. He improved accurately described the refraction of light, and discovered the laws of refraction. He dealt at length with the theory of various physical phenomena like shadows, eclipses, and the rainbow. He also attempted to explain binocular vision and the moon illusion. Through these extensive researches on optics, he is considered a pioneer of modern optics. His *Book of Optics* was later translated into Latin, and has been ranked alongside Isaac Newton's *Philosophiae Naturalis Principia Mathematica* as one of the most influential books in the history of physics, for initiating a revolution in optics and visual perception.

Avicenna (980-1037) agreed that the speed of light is finite, as he "observed that if the perception of light is due to the emission of some sort of particles by a luminous source, the speed of light must be finite." Abû Rayhân alBîrûnî (973-1048) also agreed that light has a finite speed, and he was the first to discover that the speed of light is much faster than the speed of sound. Qutb al-Din al-Shirazi (1236-1311) and Kamâl al-Dîn al-Fârisî (1260-1320) gave the first correct explanations for the rainbow phenomenon.

In mechanics, Ja'far Muhammad ibn Mûsâ ibn Shâkir (800-873) of the Banû Mûsâ hypothesized that heavenly bodies and celestial spheres were subject to the same laws of physics as Earth, and in his *Astral Motion* and *The Force of Attraction*, he also hypothesized that there was a force of attraction between heavenly bodies. Abû Rayhân al-Bîrûnî (973-1048), and later al-Khazini, developed experimental scientific methods for mechanics, especially the fields of statics and dynamics, particularly for determining specific weights, such as those based on the theory of balances and weighing. Muslim physicists unified statics and dynamics into the science of mechanics, and they combined the fields of hydrostatics with dynamics to give birth to hydrodynamics. They applied the mathematical theories of ratios and infinitesimal techniques, and introduced algebraic and fine calculation techniques into the field of statics.

They were also generalized the theory of the centre of gravity and applied it to three-dimensional bodies. They also founded the theory of the ponderable lever and created the "science of gravity" which was later further developed in medieval Europe. Al-Biruni also theorized that acceleration is connected with non-uniform motion. In mechanics, Ibn al-Haytham discussed the theory of attraction between masses, and it seems that he was aware of the magnitude of acceleration due to gravity, and he stated that the heavenly bodies "were accountable to the laws of physics". Ibn al-Haytham also enunciated the law of inertia when he stated that a body moves perpetually unless an external force stops it or changes its direction of motion.

He also developed the concept of momentum, though he did not quantify this concept mathematically. Avicenna (980-1037) developed the concept of momentum, referring to impetus as being proportional to weight times velocity. His theory of motion was also consistent with the concept of inertia in classical mechanics. In 1121, al-Khazini, in *The Book of the Balance of Wisdom*, proposed that the gravity and gravitational potential energy of a body varies depending on its distance from the centre of the Earth, and in statics, he clearly differentiated between force, mass and weight. Avempace (d. 1138) argued that there is always a reaction force for every force exerted, though he did not refer to the reaction force as being equal to the exerted force. His theory of motion had an important influence on later physicists like Galileo Galilei.

Hibat Allah Abu'l-Barakat al-Baghdaadi (1080-1165) wrote a critique of Aristotelian physics entitled *al-Mu'tabar,* where he negated Aristotle's idea that a constant force produces uniform motion, as he theorized that a force applied continuously produces acceleration. He also described acceleration as the rate of change of velocity. Averroes (1126–1198) defined and measured force as "the rate at which work is done in changing the kinetic condition of a material body" and correctly argued "that the effect and measure of force is change in the kinetic condition of a materially resistant mass." In the early 16th century, alBirjandi developed a hypothesis similar to "circular inertia." The Muslim developments in mechanics laid the foundations for the later development of classical mechanics in early modern Europe.

Zoology

In the zoology field of biology, Muslim biologists developed theories on evolution which were widely taught in medieval Islamic schools. John William Draper, a contemporary of Charles Darwin, considered the "Mohammedan theory of evolution" to be developed "much farther than we are disposed to do, extending them even to inorganic or mineral things." According to al-Khazini, ideas on evolution were widespread among "common people" in the Islamic world by the 12th century.

The first Muslim biologist to develop a theory on evolution was al-Jahiz (781-869). He wrote on the effects of the environment on the likelihood of an animal to survive, and he first described the struggle for existence. Al-Jahiz was also the first to discuss food chains, and was also an early adherent of environmental determinism, arguing that the environment can determine the physical characteristics of the inhabitants of a certain community and that the origin of different human skin colors is the result of the environment. Ibn al-Haytham wrote a book in which he argued for evolutionism (although not natural selection), and numerous other Islamic scholars and scientists, such as Ibn Miskawayh, the Brethren of Purity, al-Khazini, Abû Rayhân al-Bîrûnî, Nasir al-Din Tusi, and Ibn Khaldun, discussed and developed these ideas.

Translated into Latin, these works began to appear in the West after the Renaissance and appear to have had an impact on Western science. Ibn Miskawayh's *al-Fawz al-Asghar* and the Brethren of Purity's *Encyclopedia of the Brethren of Purity* (*The Epistles of Ikhwan al-Safa*) expressed evolutionary ideas on how species evolved from matter, into vapor, and then water, then minerals, then plants, then animals, then apes, and then humans. These works were known in Europe and likely had an influence on Darwinism.

Social Sciences

Sociology and Anthropology

Significant contributions were made to the social sciences in the Islamic civilization. Abû al-Rayhân al-Bîrûnî (973-1048) has been described as "the first anthropologist". He wrote detailed comparative studies on the anthropology of peoples, religions and cultures in the Middle East, Mediterranean and South Asia. Biruni's anthropology of religion was only possible for a scholar deeply immersed in the lore of other nations. Biruni has also been praised by several scholars for his Islamic anthropology. Biruni is also considered a pioneer of Indology. Al-Saghani (died 990) wrote some of the earliest comments on the history of science, which included a comparison between the more theoretical approach of the "ancients" (including the ancient Egyptians, Babylonians, Greeks and Indians) to that of the more experimental approach of the "modern scholars" (the Muslim scientists of his time). Al-Muqaddasi (b. 945) also made contributions to the social sciences.

Ibn Khaldun (1332-1406) is considered a forerunner of several social sciences such as demography, cultural history, and historiography, the philosophy of history, sociology, and economics. He is best known for his *Muqaddimah* (Latinized as *Prolegomenon*). Some of the ideas he introduced in the *Muqaddimah* include social philosophy, social conflict theories, social cohesion, social capital, social networks, dialectics, the Laffer curve, the historical method, systemic bias, the rise and fall of civilizations, feedback loops, systems theory, and corporate social responsibility. He also introduced the scientific method into the social sciences.

Franz Rosenthal wrote in the *History of Muslim Historiography*:

"Muslim historiography has at all times been united by the closest ties with the general development of scholarship in Islam, and the position of historical knowledge in Muslim education has exercised a decisive influence upon the intellectual level of historical writing....The Muslims achieved a definite advance beyond previous historical writing in the sociological understanding of history and the systematisation of historiography. The development of modern historical writing seems to have gained considerably in speed and substance through the utilization of a Muslim Literature which enabled western historians, from the seventeenth century on, to see a large section of the world through foreign eyes. The Muslim historiography helped indirectly and modestly to shape present day historical thinking."

Psychology

"Islamic psychology" or *Ilm-al Nafsiat* refers to the study of the *Nafs* ("self" or "psyche") in the Islamic world and encompassed a "broad range of topics including the *qalb* (heart), the *ruh* (spirit), the *aql* (intellect) and *irada* (will)." Al-Kindi (Alkindus) was the first to experiment with music therapy, and Ali ibn Sahl Rabban al-Tabari was the first to practice *'al-'ilaj al-nafs* ("psychotherapy"). The concepts of *al-tibb al-ruhani* ("spiritual health") and "mental hygiene" were introduced by Ahmed ibn Sahl al-Balkhi, who was "probably the first cognitive and medical psychologist to clearly differentiate between neuroses and psychoses, to classify neurotic disorders, and to show in detail how rational and spiritual cognitive therapies can be used to treat each one of his classified disorders." Al-Razi (Rhazes) made significant advances in psychiatry in his landmark texts *El-Mansuri* and *Al-Hawi*, which presented definitions, symptoms and treatments for mental illnesses and problems related to mental health.

He also ran the psychiatric ward of a Baghdad hospital. Such institutions could not exist in Europe at the time because of fear of demonic possessions. Al-Farabi wrote the first treatises on social psychology and dealt with consciousness studies. In al-Andalus, Abulcasis pioneered neurosurgery, while Ibn Zuhr (Avenzoar) gave the first accurate descriptions on neurological disorders and contributed to modern neuropharmacology, and Averroes suggested the existence of Parkinson's disease.

Ali ibn Abbas al-Majusi discussed "the relationship between certain psychological events to the physiological changes in the body", while Avicenna anticipated the word association test, discussed neuropsychiatry in *The Canon of Medicine*, and described the first thought experiments on self-awareness and self aconsciousness.

Ibn al-Haytham (Alhazen) is considered by some a forerunner of experimental psychology, for his experimental work on the psychology of visual perception in the *Book of Optics*, where he was the first scientist to argue that vision occurs in the brain, rather than the eyes. He pointed out that personal experience has an effect on what people see and how they see, and that vision and perception are subjective. He was also the first to combine physics and psychology to form psychophysics, and his investigations and experiments on psychology and visual perception included sensation, variations in sensitivity, sensation of touch, perception of colours, perception of darkness, the psychological explanation of the moon illusion, and binocular vision. Biruni was also a pioneer of experimental psychology, as he was the first to empirically describe the concept of reaction time.

Historiography of Islamic Science

The history of science in the Islamic world, like all history, is filled with questions of interpretation. Historians of science generally consider that the study of Islamic science, like all history, must be seen within the particular circumstances of time and place. A. I. Sabra opened a recent overview of Arabic science by noting, "I trust no one would wish to contest the proposition that all of history is local history ... and the history of science is no exception."

Some scholars avoid such local historical approaches and seek to identify essential relations between Islam and science that applies at all times and places. The Pakistani physicist, Pervez Hoodbhoy, portrayed "religious fanaticism to be the dominant relation of religion and science in Islam". Sociologist Toby Huff claimed that Islam lacked the "rationalist view of man and nature" that became dominant in Europe. The Persian philosopher and historian of science, Seyyed Hossein Nasr saw a more positive connection in "an Islamic science that was spiritual and antisecular" which "point[ed] the way to a new 'Islamic science' that would avoid the dehumanizing and despiritualizing mistakes of Western science."

Nasr identified a distinctly Muslim approach to science, flowing from Islamic monotheism and the related theological prohibition against portraying graven images. In science, this is reflected in a philosophical disinterest in describing individual material objects, their properties and characteristics and instead a concern with the ideal, the Platonic form, which exists in matter as an expression of the will of the Creator. Thus one can "see why mathematics was to make such a strong appeal to the Muslim: its abstract nature furnished the bridge that Muslims were seeking between multiplicity and unity."

Some historians of science, however, question the value of drawing boundaries that label the sciences, and the scientists who practice them, in specific cultural, civilizational, or linguistic terms. Consider the case of Nasir al-Din Tusi (1201–1274), who invented his mathematical theorem, the Tusi Couple, while he was director of Maragheh observatory. Tusi's patron and founder of the observatory was the non-Muslim Mongol conqueror of Baghdad, Hulagu Khan. The Tusi-couple "was first encountered in an Arabic text, written by a man who spoke Persian at home, and used that theorem, like many other astronomers who followed him and were all working in the "Arabic/Islamic" world, in order to reform classical Greek astronomy, and then have his theorem in turn be translated into Byzantine Greek towards the beginning of the fourteenth century, only to be used later by Copernicus and others in Latin texts of Renaissance Europe."

3

Science and Islam in the Medieval Period

Science in medieval Islam, also known as Islamic science, is a term used in the history of science to refer to the science developed in the Islamic world between 7th and 16th centuries, a period also known as the Islamic Golden Age. Most texts during this period were written in Arabic, a *lingua franca* of this period, although most scientists were Muslims but they were of diverse ethnicity (mostly Persian but also some of Arab, Berber, Moorish, and Turkic background), in addition to some from other religious backgrounds (Christian, Jewish, Sabian, Zoroastrian, and irreligious).

Early Islamic Philosophy

Early Islamic philosophy or classical Islamic philosophy is a period of intense philosophical development beginning in the 2nd century AH of the Islamic calendar (early 9th century CE) and lasting until the 6th century AH (late 12th century CE). The period is known as the Islamic Golden Age, and the achievements of this period had a crucial influence in the development of modern philosophy and science. This period starts with al-Kindi in the 9th century and ends with Averroes (Ibn Rushd) at the end of 12th century. The death of Averroes effectively marks the end of a particular discipline of Islamic philosophy usually called the *Peripatetic Arabic School*, and philosophical activity declined significantly in Western Islamic countries, namely in Islamic Spain and North Africa, though it persisted for much longer in the Eastern countries, in particular Persia and India where several schools of philosophy continued to flourish: Avicennism, Illuminationist philosophy, Mystical philosophy, and Transcendent theosophy.

Some of the significant achievements of early Muslim philosophers included the development of a strict science of citation, the isnad or "backing"; the development of a method of open inquiry to disprove claims, the ijtihad, which could be generally applied to many types of questions (although which to apply it to is an ethical question); the willingness to both accept and challenge authority within the same process; recognition that science and philosophy are both subordinate to morality, and that moral choices are prior to any investigation or concern with either; the separation of theology (kalam) and law (shariah) during the early Abbasid period, a precursor to secularism; the distinction between religion and philosophy, marking the beginning of secular thought; the beginning of a peer review process; early ideas on evolution; the beginnings of the scientific method, an important contribution to the philosophy of science; the first forms of non-Aristotelian logic and the introduction of temporal modal logic and inductive logic; the beginning of social philosophy, including the formulation of theories on social cohesion and social conflict; the beginning of the philosophy of history; the development of the philosophical novel and the concepts of empiricism and tabula rasa; and distinguishing between essence and existence.

Thomas Aquinas knew of at least some of the Mutazilite work, particularly Avicennism and Averroism, and the Renaissance and the use of empirical methods were inspired at least in part by Arabic works translated into Latin during the Renaissance of the 12th century, and taken during the Reconquista in 1492. Early Islamic philosophy can be divided into clear sets of influences, branches, schools, and fields, as described below.

Origin

Muhammad

The life of Muhammad or sira which generated both the Qur'an (revelation) and hadith (his daily utterances and discourses on social and legal matters), during which philosophy was defined by Muslims as consisting in acceptance or rejection of his message. Together the sira and hadith constitute the sunnah and are validated by isnad ("backing") to determine the likely truth of the report of any given saying of Muhammad. Key figures are Imam Ja'far al-Sadiq, Imam Bukhari, Imam Muslim, Al-Tirmidhi, Ibn Majah, Abu Dawud and Al-Nasa'i. Each sifted through literally millions of hadith to accept a list of fewer than 10,000. This work, which was not completed until the 10th century, began shortly after The Farewell Sermon in 631, after which Muhammad could not mediate disputes. After his death Abu Bakr began to collect all fragments of his sayings.

Branches

Kalam

With Kalam, questions about the sira and hadith, as well as science (Islamic science) and law (fiqh and sharia), began to be investigated beyond the scope of Muhammad's beliefs. This period is characterized by emergence of ijtihad and the first fiqh. As the Sunnah became published and accepted, philosophy separate from Muslim theology was discouraged due to a lack of participants. During this period, traditions similar to Socratic Method began to evolve, but philosophy remained subordinate to religion. "Kalam" generally referred to the Islamic tradition of seeking theological principles through dialectic.

Independent minds exploiting the methods of ijtihad sought to investigate the doctrines of the Qur'an, which until then had been accepted in faith on the authority of divine revelation. One of first debates was that between partisan of the *Qadar* (Arabic: qadaraý, to have power), who affirmed free will, and the *Jabarites* (jabar, force, constraint), who maintained the belief in fatalism. At the second century of the Hijra, a new movement arose in the theological school of Basra, Iraq. A pupil, Wasil ibn Ata, who was expelled from the school because his answers were contrary to then orthodox Islamic tradition and became leader of a new school, and systematized the radical opinions of preceding sects, particularly those of the Qadarites.

This new school was called *Mutazilite* (from i'tazala, to separate oneself, to dissent). Its principal dogmas were three:

1. God is an absolute unity, and no attribute can be ascribed to Him.
2. Man is a free agent. It is on account of these two principles that the Mu'tazilities designates them the "Partisans of Justice and Unity".
3. All knowledge necessary for the salvation of man emanates from his reason; humans could acquire knowledge before, as well as after, Revelation, by the sole light of reason. This fact makes knowledge obligatory upon all men, at all times, and in all places.

The Mutazilities, compelled to defend their principles against the orthodox Islam of their day, looked for support in philosophy, and are one of the first to pursue a rational theology called *Ilm-al-Kalam* (Scholastic theology); those professing it were called *Mutakallamin*. This appellation became the common name for all seeking philosophical demonstration in confirmation of religious principles. The first Mutakallamin had to debate both the orthodox and the non-Muslims, and they may be described as occupying the middle ground between those two parties. But subsequent generations were to large extent critical towards the Mutazilite School, especially after formation of the Asharite concepts.

Falsafa

From the 9th century onwards, owing to Caliph al-Ma'mun and his successor, Greek philosophy and Hellenistic philosophy were introduced among the Persians and Arabs, and the Peripatetic and Neoplatonic schools began to find able representatives among them; such were al-Kindi, al-Farabi, Avicenna (Ibn Sina), and Averroes (Ibn Rushd), all of whose fundamental principles were considered as criticized by the Mutakallamin.

During the Abbasid caliphate a number of thinkers and scientists, some of them heterodox Muslims or non-Muslims, played a role in transmitting Greek, Hellenistic, Indian and other pre-Islamic knowledge to the Christian West. They contributed to making Aristotle known in Christian Europe. Three speculative thinkers, the Turk al-Farabi, the Iranian Avicenna and the Arab al-Kindi, combined Aristotelianism and Neoplatonism with other ideas introduced through Islam. They were considered by many as highly unorthodox and a few even described them as non-Islamic philosophers.

From Spain Arabic philosophic literature was translated into Hebrew and Latin, contributing to the development of modern European philosophy. The philosophers Moses Maimonides (a Jew born in Muslim Spain) and Ibn Khaldun (born in modern-day Tunisia), the father of sociology and historiography, were also important philosophers, though the latter did not identify himself as a *falsafa*, but rather a *kalam* author.

Some differences between **Kalam** *and* **Falsafa**

Aristotle attempted to demonstrate the unity of God; but from the view which he maintained, that matter was eternal, it followed that God could not be the Creator of the world. To assert that God's knowledge extends only to the general laws of the universe, and not to individual and accidental things, is tantamount to denying prophecy. One other point shocked the faith of the Mutakallamin – the theory of intellect. The Peripatetics taught that the human soul was only an aptitude – a faculty capable of attaining every variety of passive perfection – and that through information and virtue it became qualified for union with the active intellect, which latter emanates from God. To admit this theory would be to deny the immortality of the soul.

Wherefore the Mutakallamin had, before anything else, to establish a system of philosophy to demonstrate the creation of matter and they adopted to that end the theory of atoms as enunciated by Democritus. They taught that atoms possess neither quantity nor extension. Originally atoms were created by God, and are created now as occasion seems to require. Bodies come into existence or die, through the aggregation or the sunderance of these atoms. But this theory did not remove the objections of philosophy to a creation of matter.

For, indeed, if it be supposed that God commenced His work at a certain definite time by His "will", and for a certain definite object, it must be admitted that He was imperfect before accomplishing His will, or before attaining His object. In order to obviate this difficulty, the Motekallamin extended their theory of the atoms to Time, and claimed that just as Space is constituted of atoms and vacuum, Time, likewise, is constituted of small indivisible moments. The creation of the world once established, it was an easy matter for them to demonstrate the existence of a Creator, and that God is unique, omnipotent, and omniscient.

Main Protagonists of Falsafa and their Critics

The twelfth century saw the apotheosis of pure philosophy and the decline of the Kalam, which latter, being attacked by both the philosophers and the orthodox, perished for lack of champions. This supreme exaltation of philosophy may be attributed, in great measure, to Al-Ghazali (1005-1111) among the Persians, and to Judah ha-Levi (1140) among the Jews. It can be argued that the attacks directed against the philosophers by Ghazali in his work, "Tahafut al-Falasifa" (The Destruction of the Philosophers), not only produced, by reaction, a current favorable to philosophy, but induced the philosophers themselves to profit by his criticism. They thereafter made their theories clearer and their logic closer.

The influence of this reaction brought forth the two greatest philosophers that the Islamic Peripatetic School ever produced, namely, Ibn Bajjah (Avempace) and Ibn Rushd (Averroes), both of whom undertook the defense of philosophy. Since no idea and no literary or philosophical movement ever germinated on Persian or Arabian soil without leaving its impress on the Jews, the Persian Ghazali found an imitator in the person of Judah ha-Levi. This poet also took upon himself to free his religion from what he saw as the shackles of speculative philosophy, and to this end wrote the "Kuzari", in which he sought to discredit all schools of philosophy alike. He passes severe censure upon the Mutakallamin for seeking to support religion by philosophy.

He says, "I consider him to have attained the highest degree of perfection that is convinced of religious truths without having scrutinized them and reasoned over them" ("Kuzari", v.). Then he reduced the chief propositions of the Mutakallamin, to prove the unity of God, to ten in number, describing them at length, and concluding in these terms: "Does the Kalam give us more information concerning God and His attributes than the prophet did?"

(Ib. iii. and iv.) Aristotelianism finds no favor in Judah ha-Levi's eyes, for it is no less given to details and criticism; Neoplatonism alone suited him somewhat, owing to its appeal to his poetic temperament.

Ibn Rushd (or Ibn Roshd or Averroës), the contemporary of Maimonides, closed the first great philosophical era of the Muslims. The theories of Ibn Rushd do not differ fundamentally from those of Ibn Bajjah and Ibn Tufail, who only follow the teachings of Ibn Sina and Al-Farabi. Like all Islamic Peripatetics, Ibn Rushd admits the hypothesis of the intelligence of the spheres and the hypothesis of universal emanation, through which motion is communicated from place to place to all parts of the universe as far as the supreme world—hypotheses which, in the mind of the Arabic philosophers, did away with the dualism involved in Aristotle's doctrine of pure energy and eternal matter. His ideas on the separation of philosophy and religion, further developed by the Averroist School of philosophy, were later influential in the development of modern secularism. Ibn Rushd is thus regarded as the founding father of secular thought in Western Europe.

But while Al-Farabi, Ibn Sina, and other Persian and Muslim philosophers hurried, so to speak, over subjects that trenched on religious dogmas, Ibn Rushd delighted in dwelling upon them with full particularity and stress. Thus he says, "Not only is matter eternal, but form is potentially inherent in matter; otherwise, it were a creation *ex nihilo*". According to this theory, therefore, the existence of this world is not only a possibility, as Ibn Sina declared—in order to make concessions to the orthodox— but also a necessity.

Driven from the Islamic schools, Islamic philosophy found a refuge with the Jews who belongs the honor of having transmitted it to the Christian world. A series of eminent men—such as the Ibn Tibbons, Narboni, Gersonides—joined in translating the Arabic philosophical works into Hebrew and commenting upon them. The works of Ibn Rushd especially became the subject of their study, due in great measure to Maimonides, who, in a letter addressed to his pupil Joseph ben Judah; spoke in the highest terms of Ibn Rushd's commentary.

It should be mentioned that this depiction of intellectual tradition in Islamic Lands is mainly dependent upon what West could understand (or was willing to understand) from this long era. In contrast, there are some historians and philosophers who do not agree with this account and describe this era in a completely different way. Their main point of dispute is on the influence of different philosophers on Islamic Philosophy, especially the comparative importance of eastern intellectuals such as Ibn Sina and of western thinkers such as Ibn Rushd.

Judeo-Islamic Philosophy

The oldest Jewish religio-philosophical work preserved is that of Saadia Gaon (892-942), *Emunot ve-Deot*, "The Book of Beliefs and Opinions". In this work Saadia treats the questions that interested the Mutakallamin, such as the creation of matter, the unity of God, the divine attributes, the soul, etc. Saadia criticizes other philosophers severely. For Saadia there was no problem as to creation: God created the world *ex nihilo*, just as the Bible attests; and he contests the theory of the Mutakallamin in reference to atoms, which theory, he declares, is just as contrary to reason and religion as the theory of the philosophers professing the eternity of matter.

To prove the unity of God, Saadia uses the demonstrations of the Mutakallamin. Only the attributes of essence (*sifat al-dhatia*) can be ascribed to God, but not the attributes of action (*sifat-ai-fi'aliya*). The soul is a substance more delicate even than that of the celestial spheres. Here Saadia controverts the Mutakallamin, who considered the soul an "accident" *'arad* (compare Guide for the Perplexed i. 74), and employs the following one of their premises to justify his position: "Only a substance can be the substratum of an accident" (that is, of a non-essential property of things). Saadia argues: "If the soul be an accident only, it can itself have no such accidents as wisdom, joy, love", etc. Saadia was thus in every way a supporter of the Kalam; and if at times he deviated from its doctrines, it was owing to his religious views; just as the Jewish and Muslim Peripatetics stopped short in their respective Aristotelianism whenever there was danger of wounding orthodox religion.

Schools

Farabism

Al-Farabi (Alfarabi) was a founder of his own school of Islamic philosophy but which was later overshadowed by Avicennism. Al-Farabi's school of philosophy "breaks with the philosophy of Plato and Aristotle [... and ...] moves from metaphysics to methodology, a move that anticipates modernity", and "at the level of philosophy, Alfarabi unites theory and practice [... and] in the sphere of the political he liberates practice from theory". His Neoplatonic theology is also more than just metaphysics as rhetoric. In his attempt to think through the nature of a First Cause, Alfarabi discovers the limits of human knowledge".

Al-Farabi had great influence on science and philosophy for several centuries, and was widely regarded to be second only to Aristotle in knowledge (alluded to by his title of "the Second Teacher") in his time. His work, aimed at synthesis of philosophy and Sufism, paved the way for the work of Ibn Sina (Avicenna).

Avicennism

Due to Avicenna's (Ibn Sina's) successful reconciliation between Aristotelianism and Neoplatonism along with Kalam, Avicennism eventually became the leading school of Islamic philosophy by the 12th century. Avicenna had become a central authority on philosophy by then, and several scholars in the 12th century commented on his strong influence at the time:

"People nowadays [believe] that truth is whatever [Ibn Sina] says, that it is inconceivable for him to err, and that whoever contradicts him in anything he says cannot be rational."

Avicennism was also influential in medieval Europe, particularly his doctrines on the nature of the soul and his existence-essence distinction, along with the debates and censure that they raised in scholastic Europe. This was particularly the case in Paris, where Avicennism was later proscribed in 1210. Nevertheless, his psychology and theory of knowledge influenced William of Auvergne and Albertus Magnus, and his metaphysics had an impact on the thought of Thomas Aquinas.

Averroism

Averroes (Ibn Rushd) is most famous for his commentaries on Aristotle's works and for writing *The Incoherence of the Incoherence* in which he defended the *falasifa* against al-Ghazali's *The Incoherence of the Philosophers.* While he had very little influence in the Islamic world, which was then dominated by Avicennian philosophy and Ash'ari theology, Averroism became very influential in medieval Europe, especially among the Scholastics. Averroism eventually led to the development of modern secularism, for which Ibn Rushd is considered as the founding father of secular thought in Western Europe. The concept of "existence precedes essence", a key foundational concept of existentialism, can also be found in the works of Averroes, as a reaction to Avicenna's concept of "essence precedes existence".

Ethics

Environmental Philosophy

Perhaps due to resource scarcity in most Islamic nations, there was an emphasis on limited (and some claim also sustainable) use of natural capital, i.e. producing land. Traditions of haram and hima and early urban planning were expressions of strong social obligations to stay within carrying capacity and to preserve the natural environment as an obligation of khalifa or "stewardship".

Muhammad is considered a pioneer of environmentalism for his teachings on environmental preservation. His hadiths on agriculture and environmental philosophy were compiled in the "Book of Agriculture" of the *Sahih Bukhari*, which included the following saying:

"There is none amongst the believers who plants a tree, or sows a seed, and then a bird, or a person, or an animal eats thereof, but it is regarded as having given a charitable gift [for which there is great recompense]."

Several such statements concerning the environment are also found in the *Qur'an*, such as the following:

"And there is no animal in the earth or bird that flies with its two wings, but that they are communities like you."

The earliest known treatises dealing with environmentalism and environmental science, especially pollution, were Arabic medical treatises written by al-Kindi, Qusta ibn Luqa, al-Razi, Ibn Al-Jazzar, al-Tamimi, al-Masihi, Avicenna, Ali ibn Ridwan, Ibn Jumay, Isaac Israeli ben Solomon, Abd-el-latif, Ibn al-Quff, and Ibn al-Nafis. Their works covered a number of subjects related to pollution such as air pollution, water pollution, soil contamination, municipal solid waste mishandling, and environmental impact assessments of certain localities. Cordoba, al-Andalus also had the first waste containers and waste disposal facilities for litter collection.

Medical Ethics

The ethical standards of Muslim physicians was first laid down in the 9th century by Ishaq bin Ali Rahawi, who wrote the *Adab al-Tabib* (*Conduct of a Physician*), the first treatist dedicated to medical ethics. He regarded physicians as "guardians of souls and bodies", and wrote twenty chapters on various topics related to medical ethics, including:

- What the physician must avoid and beware of
- The manners of visitors
- The care of remedies by the physician
- The dignity of the medical profession
- The examination of physicians
- The removal of corruption among physicians

Humanism

Many medieval Muslim thinkers pursued humanistic, rational and scientific discourses in their search for knowledge, meaning and values. A wide range of Islamic writings on love poetry, history and philosophical theology show that medieval Islamic thought was open to the humanistic ideas of individualism, occasional secularism, skepticism and liberalism.

Another reason the Islamic world flourished during the Middle Ages was an early emphasis on freedom of speech, as summarized by al-Hashimi (a cousin of Caliph al-Ma'mun) in the following letter to one of the religious opponents he was attempting to convert through reason:

"Bring forward all the arguments you wish and say whatever you please and speak your mind freely. Now that you are safe and free to say whatever you please appoint some arbitrator who will impartially judge between us and lean only towards the truth and be free from the empery of passion, and that arbitrator shall be Reason, whereby God makes us responsible for our own rewards and punishments. Herein I have dealt justly with you and have given you full security and am ready to accept whatever decision Reason may give for me or against me. For "There is no compulsion in religion" (Qur'an 2:256) and I have only invited you to accept our faith willingly and of your own accord and have pointed out the hideousness of your present belief. Peace be with you and the blessings of God!"

Certain aspects of Renaissance humanism have its roots in the medieval Islamic world, including the "art of *dictation*, called in Latin, *ars dictaminis*," and "the humanist attitude toward classical language."

Evolution

Early Muslim scientists and philosophers developed theories on evolution, and the transmutation of species, which were widely taught in medieval Islamic schools. John William Draper, a contemporary of Charles Darwin, wrote the following on what he called the "Mohammedan theory of evolution" in 1878:

"Sometimes, not without surprise, we meet with ideas which we flatter ourselves have originated in our own times. Thus our modern doctrines of evolution and development were taught in their schools. In fact, they carried them much farther than we are disposed to do, extending them even to inorganic or mineral things. The fundamental principle of alchemy was the natural process of development of metalline bodies."

Al-Jahiz and the Struggle for Existence

The Mu'tazili scientist and philosopher al-Jahiz (c.776-869) was the first of the Muslim biologists and philosophers to develop an early theory of evolution. He speculated on the influence of the environment on animals, considered the effects of the environment on the likelihood of an animal to survive, and first described the struggle for existence, a precursor to natural selection. Al-Jahiz wrote the following on the struggle for existence in his work, *Book of Animals*:

"Animals engage in a struggle for existence; for resources, to avoid being eaten and to breed. Environmental factors influence organisms to develop new characteristics to ensure survival, thus transforming into new species. Animals that survive to breed can pass on their successful characteristics to offspring."

Ibn Miskawayh and the Brethren of Purity

Ibn Miskawayh's *al-Fawz al-Asghar* and the Brethren of Purity's *Encyclopedia of the Brethren of Purity* (*The Epistles of Ikhwan al-Safa*) developed theories on evolution that possibly had an influence on Charles Darwin and his inception of Darwinism. Muhammad Hamidullah describes their evolutionary ideas as follows:

"[These books] state that God first created matter and invested it with energy for development. Matter, therefore, adopted the form of vapour which assumed the shape of water in due time. The next stage of development was mineral life. Different kinds of stones developed in course of time and their highest form being mirjan (coral). It is a stone which has in it branches like those of a tree after mineral life evolves vegetation. The evolution of vegetation culminates with a tree which bears the qualities of an animal. This is the date-palm. It has male and female genders. It does not wither if all its branches are chopped but it dies when the head is cut off. The date-palm is therefore considered the highest among the trees and resembles the lowest among animals then is born the lowest of animals. It evolves into an ape. This is not the statement of Darwin. This is what Ibn Maskawayh states and this is precisely what is written in the *Epistles of Ikhwan al-Safa*. The Muslim thinkers state that ape then evolved into a lower kind of a barbarian man. He then became a superior human being. Man becomes a saint, a prophet. He evolves into a higher stage and becomes an angel. The one higher to angels is indeed none but God. Everything begins from Him and everything returns to Him."

Eloise Hart also describes the evolutionary thought in the *Encyclopedia of the Brethren of Purity* as follows:

"Another section describes the creation of worlds and the evolution of life in details that would have impressed Darwin. It explains how manifestation unfolds through successive layers, or stratified planes down to the mineral kingdom. Where, in this lowest kingdom, the most developed mineral entities live within its highest strata and blend imperceptibly into the next higher or vegetable kingdom. Likewise the vegetable kingdom contacts, at its highest level, the animal kingdom, whose culmination is man. The most evolved men contact higher spheres and, standing between the angelic and animal orders, serve on earth as vicegerents of God."

English translations of the *Encyclopedia of the Brethren of Purity* were available from 1812, while Arabic manuscripts of the *al-Fawz al-Asghar* and *The Epistles of Ikhwan al-Safa* were also available at the University of Cambridge by the 19th century. These works likely had an influence on 19th century evolutionists, and possibly Charles Darwin, who may have been a student of Arabic.

Al-Khazini and the Transmutation of Species

In the 12th century, al-Khazini wrote the following on how evolution in alchemy and biology were perceived by natural philosophers and common people in the Islamic world at the time:

"When common people hear from natural philosophers that gold is a body which has attained to perfection of maturity, to the goal of completeness, they firmly believe that it is something which has gradually come to that perfection by passing through the forms of all other metallic bodies, so that its gold nature was originally lead, afterward it became tin, then brass, then silver, and finally reached the development of gold; not knowing that the natural philosophers mean, in saying this, only something like what they mean when they speak of man, and attribute to him a completeness and equilibrium in nature and constitution - not that man was once a bull, and was changed into an ass, and afterward into a horse, and after that into an ape, and finally became a man."

Other Supporters

The Ash'ari polymath Ibn al-Haytham later wrote a book in which he argued for evolutionism (although not natural selection), and numerous other Islamic scholars and scientists, including the polymaths Abû Rayhân al-Bîrûnî, al-Khazini, Nasir al-Din Tusi, and Ibn Khaldun, discussed and developed these ideas. Translated into Latin, these works began to appear in the West after the Renaissance and may have had an impact on Western philosophy and science.

Logic

In early Islamic philosophy, logic played an important role. Islamic law placed importance on formulating standards of argument, which gave rise to a novel approach to logic in Kalam, but this approach was later displaced by ideas from Greek philosophy and Hellenistic philosophy with the rise of the Mu'tazili philosophers, who highly valued Aristotle's *Organon*.

The works of Hellenistic-influenced Islamic philosophers were crucial in the reception of Aristotelian logic in medieval Europe, along with the commentaries on the *Organon* by Averroes. The works of al-Farabi, Avicenna, al-Ghazali and other Muslim logicians who often criticized and corrected Aristotelian logic and introduced their own forms of logic, also played a central role in the subsequent development of European logic during the Renaissance.

According to the Routledge Encyclopedia of Philosophy:

"For the Islamic philosophers, logic included not only the study of formal patterns of inference and their validity but also elements of the philosophy of language and even of epistemology and metaphysics. Because of territorial disputes with the Arabic grammarians, Islamic philosophers were very interested in working out the relationship between logic and language, and they devoted much discussion to the question of the subject matter and aims of logic in relation to reasoning and speech. In the area of formal logical analysis, they elaborated upon the theory of terms, propositions and syllogisms as formulated in Aristotle's Categories, De interpretatione and Prior Analytics. In the spirit of Aristotle, they considered the syllogism to be the form to which all rational argumentation could be reduced, and they regarded syllogistic theory as the focal point of logic. Even poetics was considered as a syllogistic art in some fashion by most of the major Islamic Aristotelians."

Important developments made by Muslim logicians included the development of "Avicennian logic" as a replacement of Aristotelian logic. Avicenna's system of logic was responsible for the introduction of hypothetical syllogism, temporal modal logic and inductive logic. Other important developments in early Islamic philosophy include the development of a strict science of citation, the isnad or "backing", and the development of a scientific method of open inquiry to disprove claims, the ijtihad, which could be generally applied to many types of questions.

Logic in Islamic Law and Theology

Early forms of analogical reasoning, inductive reasoning and categorical syllogism were introduced in Fiqh (Islamic jurisprudence), Sharia (Islamic law) and Kalam (Islamic theology) from the 7th century with the process of *Qiyas*, before the Arabic translations of Aristotle's works. Later during the Islamic Golden Age, there was a logical debate among Islamic philosophers, logicians and theologians over whether the term *Qiyas* refers to analogical reasoning, inductive reasoning or categorical syllogism.

Some Islamic scholars argued that *Qiyas* refers to inductive reasoning, which Ibn Hazm (994-1064) disagreed with, arguing that *Qiyas* does not refer to inductive reasoning, but refers to categorical syllogism in a real sense and analogical reasoning in a metaphorical sense. On the other hand, al-Ghazali (1058-1111) (and in modern times, Abu Muhammad Asem al-Maqdisi) argued that *Qiyas* refers to analogical reasoning in a real sense and categorical syllogism in a metaphorical sense. Other Islamic scholars at the time, however, argued that the term *Qiyas* refers to both analogical reasoning and categorical syllogism in a real sense.

Aristotelian Logic

The first original Arabic writings on logic were produced by al-Kindi (Alkindus) (805–873), who produced a summary on earlier logic up to his time. The first writings on logic with non-Aristotelian elements was produced by al-Farabi (Alfarabi) (873–950), who discussed the topics of future contingents, the number and relation of the categories, the relation between logic and grammar, and non-Aristotelian forms of inference. He is also credited for categorizing logic into two separate groups, the first being "idea" and the second being "proof." Averroes (1126–98) was the last major logician from al-Andalus, who wrote the most elaborate commentaries on Aristotelian logic.

Avicennian Logic

Avicenna (980-1037) developed his own system of logic known as "Avicennian logic" as an alternative to Aristotelian logic. By the 12th century, Avicennian logic had replaced Aristotelian logic as the dominant system of logic in the Islamic world. The first criticisms of Aristotelian logic were written by Avicenna (980–1037), who produced independent treatises on logic rather than commentaries. He criticized the logical school of Baghdad for their devotion to Aristotle at the time.

He investigated the theory of definition and classification and the quantification of the predicates of categorical propositions, and developed an original theory on "temporal modal" syllogism. Its premises included modifiers such as "at all times", "at most times", and "at some time". While Avicenna (980-1037) often relied on deductive reasoning in philosophy, he used a different approach in medicine. Ibn Sina contributed inventively to the development of inductive logic, which he used to pioneer the idea of a syndrome. In his medical writings, Avicenna was the first to describe the methods of agreement, difference and concomitant variation which are critical to inductive logic and the scientific method.

Ibn Hazm (994-1064) wrote the *Scope of Logic,* in which he stressed on the importance of sense perception as a source of knowledge. Al-Ghazali (Algazel) (1058–1111) had an important influence on the use of logic in theology, making use of Avicennian logic in Kalam. Despite the logical sophistication of al-Ghazali, the rise of the Ash'ari school in from the 12th century slowly suffocated original work on logic in much of the Islamic world, though logic continued to be studied in some Islamic regions such as Persia and the Levant. Fakhr al-Din al-Razi (b. 1149) criticised Aristotle's "first figure" and developed a form of inductive logic, foreshadowing the system of inductive logic developed by John Stuart Mill (1806-1873).

Systematic refutations of Greek logic were written by the Illuminationist school, founded by Shahab al-Din Suhrawardi (1155-1191), who developed the idea of "decisive necessity", an important innovation in the history of logical philosophical speculation. Another systematic refutation of Greek logic was written by Ibn Taymiyyah (1263-1328), who wrote the *ar-Radd 'ala al-Mantiqiyyin* (*Refutation of Greek Logicians*), in which he gave a proof for induction being the only true form of argument, which had an important influence on the development of the scientific method of observation and experimentation.

Metaphysics

Cosmological and Ontological Arguments

Avicenna's proof for the existence of God was the first ontological argument, which he proposed in the *Metaphysics* section of *The Book of Healing*. This was the first attempt at using the method of a priori proof, which utilizes intuition and reason alone. Avicenna's proof of God's existence is unique in that it can be classified as both a cosmological argument and an ontological argument. "It is ontological insofar as 'necessary existence' in intellect is the first basis for arguing for a Necessary Existent". The proof is also "cosmological insofar as most of it is taken up with arguing that contingent existents cannot stand alone and must end up in a Necessary Existent."

Distinction between Essence and Existence

Islamic philosophy, imbued as it is with Islamic theology, distinguishes more clearly than Aristotelianism the difference between essence and existence. Whereas existence is the domain of the contingent and the accidental, essence endures within a being beyond the accidental. This was first described by Avicenna's works on metaphysics, and was himself influenced by al-Farabi. Some *orientalists* (or those particularly influenced by Thomist scholarship) argued that Avicenna was the first to view existence (*wujud*) as an accident that happens to the essence (*mahiyya*). However, this aspect of ontology is not the most central to the distinction that Avicenna established between essence and existence.

One cannot therefore make the claim that Avicenna was the proponent of the concept of essentialism *per se*, given that existence (*al-wujud*) when thought of in terms of necessity would ontologically translate into a notion of the *Necessary-Existent-due-to-Itself* (*wajib al-wujud bidhatihi*), which is without description or definition, and particularly without quiddity or essence (*la mahiyya lahu*). Consequently, Avicenna's ontology is 'existentialist' when accounting for being qua existence in terms of necessity (*wujub*), while it is 'essentialist' in terms of thinking about being qua existence (*wujud*) in terms of contingency qua possibility (*imkan*; or *mumkin al-wujud*: contingent being).

Some argue that Avicenna anticipated Frege and Bertrand Russell in "holding that existence is an accident of accidents" and also anticipated Alexius Meinong's "view about nonexistent objects." He also provided early arguments for "a 'necessary being' as cause of all other existents." The idea of "essence precedes existence" is a concept which dates back to Avicenna and his school of Avicennism as well as Shahab al-Din Suhrawardi and his Illuminationist philosophy. The opposite idea of "existence precedes essence" was thus developed in the works of Averroes and Mulla Sadra's transcendent theosophy. More careful approaches are needed in terms of thinking about philo-sophers (and theologians) in Islam in terms of phenomenological methods of investigation in ontology (or ontotheology), or by way of comparisons that are made with Heidegger's thought and his critique of the history of metaphysics.

Resurrection

Ibn al-Nafis wrote the *Theologus Autodidactus* as a defense of "the system of Islam and the Muslims' doctrines on the missions of Prophets, the religious laws, the resurrection of the body, and the transitoriness of the world." The book presents rational arguments for bodily resurrection and the immortality of the human soul, using both demonstrative reasoning and material from the hadith corpus as forms of evidence. Later Islamic scholars viewed this work as a response to Avicenna's metaphysical argument on spiritual resurrection (as opposed to bodily resurrection), which was earlier criticized by al-Ghazali.

Soul and Spirit

The Muslim physician-philosophers, Avicenna and Ibn al-Nafis, developed their own theories on the soul. They both made a distinction between the soul and the spirit, and in particular, the Avicennian doctrine on the nature of the soul was influential among the Scholastics. Some of Avicenna's views on the soul included the idea that the immortality of the soul is a consequence of its nature, and not a purpose for it to fulfill. In his theory of "The Ten Intellects", he viewed the human soul as the tenth and final intellect.

Avicenna generally supported Aristotle's idea of the soul originating from the heart, whereas Ibn al-Nafis on the other hand rejected this idea and instead argued that the soul "is related to the entirety and not to one or a few organs." He further criticized Aristotle's idea that every unique soul requires the existence of a unique source, in this case the heart. Ibn al-Nafis concluded that "the soul is related primarily neither to the spirit nor to any organ, but rather to the entire matter whose temperament is prepared to receive that soul" and he defined the soul as nothing other than "what a human indicates by saying 'I'."

Thought Experiments

While he was imprisoned in the castle of Fardajan near Hamadhan, Avicenna wrote his famous "Floating Man" thought experiment to demonstrate human self-awareness and the substantiality of the soul. He referred to the living human intelligence, particularly the active intellect, which he believed to be the hypostasis by which God communicates truth to the human mind and imparts order and intelligibility to nature. His "Floating Man" thought experiment tells its readers to imagine themselves suspended in the air, isolated from all sensations, which includes no sensory contact with even their own bodies.

He argues that, in this scenario, one would still have self-consciousness. He thus concludes that the idea of the self is not logically dependent on any physical thing, and that the soul should not be seen in relative terms, but as a primary given, a substance. This argument was later refined and simplified by René Descartes in epistemic terms when he stated: "I can abstract from the supposition of all external things, but not from the supposition of my own consciousness."

Time

In contrast to ancient Greek philosophers who believed that the universe had an infinite past with no beginning, medieval philosophers and theologians developed the concept of the universe having a finite past with a beginning. This view was inspired by the creation myth shared by the three Abrahamic religions: Judaism, Christianity and Islam. The Christian philosopher, John Philoponus, presented the first such argument against the ancient Greek notion of an infinite past. However, the most sophisticated medieval arguments against an infinite past were developed by the Islamic philosopher, Al-Kindi (Alkindus); the Jewish philosopher, Saadia Gaon (Saadia ben Joseph); and the Islamic theologian, Al-Ghazali (Algazel). They developed two logical arguments against an infinite past, the first being the "argument from the impossibility of the existence of an actual infinite", which states:

"An actual infinite cannot exist."

"An infinite temporal regress of events is an actual infinite."

"An infinite temporal regress of events cannot exist."

The second argument, the "argument from the impossibility of completing an actual infinite by successive addition", states:

"An actual infinite cannot be completed by successive addition."

"The temporal series of past events has been completed by successive addition."

"The temporal series of past events cannot be an actual infinite."

Both arguments were adopted by later Christian philosophers and theologians, and the second argument in particular became more famous after it was adopted by Immanuel Kant in his thesis of the first antimony concerning time.

Truth

In metaphysics, Avicenna (Ibn Sina) defined truth as:

"What corresponds in the mind to what is outside it?"

Avicenna elaborated on his definition of truth in his *Metaphysics*:

"The truth of a thing is the property of the being of each thing which has been established in it."

In his *Quodlibeta,* Thomas Aquinas wrote a commentary on Avicenna's definition of truth in his *Metaphysics* and explained it as follows:

"The truth of each thing as Avicenna says in his *Metaphysica* is nothing else than the property of its being which has been established in it. So that is called true gold which has properly the being of gold and attains to the established determinations of the nature of gold. Now, each thing has properly being in some nature because it stands under the complete form proper to that nature, whereby being and species in that nature is."

Early Islamic political philosophy emphasized an inexorable link between science and religion and emphsized the process of ijtihad to find truth. Ibn al-Haytham (Alhacen) reasoned that to discover the truth about nature, it is necessary to eliminate human opinion and error, and allow the universe to speak for itself. In his *Aporias against*

Ptolemy, Ibn al-Haytham further wrote the following comments on truth:

"Truth is sought for itself [but] the truths, [he warns] are immersed in uncertainties [and the scientific authorities (such as Ptolemy, whom he greatly respected) are] not immune from error..."

"Therefore, the seeker after the truth is not one who studies the writings of the ancients and, following his natural disposition, puts his trust in them, but rather the one who suspects his faith in them and questions what he gathers from them, the one who submits to argument and demonstration, and not to the sayings of a human being whose nature is fraught with all kinds of imperfection and deficiency. Thus the duty of the man who investigates the writings of scientists, if learning the truth is his goal, is to make himself an enemy of all that he reads, and, applying his mind to the core and margins of its content, attack it from every side. He should also suspect himself as he performs his critical examination of it, so that he may avoid falling into either prejudice or leniency."

"I constantly sought knowledge and truth, and it became my belief that for gaining access to the effulgence and closeness to God, there is no better way than that of searching for truth and knowledge."

Philosophy of education

In the medieval Islamic world, an elementary school was known as a *maktab,* which dates back to at least the 10th century. Like madrasahs (which referred to higher education), a maktab was often attached to a mosque. In the 11th century, Ibn Sina (known as *Avicenna* in the West), in one of his books, wrote a chapter dealing with the *maktab* entitled "The Role of the Teacher in the Training and Upbringing of Children", as a guide to teachers working at *maktab* schools. He wrote that children can learn better if taught in classes instead of individual tuition from private tutors, and he gave a number of reasons for why this is the case, citing the value of competition and emulation among pupils as well as the usefulness of group discussions and debates. Ibn Sina described the curriculum of a *maktab* school in some detail, describing the curricula for two stages of education in a *maktab* school.

Primary Education

Ibn Sina wrote that children should be sent to a *maktab* school from the age of 6 and be taught primary education until they reach the age of 14. During which time, he wrote that they should be taught the *Qur'an*, Islamic metaphysics, language, literature, Islamic ethics, and manual skills (which could refer to a variety of practical skills).

Secondary Education

Ibn Sina refers to the secondary education stage of *maktab* schooling as the period of specialization, when pupils should begin to acquire manual skills, regardless of their social status. He writes that children after the age of 14 should be given a choice to choose and specialize in subjects they have an interest in, whether it was reading, manual skills, literature, preaching, medicine, geometry, trade and commerce, craftsmanship, or any other subject or profession they would be interested in pursuing for a future career. He wrote that this was a transitional stage and that there needs to be flexibility regarding the age in which pupils graduage, as the student's emotional development and chosen subjects need to be taken into account.

Philosophy of Science

Scientific Method

The pioneering development of the scientific method by the Arab Ash'ari polymath Ibn al-Haytham (Alhacen) was an important contribution to the philosophy of science. In the *Book of Optics* (c. 1025 AD), his scientific method was very similar to the modern scientific method and consisted of the following procedures:

1. Observation
2. Statement of problem
3. Formulation of hypothesis
4. Testing of hypothesis using experimentation
5. Analysis of experimental results
6. Interpretation of data and formulation of conclusion
7. Publication of findings

In *The Model of the Motions*, Ibn al-Haytham also describes an early version of Occam's razor, where he employs only minimal hypotheses regarding the properties that characterize astronomical motions, as he attempts to eliminate from his planetary model the cosmological hypotheses that cannot be observed from Earth.

In his *Aporias against Ptolemy*, Ibn al-Haytham commented on the difficulty of attaining scientific knowledge:

"Truth is sought for itself [but] the truths, [he warns] are immersed in uncertainties [and the scientific authorities (such as Ptolemy, whom he greatly respected) are] not immune from error..."

He held that the criticism of existing theories — which dominated this book — holds a special place in the growth of scientific knowledge:

"Therefore, the seeker after the truth is not one who studies the writings of the ancients and, following his natural disposition, puts his trust in them, but rather the one who suspects his faith in them and questions what he gathers from them, the one who submits to argument and demonstration, and not to the sayings of a human being whose nature is fraught with all kinds of imperfection and deficiency. Thus the duty of the man who investigates the writings of scientists, if learning the truth is his goal, is to make himself an enemy of all that he reads, and, applying his mind to the core and margins of its content, attack it from every side. He should also suspect himself as he performs his critical examination of it, so that he may avoid falling into either prejudice or leniency."

Ibn al-Haytham attributed his experimental scientific method and scientific skepticism to his Islamic faith. He believed that human beings are inherently flawed and that only God is perfect. He reasoned that to discover the truth about nature, it is necessary to eliminate human opinion and error, and allow the universe to speak for itself. In *The Winding Motion*, Ibn al-Haytham further wrote that faith should only apply to prophets of Islam and not to any other authorities, in the following comparison between the Islamic prophetic tradition and the demonstrative sciences:

"From the statements made by the noble Shaykh, it is clear that he believes in Ptolemy's words in everything he says, without relying on a demonstration or calling on a proof, but by pure imitation (taqlid); that is how experts in the prophetic tradition have faith in Prophets, may the blessing of God be upon them. But it is not the way that mathematicians have faith in specialists in the demonstrative sciences."

Ibn al-Haytham described his search for truth and knowledge as a way of leading him closer to God: "I constantly sought knowledge and truth, and it became my belief that for gaining access to the effulgence and closeness to God, there is no better way than that of searching for truth and knowledge."

His contemporary Abû Rayhân al-Bîrûnî also introduced an early scientific method in nearly every field of inquiry he studied. For example, in his treatise on mineralogy, *Kitab al-Jamahir* (*Book of Precious Stones*), he is "the most exact of experimental scientists", while in the intro-duction to his study of India, he declares that "to execute our project, it has not been possible to follow the geometric method" and develops comparative sociology as a scientific method in the field. He was also responsible for introducing the experimental method into mechanics, the first to conduct elaborate experiments related to astronomical phenomena, and a pioneer of experimental psychology.

Unlike his contemporary Avicenna's scientific method where "general and universal questions came first and led to experimental work", al-Biruni developed scientific methods where "universals came out of practical, experimental work" and "theories are formulated after discoveries." During his debate with Avicenna on natural philosophy, al-Biruni made the first real distinction between a scientist and a philosopher, referring to Avicenna as a philosopher and considering him to be a mathematical scientist.

Al-Biruni's scientific method was similar to the modern scientific method in many ways, particularly his emphasis on repeated experimentation. Biruni was concerned with how to conceptualize and prevent both systematic errors and random errors, such as "errors caused by the use of small instruments and errors made by human observers." He argued that if instruments produce random errors because of their imperfections or idiosyncratic qualities, then multiple observations must be taken, analyzed quali1tatively, and on this basis, arrive at a "common-sense single value for the constant sought", whether an arithmetic mean or a "reliable estimate."

Experimental Medicine

Avicenna (Ibn Sina) is considered the father of modern medicine, for his introduction of systematic experimentation and quantification into the study of physiology, the introduction of experimental medicine and clinical trials, the experimental use and testing of drugs, and a precise guide for practical experimentation in the process of discovering and proving the effectiveness of medical substances, in his medical encyclopedia, *The Canon of Medicine* (11th century), which was the first book dealing with experimental medicine. It laid out the following rules and principles for testing the effectiveness of new drugs or medications, which still form the basis of modern clinical trials:

1. "The drug must be free from any extraneous accidental quality."
2. "It must be used on a simple, not a composite, disease."
3. "The drug must be tested with two contrary types of diseases, because sometimes a drug cures one disease by its essential qualities and another by its accidental ones."
4. "The quality of the drug must correspond to the strength of the disease. For example, there are some drugs whose heat is less than the coldness of certain diseases, so that they would have no effect on them."
5. "The time of action must be observed, so that essence and accident are not confused."
6. "The effect of the drug must be seen to occur constantly or in many cases, for if this did not happen, it was an accidental effect."
7. "The experimentation must be done with the human body, for testing a drug on a lion or a horse might not prove anything about its effect on man."

Other Fields

Atomism

Atomistic philosophies are found very early in Islamic philosophy, and represent a synthesis of the Greek and Indian ideas. Like both the Greek and Indian versions, Islamic atomism was a charged topic that had the potential for conflict with the prevalent religious orthodoxy. Yet it was such a fertile and flexible idea that, as in Greece and India, it flourished in some schools of Islamic thought. The most successful form of Islamic atomism was in the Asharite

School of philosophy, most notably in the work of the philosopher al-Ghazali (1058-1111). In Asharite atomism, atoms are the only perpetual, material things in existence, and all else in the world is "accidental" meaning something that lasts for only an instant. Nothing accidental can be the cause of anything else, except perception, as it exists for a moment.

Contingent events are not subject to natural physical causes, but are the direct result of God's constant intervention, without which nothing could happen. Thus nature is completely dependent on God, which meshes with other Asharite Islamic ideas on causation, or the lack thereof. Other traditions in Islam rejected the atomism of the Asharites and expounded on many Greek texts, especially those of Aristotle. An active school of philosophers in Spain, including the noted commentator Averroes (1126-1198 AD) explicitly rejected the thought of al-Ghazali and turned to an extensive evaluation of the thought of Aristotle. Averroes commented in detail on most of the works of Aristotle and his commentaries did much to guide the interpretation of Aristotle in later Jewish and Christian scholastic thought.

Cosmology

There are several cosmological verses in the *Qur'an* (610-632) which some modern writers have interpreted as foreshadowing the expansion of the universe and possibly even the Big Bang theory:

Don't those who reject faith see that the heavens and the earth were a single entity then We ripped them apart?

And the heavens We did create with Our Hands, and We do cause it to expand. *Qur'an* 51:47

In contrast to ancient Greek philosophers who believed that the universe had an infinite past with no beginning, medieval philosophers and theologians developed the concept of the universe having a finite past with a beginning. This view was inspired by the creation myth shared by the three Abrahamic religions: Judaism, Christianity and Islam.

The Christian philosopher, John Philoponus, presented the first such argument against the ancient Greek notion of an infinite past. However, the most sophisticated medieval arguments against an infinite past were developed by the Muslim philosopher, Al-Kindi (Alkindus); the Jewish philosopher, Saadia Gaon (Saadia ben Joseph); and the Muslim theologian, Al-Ghazali (Algazel). They developed two logical arguments against an infinite past, the first being the "argument from the impossibility of the existence of an actual infinite", which states:

"An actual infinite cannot exist."

"An infinite temporal regress of events is an actual infinite."

" An infinite temporal regress of events cannot exist."

The second argument, the "argument from the impossibility of completing an actual infinite by successive addition", states:

"An actual infinite cannot be completed by successive addition."

"The temporal series of past events has been completed by successive addition."

" The temporal series of past events cannot be an actual infinite."

Both arguments were adopted by later Christian philosophers and theologians, and the second argument in particular became more famous after it was adopted by Immanuel Kant in his thesis of the first antimony concerning time. In the 10th century, the Brethren of Purity published the *Encyclopedia of the Brethren of Purity*, in which a heliocentric view of the universe is expressed in a section on cosmology:

"God has placed the Sun at the center of the Universe just as the capital of a country is placed in its middle and the ruler's palace at the center of the city."

Epistemology

Avicenna's most influential theory in epistemology is his theory of knowledge, in which he developed the concept of tabula rasa. He argued that the "human intellect at birth is rather like a tabula rasa, a pure potentiality that is actualized through education and comes to know" and that knowledge is attained through "empirical familiarity with objects in this world from which one abstracts universal concepts" which is developed through a "syllogistic method of reasoning; observations lead to prepositional statements, which when compounded lead to further abstract concepts." In the 12th century, Ibn Tufail further developed the concept of tabula rasa in his Arabic novel, *Hayy ibn Yaqzan*, in which he depicted the development of the mind of a feral child "from a tabula rasa to that of an adult, in complete isolation from society" on a desert island. The Latin translation of his work, entitled *Philosophus Autodidactus*, published by Edward Pococke the Younger in 1671, had an influence on John Locke's formulation of tabula rasa in *An Essay Concerning Human Understanding*.

Eschatology

Islamic eschatology is concerned with the *Qiyamah* (end of the world; Last Judgement) and the final judgement of humanity. Eschatology relates to one of the six articles of faith (*aqidah*) of Islam. Like the other Abrahamic religions, Islam teaches the bodily resurrection of the dead, the fulfillment of a divine plan for creation, and the immortality of the human soul (though Jews do not necessarily view the soul as eternal); the righteous are rewarded with the pleasures of *Jannah* (Heaven), while the unrighteous are punished in *Jahannam* (Hell). A significant fraction (one third, in fact) of the Quran deals with these beliefs, with many *hadith* elaborating on the themes and details.

Islamic apocalyptic literature describing the Armageddon is often known as *fitna* (a test) and *malahim* (or *ghayba* in the shi'ite tradition). Ibn al-Nafis dealt with

Islamic eschatology in some depth in his *Theologus Autodidactus,* where he rationalized the Islamic view of eschatology using reason and science to explain the events that would occur according to Islamic eschatology. He presented his rational and scientific arguments in the form of Arabic fiction; hence his *Theologus Autodidactus* may be considered the earliest science fiction work.

Legal Philosophy

Sharia refers to the body of Islamic law. The term means "way" or "path"; it is the legal framework within which public and some private aspects of life are regulated for those living in a legal system based on Islamic principles of jurisprudence. Fiqh is the term for Islamic jurisprudence, made up of the rulings of Islamic jurists. A component of Islamic studies, Fiqh expounds the methodology by which Islamic law is derived from primary and secondary sources. Mainstream Islam distinguishes *fiqh,* which means understanding details and inferences drawn by scholars, from *sharia* that refers to principles that lie behind the fiqh. Scholars hope that *fiqh* and *sharia* are in harmony in any given case, but they cannot be sure.

Phenomenology

The Ash'ari polymath Ibn al-Haytham (Alhacen) is considered a pioneer of phenomenology. He articulated a relationship between the physical and observable world and that of intuition, psychology and mental functions. His theories regarding knowledge and perception, linking the domains of science and religion, led to a philosophy of existence based on the direct observation of reality from the observer's point of view. Much of his thought on phenomenology was not further developed until the 20th century.

Philosophical Novels

The Islamic philosophers, Ibn Tufail (Abubacer) and Ibn al-Nafis, were pioneers of the philosophical novel. Ibn

Tufail wrote the first fictional Arabic novel *Hayy ibn Yaqdhan* (*Philosophus Autodidactus*) as a response to al-Ghazali's *The Incoherence of the Philosophers*, and then Ibn al-Nafis also wrote a fictional novel *Theologus Autodidactus* as a response to Ibn Tufail's *Philosophus Autodidactus*. Both of these novels had protagonists (Hayy in *Philosophus Autodidactus* and Kamil in *Theologus Autodidactus*) who were autodidactic individuals spontaneously generated in a cave and living in seclusion on a desert island, both being the earliest examples of a desert island story. However, while Hayy lives alone on the desert island for most of the story in *Philosophus Autodidactus*, the story of Kamil extends beyond the desert island setting in *Theologus Autodidactus*, developing into the first example of a science fiction novel.

Ibn al-Nafis described his book *Theologus Autodidactus* as a defense of "the system of Islam and the Muslims' doctrines on the missions of Prophets, the religious laws, the resurrection of the body, and the transitoriness of the world." He presents rational arguments for bodily resurrection and the immortality of the human soul, using both demonstrative reasoning and material from the hadith corpus to prove his case. Later Islamic scholars viewed this work as a response to the metaphysical claim of Avicenna and Ibn Tufail that bodily resurrection cannot be proven through reason, a view that was earlier criticized by al-Ghazali.

A Latin translation of *Philosophus Autodidactus* was published in 1671, prepared by Edward Pococke the Younger. The first English translation by Simon Ockley was published in 1708, and German and Dutch translations were also published at the time. *Philosophus Autodidactus* went on to have a significant influence on European literature, and became an influential best-seller throughout Western Europe in the 17th and 18th centuries. These translations later inspired Daniel Defoe to write *Robinson Crusoe,* which also featured a desert island narrative and was regarded as the first novel in English. *Philosophus Autodidactus* also had a "profound influence" on modern Western philosophy. It became "one of the most important books that heralded the Scientific Revolution" and Euro-pean Enlightenment, and the thoughts expressed in the novel can be found in "different variations and to different degrees in the books of Thomas Hobbes, John Locke, Isaac Newton, and Immanuel Kant."

The novel inspired the concept of "tabula rasa" developed in *An Essay Concerning Human Understanding* (1690) by Locke, who was a student of Pococke. *Philosophus Autodidactus* also developed the themes of empiricism, tabula rasa, nature versus nurture, condition of possibility, materialism, and Molyneux's Problem. The novel also ins-pired Robert Boyle, another acquaintance of Pococke, to write his own philosophical novel set on an island, *The Aspiring Naturalist*. Other European scholars influenced by *Philosophus Autodidactus* include Gottfried Leibniz, Mel-chisédech Thévenot, John Wallis, Christiaan Huygens, George Keith, Robert Barclay, the Quakers, and Samuel Hartlib.

Philosophy of Mind

The philosophy of mind was studied in medieval Islamic psychological thought, which refers to the study of the *nafs* (literally "self" or "psyche" in Arabic) in the Islamic world, particularly during the Islamic Golden Age (8th–15th centuries) as well as modern times (20th–21st centuries), and is related to psychology, psychiatry and the neurosciences.

Place and Space

The Arab polymath al-Hasan Ibn al-Haytham (Alhazen; d. ca. 1041) presented a thorough mathematical critique and refutation of Aristotle's conception of place (*topos*) in his *Risala/Qawl fi'l-makan* (*Treatise/Discourse on Place*). Aristotle's *Physics* (Book IV - *Delta*) stated that the place of something is the two-dimensional boundary of the containing body that is at rest and is in contact with what it contains. Ibn al-Haytham disagreed with this definition and demonstrated that place (*al-makan*) is the imagined (three-dimensional) void (*al-khala' al-mutakhayyal*) between the inner surfaces of the containing body. He showed that place was akin to space, foreshadowing Descartes's notion of place as space qua *Extensio* or even Leibniz's *analysis situs*. Ibn al-Haytham's mathematization of place rested on several geometric demonstrations, including his study on the sphere and other solids, which showed that the sphere (*al-kura*) is the largest in magnitude (volumetric) with respect to other geometric solids that have equal surface areas.

For instance, a sphere that has an equal surface area to that of a cylinder, would be larger in (volumetric) magnitude than the cylinder; hence, the sphere occupies a larger place than that occupied by the cylinder; unlike what is entailed by Aristotle's definition of place: that this sphere and that cylinder occupy places that are equal in magnitude. Ibn al-Haytham rejected Aristotle's philosophical concept of place on mathematical grounds. Later, the philosopher 'Abd al-Latif al-Baghdadi (13th century) tried to defend the Aristotelian conception of place in a treatise titled: *Fi al-Radd 'ala Ibn al-Haytham fi al-makan* (*A refutation of Ibn al-Haytham's place*), although his effort was admirable from a philosophical standpoint, it was unconvincing from the scientific and mathematical viewpoints. Ibn al-Haytham also discussed space perception and its epistemological implications in his *Book of Optics* (1021).

His experimental proof of the intromission model of vision led to changes in the way the visual perception of space was understood, contrary to the previous emission theory of vision supported by Euclid and Ptolemy. In "tying the visual perception of space to prior bodily experience, Alhacen unequivocally rejected the intuitiveness of spatial perception and therefore, the autonomy of vision without tangible notions of distance and size for correlation, sight can tell us next to nothing about such things."

Political Philosophy

Early Islamic political philosophy emphasized an inexorable link between science and religion, and the process of ijtihad to find truth - in effect *all* philosophy was "political" as it had real implications for governance. This view was challenged by the Mutazilite philosophers, who held a more secular view and were supported by secular aristocracy who sought freedom of action independent of the Caliphate. The only Greek political treatise known to medieval Muslims at the time was Plato's *Re-public*. By the end of the Islamic Golden Age, however, the Asharite view of Islam had in general triumphed.

Islamic political philosophy, was, indeed, rooted in the very sources of Islam, i.e. the Qur'an and the Sunnah, the words and practices of Muhammad. However, in the Western thought, it is generally known that it was a specific area peculiar merely to the great philosophers of Islam: al-Kindi (Alkindus), al-Farabi (Alfarabi), Ýbn Sina (Avicenna), Ibn Bajjah (Avempace), Ibn Rushd (Averroes), and Ibn Khaldun. The political conceptions of Islam such as kudrah, sultan, ummah, cemaa -and even the "core" terms of the Qur'an, i.e. ibada, din, rab and ilah- is taken as the basis of an analysis. Hence, not only the ideas of the Muslim political philosophers but also many other jurists and ulama posed political ideas and theories. For example, the ideas of the Khawarij in the very early years of Islamic history on Khilafa and Ummah, or that of Shia Islam on the concept of Imamah is considered proofs of political thought. The clashes between the Ehl-i Sunna and Shia in the 7th and 8th centuries had a genuine political character. The 14th century Arab scholar Ibn Khaldun is considered one of the greatest political theorists. The British philosopher-anthropologist Ernest Gellner considered Ibn Khaldun's definition of government, "an institution which prevents injustice other than such as it commits itself", the best in the history of political theory.

4

Ethical Theories in Islam

Since Donaldson's book, the discussion of the subject has gained in sophistication. Philosophical precision in the definition and analysis of concepts and areas of Islamic ethical literature was achieved in the works of George F. Hourani and his path-breaking study of Abd al-Gabbar. The criteria for the study of Islamic ethical texts which he adumbrated in his opening chapter Hourani later published in a seminal article, "Ethics in Medieval Islam: A Conspectus." In this article he developed two sets of two criteria, based on method and sources, in order to classify types of Islamic ethical thinking. The two criteria based on method determine whether ethical positions are arrived at through the prescription of a higher authority or through analytical thinking ("normative" and "analytical" ethics), while the two criteria based on the sources of ethical knowledge determine whether it comes from secular or religious sources ("secular" and "religious" ethics). "Thus we can derive a fourfold scheme of types of writing on ethics: (A) Normative religious ethics. (B) Normative secular ethics. (C) Ethical analysis in the religious tradition. (D) Ethical analysis by [secular] philosophers".

Hourani's typology was accepted by Mohammed Arkoun, a scholar who has worked with consistency on Islamic ethical traditions. Arkoun went beyond a purely philosophical analysis and enriched the discussion by incorporating into it social, political, and cultural dimensions; specifically, he wanted to question the relevance and significance of the traditional material for contemporary Islamic societies. This latter interest is paramount also in the concise study of Peter Antes. Finally, various aspects of Islamic ethical traditions, and especially the legal ramifications, were extensively studied in the Ninth Giorgio Levi della Vida Biennial Conference held in 1983. With all this preliminary work at his disposal, Fakhry had an excellent opportunity in the book under review - indeed, with the second printing of the book, two opportunities - to contribute significantly to a serious discussion of the subject. Instead, he chose to go back to the model of Donaldson and produce a book that is essentially a series of summaries of the ethical writings already covered in Donaldson's anthology.

Fakhry's version, however, is deliberately narrower in scope: he left out the Sufis, the Persian poets, and all Muslim authors, whatever the nature of their ethical writings, who wrote after the fifteenth century. In the preface to the second printing of the book in 1994, and in answer to criticism of this latter omission in the first printing, he justified his decision with this astounding statement: "The fact is that if we scour the literature beyond the fifteenth century, we would be hard put to produce a single ethical treatise which adds substantially to our knowledge of Islamic ethics, and this applies to modern ethical writings as well".

The work of all Muslim reformers from the eighteenth century to the present, most of which is predicated on ethical categories of thought in a primary sense, is dismissed by this statement which hides either ignorance of the subject or extreme bias against it. Fakhry organizes his material according to a typology of ethical theories he tries to develop in the introduction, while completely ignoring the work of Hourani presented above. He comes up with four types: "scriptural morality," "theological theories," "philosophical theories," and "religious theories."

Other than the philosophical theories, which Fakhry says stem "ultimately from the ethical writings of Plato and Aristotle", and hence differentiated from the rest on the basis of the source of ethical knowledge, it is very difficult to set the other three apart and understand how they are meant to be substantially different. "Scriptural morality," says Fakhry, is "exhibited in the moral and quasi-moral pronouncements of the Koran and the Traditions" (what is a "quasi-moral pronouncement"?) "in partial abstraction from their elaboration . . . by . . . the theologians in the light of the discursive methods and categories developed in the eighth and ninth centuries"; while "theological theories" have "their ultimate grounding in the Koran and the Traditions, and a heavy reliance on these categories and methods" (emphasis added). In other words, these two types differ only in quantity, not quality. One wonders when "partial abstraction" becomes "heavy reliance," and who determines the cut-off point.

The third inchoate type, "religious theories," is also "grounded ultimately in the Koran" but differs from the first type, scriptural morality, "in that their protagonists had received the impact of Greek philosophy and Islamic theology." This may set it apart in a certain rudimentary way from the first type, but it is hardly different from the second, "theological theories." For the two major protagonists of the second type, says Fakhry, are the Mutazilites and the Asarites, and one wonders whether Fakhry would claim that the Mutazilites had not "received the impact of Greek philosophy and Islamic theology."

It gets even more turbid. Of the four types, Fakhry says that the "religious theories" type of ethics is "the most charac-teristically Islamic" and al-Gazali its "most representative example". By this logic, then, this type turns out to be more characteristically Islamic than the Quran and the hadit (representatives of the first type), and al-Gazali a better source for Islamic ethics than both the Quran and the hadit! I wonder what the Maliki fuqaha who burned al-Gazali's books as heretical would have thought of this evaluation.

Fakhry, however, is undaunted in this exercise of pontificating on who is a "thorough" Muslim and who is not. "The Sufis and the philosophers," he says, "cannot be said to have developed a thoroughly Islamic view of the universe and of man, owing to the extraneous influences, Indian, Greek, Christian, and other, which conditioned their thought". On this analogy, the view of the universe and of man held by somebody like Thomas Aquinas would not be "thoroughly" Christian because he was influenced by the Greeks and the Arabs. I did not select Aquinas here arbitrarily; Fakhry himself introduces him, at the end of his book on Islamic ethical theories, as the thinker [in Islam? in Christianity and Islam together? in world civilization?] who best combined the humanism of "a Greek philosopher like Aristotle" and the "Semitic conception of God's ever presence to man" to fashion the most satisfactory theory of the contemplative ideal, the pinnacle of beatitude.

The roots of the problem in Fakhry's thinking are very deep and sufficiently adumbrated by my emphasizing some of his words in the preceding quotations. Explicitly I will mention only one of them, and that is the essentialist, a historical, and in the final analysis, utterly invalid view of Islam held by Fakhry, which assumes that an arbitrarily selected version of "Islam" can be idealized and presented as normative and as the criterion by which not only to understand intellectual developments in history (like ethical theories), but also to judge the "orthodoxy" or "originality" of historical figures and on that basis to include them in the discussion or exclude them altogether (as all post-fifteenth-century Muslims).

Within this framework, then, in the rest of the book Fakhry assigns proponents of ethical theories to one of his four types and summarizes their writings. However, the usefulness of the book, even as a series of summaries, is reduced by gross inconsistencies of style and composition and by the woefully inadequate and outdated bibliographical apparatus. The style suffers because the book was apparently written over the past few decades and was never editorially revised to bring the various parts into a consistent whole. The first printing appeared in 1991 but its preface is dated November 1985, while the same preface mentions that it was researched ten years before that, in 1974-75. Some parts, however, may have been written even before that; Fakhry refers to Richard Walzer's article on Miskawayh in the Levi della Vida Festschrift, which appeared in 1956, "as Walzer has shown recently." It is amazing that the word "recently" was retained in the second printing of 1994.

The book bears every sign of hasty and careless composition; it appears as a haphazard collage of various pieces written at sundry times. For example, here is a far from exhaustive list: al-Kindi's al-Hila fi daf al-ahzan is summarized at length on pp. 68-70 and the claim is made that it exhibits the "Stoic, Cynic ideal of moral fortitude and apatheia". Four chapters down the line. Fakhry refers to the same treatise by al-Kindi as if it had never been mentioned before and this time he calls it "an essentially Socratic tract." On pp. 61-62 Fakhry introduces the Arabic gnomological literature in considerable detail; he refers to it as if for the first time without cross-reference to the earlier passage. The bibliographical information on the Arabic translation of the Nicomachean Ethics should have been given in its proper place on pp. 65-66 and not in note 2 on p. 78. The dates of death of al-Amiri and Abu Sulayman as-Sigistani are listed as "991" and "ca. 988" respectively on p. 61, but as "993" and "1000" on p. 78. Some statements generate the impression that Fakhry never looked at the book he is talking about: Hunayn's Nawadir al-falasifa, Fakhry says, "contains a vast amount of ethical dicta by the Greek philosophers"; in fact, in Badawi's 1985 edition of the work (Kuwayt; not mentioned by Fakhry), the Greek dicta occupy only 113 small pages (37-149), over a fourth of which contains not dicta but Alexander's apocryphal correspondence with Aristotle.

The bibliography also suffers apparently for the same reason. It is obvious that Fakhry was not interested in keeping up with new publications or using constructively the publications he does cite. As already mentioned, Hourani's analyses, so pertinent to Fakhry's purpose, are basically ignored, as are the numerous insights offered in the papers contained in the Levi della Vida conference volume, though Fakhry does list Hourani's 1985 collection of articles in his bibliography and does refer to the Levi della Vida. As for the omissions, there is barely space to mention even the most egregious: during the discussion of al-Hasan al-Basri's letter on the question of qadar, and note 13, Fakhry refers to the articles by Ritter (1933) and Obermann (1935), the two works also referred to by Donaldson, but amazingly not to the series of studies, dealing at great length with that very work, initiated by Josef van Ess's Anfange muslimischer Theologie and continued by Michael Cook's rejoinder in his Early Muslim Dogma, van Ess's review of Cook in Der Islam 60 (1983): 311-13, and finally van Ess's most recent synthesis in his Theologie und Gesellschaft im 2. und 3. Jahrhundert Hidschra.

The incredibly superficial discussion of kasb does not benefit from the studies by R. M. Frank and D. Gimaret, among others, which have appreciably deepened our understanding of this difficult concept. The work by Ibn Sina which Fakhry cites as Ethics and Psychological Affections (Fi l-ahlaq wa-l-infialat an-nafsaniyya), properly to be translated as "Natural dispositions and affections of the soul," is not a treatise on ethics but a summary of Aristotie's Rhetoric II.i-x, as I discussed in my Avicenna and the Aristotelian Tradition, 89, 92-93. The work, moreover, was edited and translated into French by D. Remon-don already in 1954. On pp. 176-85 Fakhry discusses ar-Ragib al-Isfahani's Daria as a representative of the "religious ethics" typology, which, according to Fakhry, "firmly grounded in the Koran and the Traditions, tended . . . to dispense with 'dialectical' or 'methodological' subtleties and to concentrate on eliciting the spirit of Islamic morality in a more direct way". Wilferd Madelung, however, had previously established that ar-Ragib's ethics was indeed that of the philosophical tradition though "dressed in Islamic clothing." Unaware of Madelung's article, Fakhry is thus misled by ar-Ragib's style and wrongly categorizes the Daria as a work in "religious ethics."

But then this is not the only German publication that was not consulted; German bibliography is almost completely missing. There are only thirteen references to German publications in the entire book, eight of which are to publications by Hans Daiber, the editor of the series in which Fakhry's book appeared. I have been referring to the self-styled second "edition" of the book in 1994 as the second "printing" because that is precisely what it is. In the hope of forestalling yet another book purporting to discuss ethics in "Islam" along the same lines, I have provided a comparative chart (at left) of the contents of the books by Fakhry and Donaldson. I have classified the material according to the four categories developed by Hourani and discussed above. The classification of certain works under each category is necessarily provisional; whether they are analytical or normative will have to be ascertained after a serious study of ethical theories in the Islamic world, a study that has yet to be undertaken.

Medical Ethics from Maqasid Al Shari'at

Secularized European law denied moral considerations associated with 'religion' and therefore failed to solve issues in modern medicine requiring moral considerations. This led to the birth of the discipline of medical ethics that is neither law enforceable by government nor morality enforceable by conscience. On the other hand, Islamic Law is comprehensive and encompasses moral principles directly applicable to medicine. This chapter proposes that the theory of medical ethics in Islam should be based on the 5 purposes of the Law, maqasid al shari'at, that are also considered the 5 purposes of medicine. The 5 purposes are preservation of religion and morality, hifdh al ddiin; preservation of life and health, hifdh al nafs; preservation of progeny, hifdh al nasl; preservation of intellect, hifdh al 'aql; and preservation of wealth, hifdh al maal.

Any medical action must fulfill one of the above purposes if it is to be considered ethical. If any medical procedure violates any of the 5 purposes it is deemed unethical. This chapter proposes that the basic ethical principles of Islam relevant to medical practice be derived from the 5 principles of the Law, qawa'id al shari'at, that are: intention, qasd; certainty, yaqeen; injury, dharar; hardship, mashaqqat; and custom or precedent, 'aadat. The maqasid and qawa'id are used in a synergistic way. The basic purpose of qawa'id is to provide robust rules for resolving situations of conflict between or among different maqasid.

The challenge before Muslim physicians is to liberate themselves from confusing and inconsistent European ethical theories and principles and instead to work hard to develop specific regulations for various medical interventions, dhawaabit al tibaabat, by a renewal of ijtihad. This ijtihad will be based on primary sources of the Law (Qur'an and sunnat), secondary sources of the Law based on transmission, masaadir naqliyyat (ijma and qiyaas); secondary sources of the Law based on reason, masaadir 'aqliyyat (istishaab, istihsaan, & istilaah); the purposes of the Law, maqasid al shari'at; principles of the Law, qawa'id al fiqh; as well as regulations of the Law, dhawaabit al fiqh.

In the early period of medical jurisprudence (0-1400 H) most issues could be resolved by direct reference to the primary sources. In the middle period (1401 – 1420 H) issues were resolved by using ijma, qiyaas, istishaab, istihsaan, & istilaah. In the modern period (1420 -) medical technology is creating so many issues whose resolution will require a broad bird's eye-view approach that can only be found in the theory of maqasid al shari'at. Medical ethics is both old and new. Some statements in the Hippocratic Oath deal with professional medical ethics and Ibn Sina wrote about ethics. Concern with ethics in the past was not as intensive as it is at the moment. It was assumed that physicians would be ethical and moral in their work and this was true to a large extent because religiosity was a leading characteristic of life in the past.

Towards the end of the 14th hijri century ethical considerations became a major concern for two reasons. The first reason was that developments in medical technology gave rise to problems such as life-support, invitro fertilization and others that had moral dimensions. The second reason was the increase in moral violations by medical practitioners. The European medical profession found itself in a dilemma because moral values were not part of the secular medical tradition. The rebirth (renaissance) of the discipline of ethics thus became inevitable. Muslims did not face a similar dilemma because Islamic Law, unlike European secular law, is based on a complete system of morality and can therefore handle all moral problems that arise in medicine from a legal perspective. It also is very flexible being adaptable to many new and novel situations.

Strictly speaking, Muslims do not need to talk of ethics as a separate discipline because it is already included in their Law. Muslim physicians trained in the European tradition tended in the past to employ European ethical theories and principles in dealing with ethical problems in medicine. This chapter proposes that Muslims should turn to their intellectual and legal heritage as a source of ethical guidelines. The chapter critiques European ethics by pointing out conceptual and practical defects. It then presents Islamic ethical system as a more robust and consistent guideline for ethical dilemmas in medicine.

Critique of European Ethics

European Morality

The term European in this chapter is used in a cultural and not a geographical sense to refer to people of European origin who live in the European continent, North and South America, Australasia, and other parts of the world colonized by Europeans over the past 500 years. The European civilization has its roots in the Greco-Roman and Judeo-Christian traditions. Europeans have had a problem dealing consis-tently with moral issues after removing religion from public life over the past 5 centuries of secularism that followed the European renaissance. Morality to them is communal consensus about what is right and what is wrong. For example codes of professional conduct are a consensus reached within each profession. Ethical guidelines are developed while reasoning through ethical or practical dilemmas.

This reasoning can be weak and inconsistent if not based on an underlying coherent system of moral values. European law is not always consistent in dealing with issues of a moral nature. Unlike Islamic Law, European law is not the expression and practical manifestation of a definable system of immorality. As a consequence European law does not always permit all morally acceptable practices and neither does it automatically ban all immoral activities. It sometimes bans morally acceptable practices. It also deals paradoxically with some situations. For example a man who marries 2 wives is punished severely for the crime of bigamy. If on the other hand he co-habits with 4 women as girl friends and has children with them, he will not be penalized. The law recognizes his paternity. It also recognizes specific financial rights of inheritance and maintenance for the women and the children.

An ethical theory provides a framework within which moral reasoning and judgment can be undertaken. There is no one coherent European theory of ethics because of historical reasons. Judeo-Christian concepts were Europeanized when the Roman Empire opted for Christianity and the system of moral values developed in Europe became a syncretic compromise between the pagan European polytheistic Greco-roman religion on one hand and the Judeo-christian religion on the other hand. During the renaissance the Christian church was relatively marginalized. There was a partial return to Grecoroman ideas and practices starting with the renaissance. This resulted into a complex mosaic of moral and philosophical concepts of secular Europe. In these circumstances it became difficult to define or follow one coherent ethical theory. Secularism gradually encroached on civil life starting with the renaissance. By the 20th century, all aspects of European life including medicine had become secularized.

The practical manifestation of this secularization was the marginalization of religious and moral values and confining them to the private arena of individual belief. Secularized European law is in essence a denial of moral considerations in law because morality is associated with 'religion'. However application of the secularized law in medicine showed its deficiencies because issues arose that required moral considerations. The medical profession and society at large were not ready to face the new challenges. The existing positive secular laws lacked a moral spine. It became necessary to develop secular medical ethics as a new discipline to deal with the challenges. Unfortunately this discipline was not wholly effective because it neither law enforced by the authority of the state and neither morality enforced by conscience.

It was unfortunate that Muslims with the rich intellectual heritage of usual al fiqh followed the European into the lizard hole by copying and using inferior European ethical theories, principles, and rules. Europeans consider the Hippocratic Oath as the starting point of ethical reasoning. This is supplemented by views of European philosophers and thinkers to develop ethical theories used to solve practical problems. Starting in about 1976M TL Beauchamps and JF Childress were pioneers in systematically laying down theories and principles of European medical ethics.

European Ethical Theory

According to Beauchamp and Childress there are eight ethical theories. None of them can singly explain all ethical or moral dilemmas. None of them taken singly has the attributes of a good ethical theory: clear, coherent, complete, comprehensive, simple, practicable, and able to explain and justify. In practice more than one theory may have to be combined to solve a specific ethical issue. This is cumbersome and confusing. According to the utilitarian con-sequence-based theory, an act is judged as good or bad according to the balance of its good and bad consequences. Utilitarianism aims at attaining the greatest positive with the least negative. Utilitarianism has the disadvantage of permitting acts that are clearly immoral on the basis of utility. The obligation-based theory is based on Kantian philosophy. Immanuel Kant (1724-1804M) argued that morality was based on pure reasoning.

He rejected tradition, intuition, conscience, or emotions as sources of moral judgment. He argued that a morally valid reason justifies action and that acts are based on moral obligations. The problem with the Kantian theory is that it has no solution for conflicting obligations because it considers moral rules as absolute. The rights-based theory is based on respect for human rights of property, life, liberty, and expression. The problem of the rights-based theory is that emphasis on individual rights creates an adversarial atmosphere. Individual rights may conflict with communal rights. Rights of one individual may conflict with those of another one. According to the community-based theory, ethical judgments are controlled by community values that include considerations of the common good, social goals, and tradition.

This theory repudiates the rights-based theory that is based on individualism. The problem with this theory is that it is difficult to reach a consensus on what constitutes a community value in today's complex and diverse society. The relation-based theory gives emphasis to family relations and the special physician-patient relation. For example a moral judgment may be based on the consideration that nothing should be done to disrupt the normal functioning of the family unit. The problem of this theory is that it is difficult to deal with and analyze emotional and psychological factors that are involved in relationships. The casebased theory is practical decision-making on each case as it arises. It does have fixed philosophical prior assumptions. It can give contradictory conclusions for cases of a similar nature and is very vulnerable to bias.

European Ethical Principles

Ethical principles are specific axioms that simplify ethical reasoning. There are 4 basic European ethical principles according to Beauchamp and Childress. The principle of autonomy is the power of the patient to decide on medical procedures. The principle of non-malfeasance is avoiding causation of harm. The principle of beneficence is the providing benefits and balancing them against risks and costs. The principle of justice is distribution of benefits, costs, and risks fairly. European ethical principles are not based on a comprehensive ethical theory comparable to the theory of purposes of the Law, maqasid al shari'at, found in Islam. There is correspondence between these principles and some of the qawai'd al shari'at. Compared to the qawa'id the principles of Beauchamp and Childress are limited in scope of coverage.

European Ethical Rules

According to Beauchamp and Childress, application of the above principles requires ethical rules. The European ethical rules may be substantive rules, authority rules, or procedural rules. The substantive rules deal with veracity, confidentiality, privacy, and fidelity. The authority rules deal with surrogacy, professional authority, and rationing. The procedure rules are specific on procedures to be followed. The European ethical rules can be related to regulations of Islamic Law, dhawaabit al fiqh. The European rules are very narrow in scope compared to the dhawaabit al fiqh.

Islamic Ethics

Morality and ethics in Islam are absolute and are of divine origin. Human consensus not deriving from divine legislation cannot be a source of binding ethical guidelines. All what humans do it to apply the legal and moral teachings of Islam to practical situations? Islamic Law automatically bans all immoral actions as haram and automatically permits all what is moral as mubaah. Ethical guidelincs are both fixed and variable. The fixed moral and legal principles are broad enough to encompass the needs of all times and places. The detailed applications are variable and change with the growth of science and technology. The fixed principles set the parameters beyond which it is absolutely immoral to operate. Within these parameters, consensus can be reached on specific moral issues.

Islam holds that ethics cannot be divorced from morality. Ethics can also not be divorced from Law. Islamic Law is a compendium of ethics, morality, and legal rules. The purposes of the Law, maqasid al shari'at, the principles of the Law, qawa'id al fiqh, and the regulations of the Law, dhawaabit al fiqh, are therefore the basis of ethics. Islam holds that the human mind, unless corrupted by shaitan, is capable to working out rationally what is right and what is wrong for most problems of life. There are however a few gray areas for which moral reasoning needs to be guided by revelation, wahy, to reach correct conclusions. Islam considers medical ethics the same as ethics in other areas of life. There is no special code for physicians. What we call medical ethics is restating general ethical principles using medical terminology and with medical applications. The medical ethical codes can be derived from the basic law but the detailed applications require further intellectual effort, ijtihad, by physicians.

Strange as it may sound, some ethical problems are solved by avoiding them. This is part of the Islamic teaching of avoiding doubtful things. The prophet taught us to leave what causes us doubts to what does not cause such doubt, da' ma yuribuuka ila ma la yuriibuka. The ethical theory of Islam is found in the 5 purposes of the Law, maqasid al shari'at. The five purposes are preservation of ddiin, life, progeny, intellect, and wealth. Any medical action must fulfill one of the above purposes if it is to be considered ethical. The basic ethical principles of Islam relevant to medical practice are derived from the 5 principles of the Law are: intention, qasd; certainty, yaqeen; harm, dharar; hardship, mashaqqat; and custom, and 'aadat.

The first purpose is protection of ddiin, hifdh al ddiin. It involves both physical health and mental health. Protection of ddiin essentially involves 'ibadat in the wide sense that every human endeavor is a form of 'ibadat. Thus medical treatment makes a direct contribution to 'ibadat by protecting and promoting good health so that the worshipper will have the phusical and mental energy to undertake all the responsibilities of 'ibadat. The principal forms of physical 'ibadat are prayer, salat; fasting, siyaam; and pilgrimage, hajj. A sick or a weak body can perform them properly. Balanced mental health is necessary for understanding 'aqiidat and avoiding false ideas that violate 'aqiidat because 'aqiidat is the basis of ddiin. The second purpose is protection of life, hifdh al nafs, and the primary purpose of medicine. Medicine cannot prevent or postpone death since such matters are in the hands of Allah alone. It however tries to maintain as high a quality of life until the appointed time of death arrives. Medicine contributes to the preservation and continuation of life by making sure that physiological functions are well maintained.

It also relieves pathophysiological stress by preventive, curative, and rehabilitative measures. The third purpose is protection of progeny, hifdh al nasl. Medicine contributes to the fulfillment of this function by making sure that children are cared for well so that they grow into healthy adults who can bear children. Treatment of male and female infertility ensures successful reproduction. The care for pregnant women, perinatal medicine, and pediatric medicine all ensure that children are born and grow healthy. The fourth purpose is protection of the mind, hifdh al 'aql. Medical treatment plays a very important role in protection of the mind. Treatment of physical illnesses removes stress that affects the mental state. Treatment of neuroses and psychoses restores intellectual and emotional functions. Medical treatment of alcohol and drug abuse prevents deterioration of the intellect.

The fifth purpose is protection of wealth, hifdh al maal. The wealth of any community depends on the productive activities of its healthy citizens. Medicine contributes to wealth generation by prevention of disease, promotion of health, and treatment of any diseases and their sequel. Communities with general poor health are less productive than healthy vibrant communities. The principles of protection of life and protection of wealth may conflict in cases of terminal illness. Care for the terminally ill consumes a lot of resources that could have been used to treat other persons with treatable conditions. Resolution of such contrasts requires resort to the principles of the Law, qawa'id al shari'at that are described below.

Principle of Intention

The first principle is the principle of intention, qa'idat al qasd. It gives rise to several sub-principles applicable to medical practice. The sub-principle 'each action is judged by the intention behind it, al umuur bi maqasidiha' calls upon the physician to consult his inner conscience. There are many issues about medical procedures and medical decisions that are hidden from public view. A physician may carry out a procedure for a stated reason that seems plausible on the outside but he may have a different but hidden intention. A practical example is use of morphine for pain relief in terminal care when the actual intention may be to cause respiratory depression that will lead to death.

The sub-principle 'what matters are the intentions and not the literal meaning – maqasid wa ma'aani la alfaadh wa mabaani' is used to refute use of legal arguments based on literal translation of the text to justify immoral acts. An example is the interpretation of the hadith on embryological development to justify abortion on demand before ensoulment. The sub-principle 'means are judged with the same criteria as the intentions – al wasail laha hukm al maqasid' implies that no useful medical purpose should be achieved by using immoral methods.

Principle of Certainty

The second principle is the principle of certainty, qaidat al yaqeen. In both the diagnosis of disease and choice of treatment, modern medicine does not reach the standards of yaqeen demanded by the Law. It operates at the level of predominant conjecture, ghalabat al dhann. It cannot operate at the level of conjecture, dhann, or pure doubt, shakk. Legal certainty, yaqeen, a situation when there is no doubt, shakk, or second thoughts, taraddud, does not exist in medicine. Ghalabat al dhann is when there is preponderant evidence for one option and not the other. In dhann there is inclination to one option but there is not enough evidence for that option.

In shakk the evidence for the 2 options is of equal weight. Experimental therapies are used without cer-tainty of the effect. In many cases a presumptive diagnosis is made and treatment proceeds. Treatment may be symptomatic where there is no clue to the cause.

Everything in medicine is probabilistic and relative. Treatment decisions are best on a balance of probabilities. When a diagnosis is made, it should be treated as a working diagnosis until new information is obtained to change it. This provides for stability and a situation of quasi-certainty without which practical procedures will be taken reluctantly and inefficiently. Existing assertions should continue in force until there is compelling evidence to change them, al asl baqau ma kaana 'ala ma kaana. The principle of certainty also applies to consideration of pathological conditions. A pathological or clinical event is considered of recent occurrence unless there is evidence to the contrary, al asl idhafat al haadith ila aqrab waqtihi. An acquired attribute or change is not accepted as normal unless there is compelling evidence, al asl fi al umuur al 'aaridhat al 'adam. An existing condition whose origin or cause is not known should be left as is until there is evidence to the contrary, al qadiim yutraku ala qadamihi.

This principle protects against unnecessary medical interventions in long-standing anomalies or deformities that do not appear to cause any discomfort. What has been accepted as customary over a long time is not considered harmful unless there is evidence to the contrary, al qadiim la yakuun dhararan. According to the principle of certainty all medical procedures are considered permissible unless there is evidence to prove their prohibition, al asl fi al ashiya al ibaaha. Exceptions to this rule are conditions related to the sexual and reproductive functions. All matters related to the sexual function are presumed forbidden unless there is evidence to prove permissibility, al asl fi al abdhai al tahriim.

Principle of Injury

The third principle is the principle of injury, qa'idat al dharar. Medical intervention is justified on the basic principle that injury, if it occurs, should be relieved, al dharar yuzaal. The physician should however cause no harm in the course of his work according to the principle of la dharara wa la dhirar. Injury should be prevented or mitigated as much as is possible, al dharar yudfau bi qadr al imkaan. When an injury is found in a patient it is presumed to be of recent origin unless there is evidence to the contrary, al dharar la yakuun qadiiman, and therefore must be alleviated. An injury should not be relieved by a medical procedure that leads to an injury of the same magnitude as a side effect, al dharar la yuzaal bi mithlihi. In a situation in which the proposed medical intervention has side effects, we follow the principle that prevention of harm has priority over pursuit of a benefit of equal worth, dariu an mafasid awla min jalbi al masaalih. If the benefit has far more importance and worth than the harm, then the pursuit of the benefit has priority.

Physicians sometimes are confronted with medical interventions that are double edged; they have both prohibited and permitted effects. The guidance of the Law is that the prohibited has priority of recognition over the permitted if the two occur together and a choice has to be made, idha ijtama'a al halaal wa al haram ghalaba al haraam al halaaal. If confronted with 2 medical situations both of which are harmful and there is no way but to choose one of them, the lesser harm is committed, ikhtiyaar ahwan al sharrain. A lesser harm is committed in order to prevent a bigger harm, al dharar al ashadd yuzaalu bi al dharar al akhaff.

In the same way medical interventions that are in public interest have priority over consideration of individual interest, al maslahat al aamat muqaddamat ala al maslahat al khaassat. The individual may have to sustain harm in order to protect public interest, yatahammalu al dharar al khaas li dafu'i al dharar al aam. In the course of combating communicable diseases, the state may have to restrict movements of a citizen or even destroy his property. The state cannot infringe on the rights of the public unless there is a public benefit to be achieved, al tasarruf ala al ra'iyat manuutu bi al maslahat. Many situations, the line between benefit and injury is so fine that salat al istikharat is needed to reach a solution since no empirical methods can be used.

Principle of Hardship

The fourth principle is the principle of hardship, qa'idat al mashaqqat. Medical interventions that would otherwise be prohibited actions are permitted under the principle of hardship if there is a necessity, dharuurat. Necessity legalizes the prohibited, al dharuraat tubiihu al mahdhuuraat. In the medical setting a hardship is defined as any condition that will seriously impair physical and mental health if not relieved promptly. Hardship mitigates easing of the sharia rules and obligations, al mashaqqa tajlibu al tayseer. This is predicated on the general principle of Islam as an easy religion that cannot be made difficult and a burden for its followers, al ddiin yusr wa lan yashaada hadha al ddiin illa ghalabahu.

Some limitations of the principle of hardship need to be observed. Committing the otherwise prohibited action should not extend beyond the limits needed to preserve the Purpose of the Law that is the basis for the legalization, al dharuraat tuqaddar bi qadriha. Application of the principle of hardship is of limited duration. Necessity however does not permanently abrogate the patient's rights that must be restored or recompensed in due course; necessity only legalizes temporary violation of rights, al idhtiraar la yubtilu haqq al ghair. The temporary legalization of prohibited medical action ends with the end of the necessity that justified it in the first place, ma jaaza bi 'udhri batala bi zawaalihi. This can be stated in al alternative way if the obstacle ends, enforcement of the prohibited resumes, idha zaala al maniu, aada al mamnuu'u. It is illegal to get out of a difficulty by delegating to someone else to undertake a harmful act, ma haruma fi'iluhu, haruma talabuhu.

Principle of Custom

The fifth principle is the principle of custom or precedent, qa'idat al urf. The generally accepted standard of medical care is defined by custom. The basic principle is that custom or precedent has legal force, al aadat muhakamat. What is considered customary is what is uniform, widespread, and predominant, innama tu'utabaru al 'aadat idha atradat aw ghalabat, and not rare, al ibrat li al ghaalib al shaiu la al naadir. The customary must also be old and not a recent phenomenon to give chance for a medical consensus to be formed.

Regulations of Medicine

Dhaabit fiqhi is a general principle that applied to specific situations in one chapter of the law. Dhaabit is narrower in scope than the qaidat. The dhaabit deals with only one chapter of fiqh whereas qa'idat deals with several chapters. The dhaabit fiqhi is narrower in scope and admits fewer exceptions than the qa'idat fiqhiyyat.

Omnibus Regulations

The physician must have technical competence, itiqaan, and aim at excellence and quality work, ihsaan. He must have balance, tawazun, in actions and attitudes. He must realize that he is carrying a great trust, amanat, and must continuously undertake self-criticism, muhasabat. Imaam al Nawawi in his book al Adhkaar recorded over 30 hadiths that cover the core values around which Islam revolves, madaaru al islam. These values are general guidelines for medical work. All work is recognized according to the intention behind it. Doubtful things are better avoided. Leave alone what does not concern you. Love for others what you love for yourself. Cause no harm. Give sincerity advice.

Avoid what is prohibited and do as much as is possible of what is enjoined and avoiding too much sterile argumentation and questioning. Renounce longing for the material goods of the world and the property of other people. Do not take life except by judicial execution. Claims or allegations must be supported by evidence. In matters of right and wrong, the dictates of the conscience should be followed even if others say otherwise; the righteous act outs the heart at ease, the evil causes it distress. Excellence and quality work are needed in all endeavors. Guard the tongue. It is better to keep silent than to speak evil. Avoid anger and rage. Do not transgress limits set by Allah. Have consciousness of Allah in all circumstances. Perform good acts to wipe out bad ones and treat people with the best of manners. Exercise restraint and modesty. Maintain objectivity. Seek help from Allah. Avoid oppression or transgression.

Physician Obligation

A sole medical practitioner is a community is individually obliged to provide medical benefit and relief as fard 'ain. The obligation becomes fard kifayat is there are other equally competent caregivers. However if a patient has already started getting medical benefit from a particular physician, the individual responsibility of that physician remains even if there are other equally competent ones in the community.

Respect for Patient Autonomy

The principle of autonomy is derived from the shari'at principle of intention, qa'idat al qasd. Among all players in a medical scenario it is the individual patient who has the best and purest of intentions. He or she is best able to make decisions in the best interests of his or her life. Others may have other personal considerations that may bias their decision-making. It is for this reason that all decisions must be referred to the patient. No medical procedures can be carried out without informed consent except in cases of legal incompetence in which case the Law provides for other persons to make decisions on behalf of the incompetent patient.

Veracity and Disclosure

As part of the professional contract between the physician and the patient, the physician must tell the whole truth. Patients have the right to know the risks and benefits of medical procedure in order for them to make an autonomous informed consent. The physician should be guided in his communication by the background and understanding of a patient. Some patients can be given a lot of information and they do not get disturbed. Some types of information agitate patients. The prophet enjoined talking to each person according to his ability to understand, kalaam al naas hasba 'uquulihim.

Confidentiality

Revealing patient secrets violates fidelity which is the private and privileged relationship of trust between the patient and the caregiver. Revealing secrets harms the patient under the principle of Injury, qa'idat dharar. Under the principle of hardship, qa'idat al mashaqqa, secrets may be revealed under necessity, dharuurat. The injunction to keep secrets is binding on both the caregiver and the patient. The patient should not make unnecessary revelation of negative things about himself or herself, satr al mumin ala nafsihi. In cases of court litigation, The caregiver could testify in criminal cases that involve dhulm. The Qur'an forbids the revelation of the shameful unless there is dhulm. The caregiver cannot give false testimony.

Fidelity

The principle of fidelity requires that physicians be faithful to their patients. Fidelity includes: acting in faith, fulfilling agreements, maintaining relations, and acting in trust and confidence. Abandoning the patient at any stage of treatment without alternative arrangements is a violation of fidelity. The fidelity obligation may conflict with the obligation to protect third parties by disclosing contagious disease or dangerous behaviour of the patient. The physician may find himself in a situation of divided loyalty between the interests of the patient and the interests of the institution. The conflict may be between two patients of the physician such as when maternal and fetal interests conflict. Physicians involved in clinical trials have conflicting dual roles of physicians and investigators. These issues can be resolved by reference to the maqasid and qawa'id.

Islamic Golden Age

The Islamic Golden Age, also sometimes known as the Islamic Renaissance, was traditionally dated from the 700 A.D. to 1200 A.D.C.E., but has been extended to the 15th and 16th centuries by some scholars. During this period, artists, engineers, scholars, poets, philosophers, geographers and traders in the Islamic world contributed to the arts, agriculture, economics, industry, law, literature, navigation, philosophy, sciences, sociology, and technology, both by preserving and building upon earlier traditions and by adding inventions and innovations of their own. Howard R. Turner writes: "Muslim artists and scientists, princes and laborers together made a unique culture that has directly and indirectly influenced societies on every continent." During the Muslim conquests of the 7th and early 8th centuries, Rashidun armies established the Islamic Empire, which was one of the ten largest empires in history.

The Islamic Golden Age was soon inaugurated by the middle of the 8th century by the ascension of the Abbasid Caliphate and the transfer of the capital from Damascus to the Persian city of Baghdad illustrating the strong Persian presence in the Abbasid Caliphate. The Abbassids were influenced by the Qur'anic injunctions and hadith such as

"The ink of the scholar is more holy than the blood of martyrs" stressing the value of knowledge. During this period the Muslim world became the unrivalled intellectual centre for science, philosophy, medicine and education as the Abbasids championed the cause of knowledge and established the "House of Wisdom" in Baghdad; where both Muslim and non-Muslim scholars sought to translate and gather all the world's knowledge into Arabic. Many classic works of antiquity that would otherwise have been forgotten were translated into Arabic and later in turn translated into Turkish, Persian, Hebrew and Latin.

During this period the Muslim world was a cauldron of cultures which collected, synthesized and significantly advanced the knowledge gained from the ancient Iraqi, Roman, Chinese, Indian, Persian, Egyptian, North African, Greek and Byzantine civilizations. Rival Muslim dynasties such as the Fatimids of Egypt and the Umayyads of al-Andalus were also major intellectual centres with cities such as Cairo and Córdoba rivaling Baghdad. A major innovation of this period was paper - originally a secret tightly guarded by the Chinese. The art of papermaking was obtained from prisoners taken at the Battle of Talas (751), resulting in paper mills being built in the Persian cities of Samarkand and Baghdad. The Arabs improved upon the Chinese techniques of using mulberry bark by using starch to account for the Muslim preference for pens vs. the Chinese for brushes. By AD 900 there were hundreds of shops employing scribes and binders for books in Baghdad and even public libraries began to become established, including the first lending libraries.

From here paper-making spread west to Fez and then to al-Andalus and from there to Europe in the 13th century. Much of this learning and development can be linked to topography. Even prior to Islam's presence, the city of Mecca served as a center of trade in Arabia. The tradition of the pilgrimage to Mecca became a center for exchanging ideas and goods. The influence held by Muslim merchants over African-Arabian and Arabian-Asian trade routes was tremendous. As a result, Islamic civilization grew and expanded on the basis of its merchant economy, in contrast to their Christian, Indian and Chinese peers who built societies from agricultural landholding nobility. Merchants brought goods and their faith to China, India (the Indian subcontinent now has over 450 million followers), South-east Asia (which now has over 230 million followers), and the kingdoms of Western Africa and returned with new inventions. Merchants used their wealth to invest in textiles and plantations.

Aside from traders, Sufi missionaries also played a large role in the spread of Islam, by bringing their message to various regions around the world. The principal locations included: Persia, Ancient Mesopotamia, Central Asia and North Africa. Although, the mystics also had a significant influence in parts of Eastern Africa, Ancient Anatolia (Turkey), South Asia, East Asia and South-east Asia. Many medieval Muslim thinkers pursued humanistic, rational and scientific discourses in their search for knowledge, meaning and values. A wide range of Islamic writings on love, poetry, history and philosophical theology show that medieval Islamic thought was open to the humanistic ideas of individualism, occasional secularism, skepticism and liberalism. Religious freedom, though society was still controlled under Islamic values, helped create cross-cultural networks by attracting Muslim, Christian and Jewish intellectuals and thereby helped spawn the greatest period of philosophical creativity in the middle Ages from the 8th to 13th centuries.

Another reason the Islamic world flourished during this period was an early emphasis on freedom of speech, as summarized by al-Hashimi (a cousin of Caliph al-Ma'mun) in the following letter to one of the religious opponents he was attempting to convert through reason:

"Bring forward all the arguments you wish and say whatever you please and speak your mind freely. Now that you are safe and free to say whatever you please appoint some arbitrator who will impartially judge between us and lean only towards the truth and be free from the empary of passion, and that arbitrator shall be Reason, whereby God makes us responsible for our own rewards and punishments. Herein I have dealt justly with you and have given you full security and am ready to accept whatever decision Reason may give for me or against me. For "There is no compulsion in religion" (Qur'an 2:256) and I have only invited you to accept our faith willingly and of your own accord and have pointed out the hideousness of your present belief. Peace be upon you and the blessings of God!"

The earliest known treatises dealing with environmentalism and environmental science, especially pollution, were Arabic treatises written by al-Kindi, al-Razi, Ibn Al-Jazzar, al-Tamimi, al-Masihi, Avicenna, Ali ibn Ridwan, Abd-el-latif, and Ibn al-Nafis. Their works covered a number of subjects related to pollution such as air pollution, water pollution, soil contamination, municipal solid waste mishandling, and environmental impact assessments of certain localities. Cordoba, al-Andalus also had the first waste containers and waste disposal facilities for litter collection. A number of important educational and scientific insti-tutions previously unknown in the ancient world have their origins in the medieval Islamic world, with the most notable examples being: the public hospital (which replaced healing temples and sleep temples) and psychiatric hospital, the public library and lending library, the academic degreegranting university, and the astronomical observatory as a research institute (as opposed to a private observation post as was the case in ancient times).

The first universities which issued diplomas were the Bimaristan medical university-hospitals of the medieval Islamic world, where medical diplomas were issued to students of Islamic medicine who were qualified to be practicing doctors of medicine from the 9th century. The Guinness Book of World Records recognizes the University of Al Karaouine in Fez, Morocco as the oldest degreegranting university in the world with its founding in 859 CE. Al-Azhar University, founded in Cairo, Egypt in the 975 CE, offered a variety of academic degrees, including postgraduate degrees, and is often considered the first fullfledged university. The origins of the doctorate also dates back to the *ijazat attadris wa 'l-ifttd* ("license to teach and issue legal opinions") in the medieval Madrasahs which taught Islamic law. By the 10th century, Cordoba had 700 mosques, 60,000 palaces, and 70 libraries, the largest of which had 600,000 books. In the whole al-Andalus, 60,000 treatises, poems, polemics and compilations were published each year. The library of Cairo had two million books, while the library of Tripoli is said to have had as many as three million books before it was destroyed by Crusaders.

The number of important and original medieval Arabic works on the mathematical sciences far exceeds the combined total of medieval Latin and Greek works of comparable significance, although only a small fraction of the surviving Arabic scientific works have been studied in modern times. A number of distinct features of the modern library were introduced in the Islamic world, where libraries not only served as a collection of manuscripts as was the case in ancient libraries, but also as a public library and lending library, a centre for the instruction and spread of sciences and ideas, a place for meetings and discussions, and sometimes as a lodging for scholars or boarding school for pupils. The concept of the library catalogue was also introduced in medieval Islamic libraries, where books were organized into specific genres and categories. Several fundamental common law institutions may have been adapted from similar legal institutions in Islamic law and jurisprudence, and introduced to England by the Normans after the Norman Conquest of England and the Emirate of Sicily, and by Crusaders during the Crusades.

In particular, the "royal English contract protected by the action of debt is identified with the Islamic *Aqd*, the English assize of novel disseisin is identified with the Islamic *Istihqaq*, and the English jury is identified with the Islamic *Lafif*." Other legal institutions introduced in Islamic law include the trust and charitable trust (Waqf), and the agency and aval (Hawala), and the lawsuit and medical peer review. Other English legal institutions such as "the scholastic method, the license to teach," the "law schools known as Inns of Court in England and *Madrasas* in Islam" and the "European commenda" (Islamic *Qirad*) may have also originated from Islamic law. These influences have led some scholars to suggest that Islamic law may have laid the foundations for "the common law as an integrated whole". Another common feature during the Islamic Golden Age was the large number of Muslim polymath scholars, who were known as "Hakeems", each of whom contributed to a variety of different fields of both religious and secular learning, comparable to the later "Renaissance Men" (such as Leonardo da Vinci) of the European Renaissance period.

During the Islamic Golden Age, polymath scholars with a wide breadth of knowledge in different fields were more common than scholars who specialized in any single field of learning. Notable medieval Muslim polymaths included al-Biruni, al-Jahiz, al-Kindi, Avicenna, al-Idrisi, Ibn Bajjah, Ibn Zuhr, Ibn Tufail, Averroes, al-Suyuti, Geber, Abbas Ibn Firnas, Alhacen, Ibn al-Nafis, Ibn Khaldun, al-Khwarizmi, al-Masudi, al-Muqaddasi, and Nasîr al-Dîn al-Tûsî, among others. The Islamic Empire significantly contributed to globalization during the Islamic Golden Age, when the knowledge, trade and economies from many previously isolated regions and civilizations began integrating due to contacts with Muslim explorers, sailors, scholars, traders, and travelers.

Some have called this period the "Pax Islamica" or "Afro-Asiatic age of discovery", in reference to the Jewish (known as Radhanites), Sogdian and Muslim South-west Asian and North African traders and explorers who travelled most of the Old World, and established an early global economy across most of Asia and Africa and much of Europe, with their trade networks extending from the Atlantic Ocean and Mediterranean Sea in the west to the Indian Ocean and China Sea in the east. This helped establish the Islamic Empire (including the Rashidun, Umayyad, Abbasid and Fatimid caliphates) as the world's leading extensive economic power throughout the 7th-13th centuries. Several contemporary medieval Arabic reports also suggest that Muslim explorers from al-Andalus and the Maghreb may have travelled in expeditions across the Atlantic Ocean between the 9th and 14th centuries. The Islamic Golden Age witnessed a fundamental transformation in agriculture known as the "Muslim Agricultural Revolution" or "Arab Agricultural Revolution".

Due to the global economy established by Muslim traders across the Old World, this enabled the diffusion of many plants and farming techniques between different parts of the Islamic world, as well as the adaptation of plants and techniques from beyond the Islamic world. Crops from Africa such as sorghum, crops from China such as citrus fruits, and numerous crops from India such as mangos, rice, and especially cotton and sugar cane, were distributed throughout Islamic lands which normally would not be able to grow these crops. Some have referred to the diffusion of numerous crops during this period as the "Globalisation of Crops", which, along with an increased mechanization of agriculture, led to major changes in economy, population distribution, vegetation cover, agricultural production and income, population levels, urban growth, the distribution of the labour force, linked industries, cooking and diet, clothing, and numerous other aspects of life in the Islamic world.

During the Muslim Agricultural Revolution, sugar production was refined and transformed into a large-scale industry by the Arabs, who built the first sugar refineries and sugar plantations. The Arabs and Berbers diffused sugar throughout the Islamic Empire from the 8th century. Muslims introduced cash cropping and the modern crop rotation system where land was cropped four or more times in a two-year period. Winter crops were followed by summer ones. In areas where plants of shorter growing season were used, such as spinach and eggplants, the land could be cropped three or more times a year. In parts of Yemen, wheat yielded two harvests a year on the same land, as did rice in Iraq. Muslims developed a scientific approach to agriculture based on three major elements; sophisticated systems of crop rotation, highly developed irrigation techniques, and the introduction of a large variety of crops which were studied and catalogued according to the season, type of land and amount of water they require.

Numerous encyclopaedias on farming and botany were produced, containing accurate, precise detail. Early forms of proto-capitalism and free markets were present in the Caliphate, where an early market economy and early form of merchant capitalism was developed between the 8th-12th centuries, which some refer to as "Islamic capitalism". A vigorous monetary economy was created on the basis of the expanding levels of circulation of a stable high-value currency (the dinar) and the integration of monetary areas that were previously independent. Innovative new business techniques and forms of business organisation were introduced by economists, merchants and traders during this time. Such innovations included early trading companies, credit cards, big businesses, contracts, bills of exchange, long-distance international trade, early forms of partnership (*mufawada*) such as limited partnerships (*muda-raba*), and early forms of credit, debt, profit, loss, capital (*al-mal*), capital accumulation (*nama al-mal*), circulating capital, capital expenditure, revenue, cheques, promissory notes, trusts (*waqf*), startup companies, savings accounts, transactional accounts, pawning, loaning, exchange rates, bankers, money changers, ledgers, deposits, assignments, the double-entry bookkeeping system, and lawsuits. Organizational enterprises similar to corporations' independent from the state also existed in the medieval Islamic world.

Many of these early proto-capitalist concepts were adopted and further advanced in medieval Europe from the 13th century onwards. The systems of contract relied upon by merchants was very effective. Merchants would buy and sell on commission, with money loaned to them by wealthy investors, or a joint investment of several merchants, who were often Muslim, Christian and Jewish. Recently, a collection of documents was found in an Egyptian synagogue shedding a very detailed and human light on the life of medieval Middle Eastern merchants. Business partnerships would be made for many commercial ventures, and bonds of kinship enabled trade networks to form over huge distances. Networks developed during this time enabled a world in which money could be promised by a bank in Baghdad and cashed in Spain, creating the cheque system of today. Each time items passed through the cities along this extraordinary network, the city imposed a tax, resulting in high prices once reaching the final destination.

These innovations made by Muslims and Jews laid the foundations for the modern economic system. Though medieval Islamic economics appears to have been closer to proto-capitalism, some scholars have also found a number of parallels between Islamic economic jurisprudence and communism, including the Islamic ideas of zakat and riba. Muslim engineers in the Islamic world made a number of innovative industrial uses of hydropower, and early industrial uses of tidal power, wind power, steam power, fossil fuels such as petroleum, and early large factory complexes (*tiraz* in Arabic). The industrial uses of watermills in the Islamic world date back to the 7th century, while horizontal-wheeled and vertical-wheeled water mills were both in widespread use since at least the 9th century.

A variety of industrial mills were being employed in the Islamic world, including early fulling mills, gristmills, hullers, paper mills, sawmills, shipmills, stamp mills, steel mills, sugar mills, tide mills and windmills. By the 11th century, every province throughout the Islamic world had these industrial mills in operation, from al-Andalus and North Africa to the Middle East and Central Asia. Muslim engineers also invented crankshafts and water turbines, employed gears in mills and water-raising machines, and pioneered the use of dams as a source of water power, used to provide additional power to watermills and water-raising machines. Such advances made it possible for many industrial tasks that were previously driven by manual labour in ancient times to be mechanized and driven by machinery instead in the medieval Islamic world. The transfer of these technologies to medieval Europe had an influence on the Industrial Revolution. A number of industries were generated due to the Muslim Agricultural Revolution, including early industries for agribusiness, astronomical instruments, ceramics, chemicals, distillation technologies, clocks, glass, mechanical hydropowered and wind powered machinery, matting, mosaics, pulp and paper, perfumery, petroleum, pharmaceuticals, ropemaking, shipping, shipbuilding, silk, sugar, textiles, water, weapons, and the mining of minerals such as sulphur, ammonia, lead and iron.

Early large factory complexes (*tiraz*) were built for many of these industries and knowledge of these industries were later transmitted to medieval Europe, especially during the Latin translations of the 12th century, as well as before and after. For example, the first glass factories in Europe were founded in the 11th century by Egyptian craftsmen in Greece. The agricultural and handicraft industries also experienced high levels of growth during this period. The labour force in the Caliphate was employed from diverse ethnic and religious backgrounds, while both men and women were involved in diverse occupations and economic activities. Women were employed in a wide range of commercial activities and diverse occupations in the primary sector (as farmers for example), secondary sector (as construction workers, dyers, spinners, etc.) and tertiary sector (as investors, doctors, nurses, presidents of guilds, brokers, peddlers, lenders, scholars, etc.).

Muslim women also had a monopoly over certain branches of the textile industry. Slaves were purchased on the frontiers of the Islamic world and then imported to the major centers, where there were slave markets from which they were widely distributed. Slaves occupied an important place in the economic life of Islamic world. Large numbers of slaves were exported from eastern Africa to work in salt mines and labour-intensive plantations; the best evidence for this is the magnitude of the Zanj revolt in Iraq in the 9th century. Slaves were also used for domestic work, military service, bought for the harems, and civil administration. Central and east European slaves were generally known as Saqaliba (i.e., Slavs).

A significant number of inventions were produced by medieval Muslim engineers and inventors, such as Abbas Ibn Firnas, the Banû Mûsâ, Taqi al-Din, and most notably al-Jazari. Some of the inventions believed to have come from the Islamic Golden Age include the camera obscura, coffee, soap bar, shampoo, pure distillation, liquefaction, crystallization, purification, oxidisation, evaporation, filtration, distilled alcohol, uric acid, nitric acid, alembic, crankshaft, valve, reciprocating suction piston pump, mechanical clocks driven by water and weights, combination lock, quilting, pointed arch, scalpel, bone saw, forceps, surgical catgut, windmill, inoculation, smallpox vaccine, fountain pen, cryptanalysis, frequency analysis, three-course meal, stained glass and quartz glass, Persian carpet, celestial globe,

As urbanization increased, Muslim cities grew unregulated, resulting in narrow winding city streets and neighbourhoods separated by different ethnic backgrounds and religious affiliations. These qualities proved efficient for transporting goods to and from major commercial centres while preserving the privacy valued by Islamic family life. Suburbs lay just outside the walled city, from wealthy residential communities, to working class semislums. City garbage dumps were located far from the city, as were clearly defined cemeteries which were often homes for criminals. A place of prayer was found just near one of the main gates, for religious festivals and public executions. Similarly, Military Training grounds were found near a main gate. Muslim cities also had advanced domestic water systems with sewers, public baths, drinking fountains, piped drinking water supplies, and widespread private and public toilet and bathing facilities. By the 10th century, Cordoba had 700 mosques, 60,000 palaces, and 70 libraries.

The traditional view of Islamic science was that it was chiefly a preserver and transmitter of ancient knowledge. For example, Donald Lach argues that modern science originated in Europe as an amalgam of medieval technology and Greek learning. These views have been disputed in recent times, with some scholars suggesting that Muslim scientists laid the foundations for modern science, for their development of early scientific methods and an empirical, experimental and quantitative approach to scientific inquiry. Some scholars have referred to this period as a "Muslim scientific revolution", a term which expresses the view that Islam was the driving force behind the Muslim scientific achievements, and should not to be confused with the early modern European Scientific Revolution leading to the rise of modern science. Edward Grant argues that modern science was due to the cumulative efforts of the Hellenic, Islamic and Latin civilizations.

Early scientific methods were developed in the Islamic world, where significant progress in methodology was made, especially in the works of Ibn al-Haytham (Alhazen) in the 11th century, who is considered the pioneer of experimental physics. The most important development of the scientific method was the use of experimentation and quantification to distinguish between competing scientific theories set within a generally empirical orientation. Ibn al-Haytham (Alhazen) wrote the *Book of Optics*, in which he significantly reformed the field of optics, empirically proved that vision occurred because of light rays entering the eye, and invented the camera obscura to demonstrate the physical nature of light rays. Ibn al-Haytham has also been described as the "first scientist" for his introduction of the scientific method, and his pioneering work on the psychology of visual perception is considered a precursor to psychophysics and experimental psychology.

Some have referred to the achievements of the Maragha school and their predecessors and successors in astronomy as a "Maragha Revolution", "Maragha School Revolution" or "Scientific Revolution before the Renaissance". Advances in astronomy by the Maragha school and their predecessors and successors include the construction of the first observatory in Baghdad during the reign of Caliph al-Ma'-mun, the collection and correction of previous astronomical data, resolving significant problems in the Ptolemaic model, the development of universal astrolabes, the invention of numerous other astronomical instruments, the beginning of astrophysics and celestial mechanics after Ja'far Muhammad ibn Mûsâ ibn Shâkir discovered that the heavenly bodies and celestial spheres were subject to the same physical laws as Earth, the first elaborate experiments related to astronomical phenomena and the first semantic distinction between astronomy and astrology by Abû al-Rayhân al-Bîrûnî, the use of exacting empirical observations and experimental techniques, the discovery that the celestial spheres are not solid and that the heavens are less dense than the air by Ibn al-Haytham, the separation of natural philosophy from astronomy by Ibn al-Haytham and Ibn al-Shatir, the first non-Ptolemaic models by Ibn al-Haytham and Mo'ayyeduddin Urdi, the rejection of the Ptolemaic model on empirical rather than philosophical grounds by Ibn a l-Shatir, the first empirical observational evidence of the Earth's rotation by Nasîr al-Dîn al-Tûsî and Ali al-Qushji, and al-Birjandi's early hypothesis on "circular inertia."

Several Muslim astronomers also considered the possibility of the Earth's rotation on its axis and perhaps a heliocentric solar system. It is known that the Copernican heliocentric model in Nicolaus Copernicus' *De revolutionibus* was adapted from the geocentric model of Ibn al-Shatir and the Maragha school (including the Tusi-couple) in a heliocentric context, and that his arguments for the Earth's rotation were similar to those of Nasîr al-Dîn al-Tûsî and Ali al-Qushji.

Geber (Jabir ibn Hayyan) is considered a pioneer of chemistry, as he was responsible for introducing an early experimental scientific method within the field, as well as the alembic, still, retort, and the chemical processes of pure distillation, filtration, sublimation, liquefaction, crystallisation, purification, oxidisation and evaporation. The study of traditional alchemy and the theory of the transmutation of metals were first refuted by al-Kindi, followed by Abû Rayhân al-Bîrûnî, Avicenna, and Ibn Khaldun. In his *Doubts about Galen*, al-Razi was the first to prove both Aristotle's theory of classical elements and Galen's theory of humorism false using an experimental method. Nasîr al-Dîn al-Tûsî stated an early version of the law of conservation of mass, noting that a body of matter is able to change, but is not able to disappear. Alexander von Humboldt and Will Durant consider medieval Muslim chemists to be founders of chemistry.

Among the achievements of Muslim mathematicians during this period include the development of algebra and algorithms by the Persian and Islamic mathematician Muhammad ibn Mûsâ al-Khwârizmî, the invention of spherical trigonometry, the addition of the decimal point notation to the Arabic numerals, the discovery of all the trigonometric functions besides sine, al-Kindi's introduction of cryptanalysis and frequency analysis, al-Karaji's introduction of algebraic calculus and proof by mathematical induction, the development of analytic geometry and the earliest general formula for infinitesimal and integral calculus by Ibn al-Haytham, the beginning of algebraic geometry by Omar Khayyam, the first refutations of Euclidean geometry and the parallel postulate by Nasîr al-Dîn al-Tûsî, the first attempt at a non-Euclidean geometry by Sadr al-Din, the development of symbolic algebra by Abû al-Hasan ibn Alî al-Qalasâdî, and numerous other advances in algebra, arithmetic, calculus, cryptography, geometry, number theory and trigonometry.

Islamic medicine was a genre of medical writing that was influenced by several different medical systems. The works of ancient Greek and Roman physicians Hippocrates, Dioscorides, Soranus, Celsus and Galen had a lasting impact on Islamic medicine. Muslim physicians made many significant contributions to medicine, including anatomy, experimental medicine, ophthalmology, pathology, the pharmaceutical sciences, physiology, surgery, etc. They also set up some of the earliest dedicated hospitals, including the first medical schools and psychiatric hospitals. Al-Kindi wrote the *De Gradibus*, in which he first demonstrated the application of quantification and mathematics to medicine and pharmacology, such as a mathematical scale to quantify the strength of drugs and the determination in advance of the most critical days of a patient's illness. Al-Razi (Rhazes) discovered measles and smallpox, and in his *Doubts about Galen*, proved Galen's humorism false.

Abu al-Qasim (Abulcasis) helped lay the foudations for modern surgery, with his *Kitab al-Tasrif*, in which he invented numerous surgical instruments, including the first instruments unique to women, as well as the surgical uses of catgut and forceps, the ligature, surgical needle, scalpel, curette, retractor, surgical spoon, sound, surgical hook, surgical rod, and specula, and bone saw. Ibn al-Haytham (Alhacen) made important advances in eye surgery, as he correctly explained the process of sight and visual perception for the first time in his *Book of Optics*. Avicenna helped lay the foundations for modern medicine, with *The Canon of Medicine*, which was responsible for introducing systematic experimentation and quantification in physiology, the discovery of contagious disease, introduction of quarantine to limit their spread, introduction of experimental medicine, evidence-based medicine, clinical trials, randomized controlled trials, efficacy tests, and clinical pharmacology, the first descriptions on bacteria and viral organisms, distinction of mediastinitis from pleurisy, contagious nature of tuberculosis, distribution of diseases by water and soil, skin troubles, sexually transmitted diseases, perversions, nervous ailments, use of ice to treat fevers, and separation of medicine from pharmacology.

Ibn Zuhr (Avenzoar) was the earliest known experimental surgeon. In the 12th century, he was responsible for introducing the experimental method into surgery, as he was the first to employ animal testing in order to experiment with surgical procedures before applying them to human patients. He also performed the first dissections and postmortem autopsies on humans as well as animals. Ibn al-Nafis laid the foundations for circulatory physiology, as he was the first to describe the pulmonary circulation and coronary circulation, which form the basis of the circu-latory system, for which he is considered "the greatest physiologist of the Middle Ages."

He also described the earliest concept of metabolism, and developed new systems of physiology and psychology to replace the Avicennian and Galenic systems, while discrediting many of their erroneous theories on humorism, pulsation, bones, muscles, intestines, sensory organs, bilious canals, esophagus, stomach, etc. Ibn al-Lubudi rejected the theory of humorism, and discovered that the body and its preservation depend exclusively upon blood, women cannot produce sperm, the movement of arteries is not dependent upon the movement of the heart, the heart is the first organ to form in a fetus' body, and the bones forming the skull can grow into tumors. Ibn Khatima and Ibn al-Khatib discovered that infectious diseases are caused by microorganisms which enter the human body. Mansur ibn Ilyas drew comprehensive diagrams of the body's structural, nervous and circulatory systems.

The study of experimental physics began with Ibn al-Haytham, a pioneer of modern optics, who introduced the experimental scientific method and used it to drastically transform the understanding of light and vision in his *Book of Optics*, which has been ranked alongside Isaac Newton's *Philosophiae Naturalis Principia Mathematica* as one of the most influential books in the history of physics, for initiating a scientific revolution in optics and visual perception. The experimental scientific method was soon introduced into mechanics by Biruni, and early precursors to Newton's laws of motion were discovered by several Muslim scientists. The law of inertia, known as Newton's first law of motion, and the concept of momentum were discovered by Ibn al-Haytham (Alhacen) and Avicenna.

The proportionality between force and acceleration, considered "the fundamental law of classical mechanics" and foreshadowing Newton's second law of motion, was discovered by Hibat Allah Abu'l-Barakat al-Baghdaadi, while the concept of reaction, foreshadowing Newton's third law of motion, was discovered by Ibn Bajjah (Avempace). Theories foreshadowing Newton's law of universal gravitation were developed by Ja'far Muhammad ibn Mûsâ ibn Shâkir, Ibn al-Haytham, and al-Khazini. Galileo Galilei's mathematical treatment of accelcration and his concept of impetus was enriched by the commentaries of Avicenna and Ibn Bajjah to Aristotle's *Physics* as well as the Neoplatonist tradition of Alexandria, represented by John Philoponus.

Many other advances were made by Muslim scientists in biology (anatomy, botany, evolution, physiology and zoology), the earth sciences (anthropology, cartography, geodesy, geography and geology), psychology (experimental psychology, psychiatry, psychophysics and psychotherapy), and the social sciences (demography, economics, sociology, history and historiography). Other famous Muslim scientists during the Islamic Golden Age include al-Farabi (a polymath), Biruni (a polymath who was one of the earliest anthropologists and a pioneer of geodesy), Nasîr al-Dîn al-Tûsî (a polymath), and Ibn Khaldun (considered to be a pioneer of several social sciences such as demography, economics, cultural history, historiography and sociology), among others.

The Great Mosque of Xi'an in China was completed *circa* 740, and the Great Mosque of Samarra in Iraq was completed in 847. The Great Mosque of Samarra combined the hypostyle architecture of rows of columns supporting a flat base above which a huge spiraling minaret was constructed.

The Spanish Muslims began construction of the Great Mosque at Cordoba in 785 marking the beginning of Islamic architecture in Spain and Northern Africa. The mosque is noted for its striking interior arches. Moorish architecture reached its peak with the construction of the Alhambra, the magnificent palace/fortress of Granada, with its open and breezy interior spaces adorned in red, blue, and gold. The walls are decorated with stylized foliage motifs, Arabic inscriptions, and arabesque design work, with walls covered in glazed tiles.

Another distinctive sub-style is the architecture of the Mughal Empire in India in the 15-17th centuries. Blending Islamic and Hindu elements, the emperor Akbar constructed the royal city of Fatehpur Sikri, located 26 miles (42 km) west of Agra, in the late 1500s and his grandson Shah Jahan had constructed the mausoleum of Taj Mahal for Mumtaz Mahal in the 1650s, though this time period is well after the Islamic Golden Age.

In the Sunni Muslim Ottoman Empire massive mosques with ornate tiles and calligraphy were constructed by a series of sultans including the Süleymaniye Mosque, Sultanahmet Mosque, Selimiye Mosque, and Bayezid II Mosque. An Arabic manuscript from the 13th century depicting Socrates (*Soqrât*) in discussion with his pupils.

The golden age of Islamic (and/or Muslim) art lasted from 750 to the 16th century, when ceramics, glass, metalwork, textiles, illuminated manuscripts, and woodork flourished. Lustrous glazing was an Islamic contribution to ceramics. Islamic luster-painted ceramics were imitated by Italian potters during the Renaissance. Manu-script illumination developed into an important and greatly respected art, and portrait miniature painting flourished in Persia. Calligraphy, an essential aspect of written Arabic, developed in manuscripts and architectural decoration. The most well known fiction from the Islamic world was *The Book of One Thousand and One Nights* (*Arabian Nights*), which was a compilation of many earlier folk tales told by the Persian Queen Scheherazade. The epic took form in the 10th century and reached its final form by the 14th century; the number and type of tales have varied from one manuscript to another. All Arabian fantasy tales were often called "Arabian Nights" when translated into English, regardless of whether they appeared in *The Book of One Thousand and One Nights*, in any version, and a number of tales are known in Europe as "Arabian Nights" despite existing in no Arabic manuscript.

This epic has been influential in the West since it was translated in the 18th century, first by Antoine Galland. Many imitations were written, especially in France. Various characters from this epic have themselves become cultural icons in Western culture, such as Aladdin, Sinbad and Ali Baba. However, no medieval Arabic source has been traced for Aladdin, which was incorporated into *The Book of One Thousand and One Nights* by its French translator, Antoine Galland, who heard it from an Arab Syrian Christian storyteller from Aleppo. Part of its popularity may have sprung from the increasing historical and geographical knowledge, so that places of which little was known and so marvels were plausible had to be set further "long ago" or farther "far away"; this is a process that continues, and finally culminate in the fantasy world having little connection, if any, to actual times and places. A number of elements from Arabian mythology and Persian mythology are now common in modern fantasy, such as genies, bahamuts, magic carpets, magic lamps, etc. When L. Frank Baum proposed writing a modern fairy tale that banished stereo-typical elements, he included the genie as well as the dwarf and the fairy as stereotypes to go.

Ferdowsi's *Shahnameh*, the national epic of Iran, is a mythical and heroic retelling of Persian history. *Amir Arsalan* was also a popular mythical Persian story, which has influenced some modern works of fantasy fiction, such as *The Heroic Legend of Arslan*. A famous example of Arabic poetry and Persian poetry on romance (love) is *Layla and Majnun*, dating back to the Umayyad era in the 7th century. It is a tragic story of undying love much like the later *Romeo and Juliet*, which was itself said to have been inspired by a Latin version of *Layli and Majnun* to an extent.

Ibn Tufail (Abubacer) and Ibn al-Nafis were pioneers of the philosophical novel. Ibn Tufail wrote the first fictional Arabic novel *Hayy ibn Yaqdhan* (*Philosophus Autodidactus*) as a response to al-Ghazali's *The Incoherence of the*

Philosophers, and then Ibn al-Nafis also wrote a fictional novel *Theologus Autodidactus* as a response to Ibn Tufail's *Philosophus Autodidactus*. Both of these narratives had protagonists (Hayy in *Philosophus Autodidactus* and Kamil in *Theologus Autodidactus*) who were autodidactic feral children living in seclusion on a desert island, both being the earliest examples of a desert island story. However, while Hayy lives alone with animals on the desert island for the rest of the story in *Philosophus Autodidactus,* the story of Kamil extends beyond the desert island setting in *Theologus Autodidactus,* developing into the earliest known coming of age plot and eventually becoming the first example of a science fiction novel.

Theologus Autodidactus, written by the Arabian polymath Ibn al-Nafis (1213-1288), is the first example of a science fiction novel. It deals with various science fiction elements such as spontaneous generation, futurology, the end of the world and doomsday, resurrection, and the afterlife. Rather than giving supernatural or mythological explnations for these events, Ibn al-Nafis attempted to explain these plot elements using the scientific knowledge of biology, astronomy, cosmology and geology known in his time. His main purpose behind this science fiction work was to explain Islamic religious teachings in terms of science and philosophy through the use of fiction.

A Latin translation of Ibn Tufail's work, *Philosophus Autodidactus,* first appeared in 1671, prepared by Edward Pococke the Younger, followed by an English translation by Simon Ockley in 1708, as well as German and Dutch translations. These translations later inspired Daniel Defoe to write *Robinson Crusoe,* regarded as the first novel in English. *Philosophus Autodidactus* also inspired Robert Boyle to write his own philosophical novel set on an island, *The Aspiring Naturalist*. The story also anticipated Rousseau's *Emile: or, On Education* in some ways, and is also similar to Mowgli's story in Rudyard Kipling's *The Jungle Book* as well as Tarzan's story, in that a baby is abandoned but taken care of and fed by a mother wolf.

Dante Alighieri's *Divine Comedy*, considered the greatest epic of Italian literature, derived many features of and episodes about the hereafter directly or indirectly from Arabic works on Islamic eschatology: the *Hadith* and the *Kitab al-Miraj* (translated into Latin in 1264 or shortly before as *Liber Scale Machometi*, "The Book of Muhammad's Ladder") concerning Muhammad's ascension to Heaven, and the spiritual writings of Ibn Arabi. The Moors also had a noticeable influence on the works of George Peele and William Shakespeare. Some of their works featured Moorish characters, such as Peele's *The Battle of Alcazar* and Shakespeare's *The Merchant of Venice, Titus Andronicus* and *Othello*, which featured a Moorish Othello as its title character. These works are said to have been inspired by several Moorish delegations from Morocco to Elizabethan England at the beginning of the 17th century.

A number of musical instruments used in Western music are believed to have been derived from Arabic musical instruments: the lute was derived from the *al'ud*, the rebec (ancestor of violin) from the *rebab*, the guitar from *qitara*, naker from *naqareh*, adufe from *al-duff*, alboka from *al-buq*, anafil from *al-nafir*, exabeba from *al-shabbaba* (flute), atabal (bass drum) from *al-tabl*, atambal from *al-tinbal*, the balaban, the castanet from *kasatan*, sonajas de azófar from *sunuj al-sufr*, the conical bore wind instruments, the xelami from the *sulami* or *fistula* (flute or musical pipe), the shawm and dulzaina from the reed instruments *zamr* and *al-zurna*, the gaita from the *ghaita*, rackett from *iraqya* or *iraqiyya*, the harp and zither from the *qanun*, canon from *qanun*, geige (violin) from *ghichak*, and the theorbo from the *tarab*.

A theory on the origins of the Western Solfège musical notation suggests that it may have also had Arabic origins.

It has been argued that the Solfège syllables (*do, re, mi, fa, sol, la, ti*) may have been derived from the syllables of the Arabic solmization system *Durr-i-Mufassal* ("Separated Pearls") (*dal, ra, mim, fa, sad, lam*). This origin theory was first proposed by Meninski in his *Thesaurus Linguarum Orientalum* (1680) and then by Laborde in his *Essai sur la Musique Ancienne et Moderne* (1780).

Arab philosophers like al-Kindi (Alkindus) and Ibn Rushd (Averroes) and Persian philosophers like Ibn Sina (Avicenna) played a major role in preserving the works of Aristotle, whose ideas came to dominate the non-religious thought of the Christian and Muslim worlds. They would also absorb ideas from China, and India, adding to them tremendous knowledge from their own studies. Three speculative thinkers, al-Kindi, al-Farabi, and Avicenna (Ibn Sina), fused Aristotelianism and Neoplatonism with other ideas introduced through Islam, such as Kalam and Qiyas. This led to Avicenna founding his own Avicennism school of philosophy, which was influential in both Islamic and Christian lands. Avicenna was also a critic of Aristotelian logic and founder of Avicennian logic, and he developed the concepts of empiricism and tabula rasa, and distinguished between essence and existence. From Spain the Arabic philosophic literature was translated into Hebrew, Latin, and Ladino, contributing to the development of modern European philosophy.

The Jewish philosopher Moses Maimonides, Muslim sociologist-historian Ibn Khaldun, Carthage citizen Constantine the African who translated Greek medical texts, and the Muslim Al-Khwarzimi's collation of mathematical techniques were important figures of the Golden Age. One of the most influential Muslim philosophers in the West was Averroes (Ibn Rushd), founder of the Averroism School of philosophy, whose works and commentaries had an impact on the rise of secular thought in Western Europe. He also developed the concept of "existence precedes essence". Another influential philosopher who had a significant influence on modern philosophy was Ibn Tufail.

His philosophical novel, *Hayy ibn Yaqdhan*, translated into Latin as *Philosophus Autodidactus* in 1671, developed the themes of empiricism, tabula rasa, nature versus nurture, condition of possibility, materialism, and Molyneux's Problem. European scholars and writers influenced by this novel include John Locke, Gottfried Leibniz, Melchisédech Thévenot, John Wallis, Christiaan Huygens, George Keith, Robert Barclay, the Quakers, and Samuel Hartlib. Al-Ghazali also had an important influence on Jewish thinkers like Maimonides and Christian medieval philosophers such as Thomas Aquinas and René Descartes, who expressed similar ideas to that of al-Ghazali in *Discourse on the Method*. However, al-Ghazali also wrote a devastating critique in his *The Incoherence of the Philosophers* on the speculative theological works of Kindi, Farabi and Ibn Sina. The study of metaphysics declined in the Muslim world due to this critique, though Ibn Rushd (Averroes) responded strongly in his *The Incoherence of the Incoherence* to many of the points Ghazali raised.

Nevertheless, Avicennism continued to flourish long after and Islamic philosophers continued making advances in philosophy through to the 17th century, when Mulla Sadra founded his school of Transcendent Theosophy and developed the concept of existentialism. Other influential Muslim philosophers include al-Jahiz, a pioneer of evolutionary thought and natural selection; Ibn al-Haytham (Alhacen), a pioneer of phenomenology and the philosophy of science and a critic of Aristotelian natural philosophy and Aristotle's concept of place (tcpos); Biruni, a critic of Aristotelian natural philosophy; Ibn Tufail and Ibn al-Nafis, pioneers of the philosophical novel; Shahab al-Din Suhrawardi, founder of Illuminationist philosophy; Fakhr al-Din al-Razi, a critic of Aristotelian logic and a pioneer of inductive logic; and Ibn Khaldun, a pioneer in the philosophy of history and social philosophy.

End of the Golden Age

Mongolian Invasion

After the Crusades from the West that resulted in the instability of the Islamic world during the 11th century, a new threat came from the East during the 13th century: the Mongol invasions. In 1206, Genghis Khan from Central Asia established a powerful Mongol Empire. A Mongolian ambassador to the Abbasid Caliph in Baghdad is said to have been murdered, which may have been one of the reasons behind Hulagu Khan's sack of Baghdad in 1258. The Mongols conquered most of the Eurasian land mass, including both China in the east and parts of the old Islamic Caliphate and Persian Islamic Khwarezm, as well as Russia and Eastern Europe in the west, and subsequent invasions of the Levant. Later Mongol leaders, such as Timur, though he himself became a Muslim, destroyed many cities, slaughtered thousands of people and did irreparable da-mage to the ancient irrigation systems of Mesopotamia. These invasions transformed a civil society to a nomadic one.

Traditionalist Muslims at the time, including the polymath Ibn al-Nafis, believed that the Crusades and Mongol invasions were a divine punishment from God against Muslims deviating from the Sunnah. As a result, the falsafa, some of whom held ideas incompatible with the Sunnah, became targets of criticism from many traditionalist Muslims, though other traditionalists such as Ibn al-Nafis made attempts at reconciling reason with revelation and blur the line between the two. Eventually, the Mongols that settled in parts of Persia, Central Asia and Russia converted to Islam, and as a result, the Ilkhanate, Golden Horde and Chagatai Khanates became Islamic states. In many instances, Mongols assimilated into various Muslim Iranian or Turkic peoples (for instance, one of the greatest Muslim astronomers of the 15th century, Ulugh Beg, was a grandson of Timur). By the time the Ottoman Empire rose from the ashes, the Golden Age is considered to have come to an end.

Causes of Decline

"The achievements of the Arabic speaking peoples between the ninth and twelfth centuries are so great as to baffle our understanding. The decadence of Islam and of Arabic is almost as puzzling in its speed and completeness as their phenomenal rise. Scholars will forever try to explain it as they try to explain the decadence and fall of Rome. Such questions are exceedingly complex and it is impossible to answer them in a simple way."

— *George Sarton, The Incubation of Western Culture in the Middle East'*

Islamic civilization, which had at the outset been creative and dynamic in dealing with issues, began to struggle to respond to the challenges and rapid changes it faced from the 12th century onwards, towards the end of the Abbassid rule. Despite a brief respite with the new Ottoman rule, the decline continued until its eventual collapse and subsequent stagnation in the 20th century. Despite a number of attempts by many writers, historical and modern, none seem to agree on the causes of decline. The main views on the causes of decline comprise the following: political mismanagement after the early Caliphs (10th century onwards), closure of the gates of ijtihad (12th century), institutionalisation of taqlid rather than bid'ah (13th century), foreign involvement by invading forces and colonial powers (11th century Crusades, 13th century Mongol Empire, 15th century Reconquista, 19th century European colonial empires), and the disruption to the cycle of equity based on Ibn Khaldun's famous model of Asabiyyah (the rise and fall of civilizations) which points to the decline being mainly due to political and economic factors.

The North Africa's Islamic civilization collapsed after exhausting its resources in internal fighting and suffering devastation from the invasion of the Bedouin tribes of Banu Sulaym and Banu Hilal. The Black Death ravaged much of the Islamic world in the mid-14th century. Plague epidemics kept returning to the Islamic world up to the 19th century. There was an increasing lack of tolerance of intellectual debate and freedom of thought, with some seminaries systematically forbidding speculative philosophy, while polemic debates appear to have been abandoned in the 14th century. A significant intellectual shift in Islamic philosophy is perhaps demonstrated by al-Ghazali's late 11th century polemic work *The Incoherence of the Philosophers*, which lambasted metaphysical philosophy in favor of the primacy of scripture, and was later criticized in *The Incoherence of the Incoherence* by Averroes. Institutions of science comprising Islamic universities, libraries (including the House of Wisdom), observatories, and hospitals, were later destroyed by foreign invaders like the Crusaders and particularly the Mongols, and were rarely promoted again in the devastated regions.

Not only wasn't new publishing equipment accepted but also wide illiteracy overwhelmed the devastated lands, especially in Mesopotamia. Meanwhile in Persia, due to the Mongol invasions and the plague, the average life expectancy of the scholarly class in Persia had declined from 72 years in 1209 to 57 years by 1242. American economist Timur Kuran proposed an answer why economic development in the Middle East lagged that of the West: Islamic partnership law and inheritance law interacted to keep Middle Eastern enterprises small, never allowing the development of corporate forms. Some scholars have come to question the traditional picture of decline, pointing to continued astronomical activity as a sign of a continuing and creative scientific tradition through to the 15th and 16th centuries, with the works of Ibn al-Shatir, Ulugh Beg, Ali Kuþçu, al-Birjandi and Taqi al-Din considered noteworthy examples. This was also the case for other fields, such as medicine, notably the works of Ibn al-Nafis, Mansur ibn Ilyas and Þerafeddin Sabuncuoðlu; mathematics, notably the works of al-Kashi and al-Qalasadi; philosophy, notably Mulla Sadra's transcendent theosophy; and the social sciences, notably Ibn Khaldun's *Muqaddimah* (1370), which itself points out that though science was declining in Iraq, Al-Andalus and Maghreb, it continued to flourish in Persia, Syria and Egypt during his time.

5

Sociology in Medieval Islam

Medieval Islamic sociology refers to the study of sociology and the social sciences in the medieval Islamic world. Early Islamic sociology responded to the challenges of social organization of diverse peoples all under common religious organization in the Islamic Caliphate, including the Rashidun, Umayyad, Abbasid and Fatimid periods, as well as the Mamluk period in Egypt. It was rooted in methods from early Islamic philosophy and science in medieval Islam, and it reflected the strong concern of Islam with social cohesion.

Early Islamic Period

Sociologist Robert Bellah (*Beyond belief*) argues that Islam in its seventh-century origins was, for its time and place, "remarkably modern...in the high degree of commitment, involvement, and participation expected from the rank-and-file members of the community." This because, he argues, that Islam emphasized on the equality of all Muslims. Leadership positions were open to all men. However, there were restraints on the early Muslim community that kept it from exemplifying these principles, primarily from the "stagnant localisms" of tribe and kinship. Dale Eickelman writes that Bellah suggests "the early Islamic community placed a particular value on individuals, as opposed to collective or group responsibility." The Islamic idea of community (that of *umma*), established by Muhammad, is flexible in social, religious, and political terms and includes a diversity of Muslims who share a general sense of common cause and consensus concerning beliefs and individual and communal actions.

Corporate Social Responsibility in Commerce

Social responsibility and corporate social responsibility in commerce was stressed in early Islamic sociology during Muhammad's time. The development of Islamic banks and Islamic economics was a side effect of this sociology: usury was rather severely restrained, no interest rate was allowed, and investors were not permitted to escape the consequences of any failed venture - all financing was equity financing (*Musharaka*). In not letting borrowers bear all the risk/cost of a failure, an extreme disparity of outcomes between "partners" is thus avoided. Ultimately this serves a social harmony purpose. Muslims also could not and cannot (in shariah) finance any dealings in forbidden goods or activities, such as wine, pork, gambling, etc. Thus ethical investing is the only acceptable investing, and moral purchasing is encouraged.

Ecological Responsibility and Environmentalism

Perhaps due to resource scarcity in most Islamic nations, there was an emphasis on limited (and some claim also sustainable) use of natural capital, i.e. producing land. Traditions of haram and hima and early urban planning were expressions of strong social obligations to stay within carrying capacity and to preserve the natural environment as an obligation of khalifa or "stewardship". Muhammad is considered a pioneer of environmentalism for his teachings on environmental preservation. His hadiths on agriculture and environmental philosophy were compiled in the "Book of Agriculture" of the *Sahih Bukhari*, which included the following saying:

"There is none amongst the believers who plants a tree, or sows a seed, and then a bird, or a person, or an animal eats thereof, but it is regarded as having given a charitable gift [for which there is great recompense]."

Several such statements concerning the environment are also found in the Qur'an, such as the following: "And there is no animal in the earth nor bird that flies with its two wings, but that they are communities like yourselves."

Comparative Sociology

Abû al-Rayhân al-Bîrûnî (973-1048), in the introduction to his study of India, declares that "to execute our project, it has not been possible to follow the geometric method" and develops comparative sociology as a scientific method in the field. Al-Biruni is considered the "father of Indology". In the 12th century, Muhammad al-Idrisi wrote the *Nozhat al-mushtaq fi ikhtiraq al-afaq*, a compendium of the geographic and sociological knowledge of his time as well as descriptions of his own travels illustrated with over seventy maps.

Ibn Khaldun

Tunisian statue of Ibn Khaldun, the father of demography, modern economics, cultural history, historiography, the philosophy of history, sociology, and the social sciences without doubt the most important figure in early Muslim sociology was Ibn Khaldun (1332-1406), who is regarded as the father of demography, cultural history, historiography, the philosophy of history, sociology, and the social sciences, and is viewed as a father of modern economics. He is best known for his *Muqaddimah "Prolegomenon"*. Sati' al-Husri suggested that Ibn Khaldun's *Muqaddimah* is essentially a sociological work, sketching over its six books a general sociology; a sociology of politics; a sociology of urban life; a sociology of economics; and a sociology of knowledge.

Scientific Method

Ibn Khaldun often criticized "idle superstition and uncritical acceptance of historical data." As a result, he introduced the scientific method to the social sciences, which was considered something "new to his age", and he often referred to it as his "new science" and developed his own new terminology for it. His historical method also laid the groundwork for the observation of the role of state, communication, propaganda and systematic bias in history, leading to his development of historiography.

Conflict Theory

Ibn Khaldun conceived both a central social conflict ("town" versus "desert") as well as a theory (using the concept of a "generation") of the necessary loss of power of city conquerors coming from the desert.

Asibiyah

Khaldun's central concept of *asabiyah*, or "social cohesion", seems to anticipate modern conceptions of social capital arising in social networks:

This cohesion arises spontaneously in tribes and other small kinship groups; and it can be intensified and enlarged by a religious ideology. Khaldun's analysis looks at how this cohesion carries groups to power but contains within itself the seeds - psychological, sociological, economic, political - of the group's downfall, to be replaced by a new group, dynasty or empire bound by a stronger (or at least younger and more vigorous) cohesion.

Interestingly, Khaldun's concept is instinctive and does not involve any social contract or explicit forms of constitution or other instructional capital that would provide a basis for appeals, in law or otherwise.

Economic Thought

The *Muqaddimah* emphasized the role of systemic bias in affecting the standard of evidence. Khaldun was quite concerned with the effect of raising standard of evidence when confronted with uncomfortable claims, and relaxing it when given claims that seemed reasonable or comfortable. He was a jurist, and sometimes participated reluctantly in rulings that he felt were coerced, based on arguments he didn't respect. His *Muqaddimah* also laid the groundwork for the observation of the role of state, communication, propaganda and systematic bias in history, and he discussed the rise and fall of civilizations in his theory of Asabiyyah. Ibn Khaldun had few successors in his thinking about history until Arnold J. Toynbee, a 20th century British historian.

In the *Muqaddimah,* Ibn Khaldun warned of seven mistakes that he thought that historians regularly committed. In this criticism, he approached the past as strange and in need of interpretation. The originality of Ibn Khaldun was to claim that the cultural difference of another age must govern the evaluation of relevant historical material, to distinguish the principles according to which it might be possible to attempt the evaluation, and lastly, to feel the need for experience, in addition to rational principles, in order to assess a culture of the past. Ibn Khaldun often criticized "idle superstition and uncritical acceptance of historical data." As a result, he introduced a scientific method to the study of history, which was considered something "new to his age", and he often referred to it as his "new science", now associated with historio-graphy. His historical method also laid the groundwork for the observation of the role of state, communication, propaganda and systematic bias in history, and he is thus considered to be the "father of historiography" or the "father of the philosophy of history".

Similarities to Modern Sociology

Early Muslim sociology is more similar to the theories developed by Hegel or Marx in emphasizing dialectic or feedback loops, or systems theory as applied to fields such as corporate social responsibility, than to the theories of Durkheim and others who emphasized structures. There is a remarkable similarity between modern economic ideas and some ideas developed by the thinkers evoked here, especially Ibn Khaldun.

Anthropology

Abû al-Rayhân al-Bîrûnî (973-1048) has been described as "the first anthropologist". Like modern anthropologists, he engaged in extensive participant observation with a given group of people, learnt their language and studied their primary texts, and presented his findings with objectivity and neutrality using cross-cultural comparisons. He wrote detailed comparative studies on the anthropology of religions, peoples and cultures in the Middle East, Mediterranean and South Asia, especially in India's case, for which he is considered the "father of Indology". Biruni's anthropology of religion was only possible for a scholar deeply immersed in the lore of other nations. Biruni and Ibn Khaldun have also been praised by several scholars for his Islamic anthropology.

Biruni developed a sophisticated methodology for his anthropological studies. For example, he wrote the following in the opening passages of his *Indica*:

"No one will deny that in questions of historic authenticity hearsay does not equal eyewitness; for in the latter the eye of the observer apprehends the substance of that which is observed, both in the time when and in the place where it exists, whilst hearsay has its peculiar drawbacks."

He was also aware that there are limitations to eyewitness accounts:

"The object of eye-witness can only be actual momentary existence, whilst hearsay comprehends alike the present, the past and the future".

Comparative Religion

Biruni was a pioneer in comparative religion and the anthropology of religion. According to Arthur Jeffery, "It is rare until modern times to find so fair and unprejudiced a statement of the views of other religions, so earnest an attempt to study them in the best sources, and such care to find a method which for this branch of study would be both rigorous and just." In the introduction to his *Indica*, Biruni himself writes that his intent behind the work was to engage dialogue between Islam and the Indian religions, particularly Hinduism as well as Buddhism. He writes:

"Abu-Sahl at--Tiflisi incited me to write down what I know about the Hindus as a help to those who want to discuss religious questions with them, and as a repertory of information to those who want to associate with them. We think now that what we have related in this book will be sufficient for anyone who wants to converse with the Hindus, and to discuss with them questions of religion, science or literature, on the very basis of their own civilisation."

Biruni was aware that statements about a religion would be open to criticism by its adherents, and insisted that a scholar should follow the requirements of a strictly scientific method. According to William Montgomery Watt, Biruni "is admirably objective and unprejudiced in his presentation of facts" but "selects facts in such a way that he makes a strong case for holding that there is a certain unity in the religious experience of the peoples he considers, even though he does not appear to formulate this view explicitly." Biruni's tradition of comparative cross-cultural study continued in the Muslim world through to Ibn Khaldun's work in the 14th century.

Economics

To some degree, the early Muslims based their economic analyses on the Qu'ran (such as opposition to *riba,* meaning usury or interest), and from Sunnah, the sayings and doings of Muhammad. Perhaps the most well known Islamic scholar who wrote about economics was Ibn Khaldun of Tunisia (1332–1406), who is considered a father of modern economics. Ibn Khaldun wrote on economic and political theory in the introduction, or *Muqaddimah* (*Prolegomena*), of his *History of the World* (*Kitab al-Ibar*). In the book, he discussed what he called *asabiyya* (social cohesion), which he sourced as the cause of some civilizations becoming great and others not. Ibn Khaldun felt that many social forces are cyclic, although there can be sudden sharp turns that break the pattern.

His idea about the benefits of the division of labor also relate to *asabiyya,* the greater the social cohesion, the more complex the successful division may be, the greater the economic growth. He noted that growth and development positively stimulates both supply and demand, and that the forces of supply and demand are what determines the prices of goods. He also noted macroeconomic forces of population growth, human capital development, and technological developments effects on development. In fact, Ibn Khaldun thought that population growth was directly a function of wealth. Other important early Muslim scholars who wrote about economics include Abu Hanifa an-Nu'man (699-767), Abu Yusuf (731-798), Ishaq bin Ali al-Rahwi (854–931), al-Farabi (873–950), Qabus (d. 1012), Ibn Sina (Avicenna) (980–1037), Ibn Miskawayh (b. 1030), al-Ghazali (1058–1111), al-Mawardi (1075–1158), Nasîr al-Dîn al-Tûsî (1201-1274), Ibn Taymiyyah (1263–1328) and al-Maqrizi (1364-1442).

Science of Hadith

The "science of hadith" is the process that Muslim scholars use to evaluate hadith. The classification of Hadith into Sahih (sound), Hasan (good) and Da'if (weak) was firmly established by Ali ibn al-Madini (161-234 AH). Later, al-Madini's student Muhammad al-Bukhari (810-870) authored a collection that he believed contained only Sahih hadith, which is now known as the *Sahih Bukhari*. Al-Bukhari's historical methods of testing hadiths and isnads are seen as the beginning of the method of citation and a precursor to the scientific method which was developed by later Muslim scientists. I. A. Ahmad writes:

The study of world history in the Islamic world was inspired by the concept of the oneness of humanity emphasized in the Qur'an and hadiths. A sense of common origin motivated early Muslim historians such as Wahb ibn Munabbih (d. 732) and Al-Asma'i (c. 740-828) to collect historical materials on pre-Islamic Arabian kings. The Qur'an also treats historical narrative as "eternally present, thereby forming the foundation which distinguishes Arabic historiography - its universality, a genre which is to be understood within the concept of the oneness of humanity as well as within the valued diversity of its ways." The Qur'an (Sura 49:13) states:

"O human beings, We (God) created you of a male and a female (from a single pair) and made you into (different) nations and tribes that you may (seek to) know each other."

Other verses in the Qur'an urge Muslims to visit and study other lands, cultures and languages, and specifically to study ancient civilizations, such as:

"Do they not travel through the land, so that their hearts (minds) may thus learn wisdom and their ears may thus learn wisdom and their ears may thus leam to hear? For it is not the eyes which are blind, but the heart in the breast." (Sura 22:46)

"Say: Travel through the earth and see how creation started." (Sura 29:20)

"Do they not travel through the earth and see what was the end of those before them (who) were more numerous and superior in strength and monuments in the land?" (Sura 40:82)

Some early Muslim scholars regarded the study of history as a human necessity, as noted by the Afro-Arab scholar Al-Jahiz in the 9th century:

"God made inherent in us the need for knowledge of the history of our predecessors, just as was the need of our predecessors for history of their predecessors, and just as will be the need of those who shall come after us for our history."

Said Al-Andalusi (1029-1168) stated that people in all corners of the world have a common origin but differ in certain aspects: "ethics, appearance, landscape and language". He treated the history of Egypt as part of the universal history of all humanity, and he linked Egypt and Sudan to the history of the Arabs through a common ancestry.

Early writers on world history include Muhammad ibn Jarir al-Tabari (838-923), who is known for writing a detailed and comprehensive chronicle of Mediterranean and Middle Eastern history in his *History of the Prophets and Kings* in 915. Abu al-Hasan 'Alî al-Mas'ûdî (896-956), known as the "Herodotus of the Arabs", was the first to combine history and scientific geography in a large-scale work, *Muruj adhdhahab wa ma'adin al-jawahir* (*The Meadows of Gold and Mines of Gems*), a book on world history. Along with his *Researches on India,* Biruni (973-1048) discussed more on his idea of history in his chronological work *The Chronology of the Ancient Nations.*

While it is sometimes assumed that Muslims were intent on destroying pagan monuments, such destruction was in fact very rare in Muslim history. In reality, Muslim rulers most often preserved and protected pre-Islamic artifacts and monuments, for which the 12th-century Muslim historian Abd al-Latif al-Baghdadi (1162–1231), who was well aware of the value of ancient monuments, praised them for. He noted that the preservation of antiquities presented a number of benefits for Muslims:

- "monuments are useful historical evidence for

chronologies;"

- "they furnish evidence for Holy Scriptures, since the Qur'an mentions them and their people;"
- "they are reminders of human endurance and fate;"
- "they show, to a degree, the politics and history of ancestors, the richness of their sciences, and the genius of their thought."

The following verse in the Qur'an also urges Muslims to study the remains of ancient civilizations:

"Do they not travel through the earth and see what was the end of those before them (who) were more numerous and superior in strength and monuments in the land?" (Sura 40:82)

Antiquarianism and Treasure Hunting

The Egyptian historian Al-Maqrizi (1364–1442) wrote a chapter on archeology entitled "Hidden Treasures", in which he gave a religious justification for archeological excavations of pre-Islamic ancient Near Eastern sites. He cites a hadith narration which reports that Muhammad passed by a tomb of Abu Righal, a chief of the Banu Thaqif tribe, and stated that there was a gold sceptre with him; his companions then excavated the tomb and found the object. Al-Maqrizi cited this incident as proof that the excavations of pre-Islamic sites were sanctioned. The archeological professions of antiquarianism and treasure hunting were established as careers in the 9th century by Ahmad ibn Tulun, founder of the Tulunid dynasty. Since then, treasure hunting was studied as a serious topic by Islamic scholars, beginning with Al-Kindi (Alkindus).

In the 11th century, the Egyptian caliph, Ma'ad al-Mustansir Billah, established the profession of *Emir al-Matalabin* ("Overseer of Treasure Hunters"), whose role was described in 1050 by the Persian traveller Nasir Khusraw while he was in Egypt as follows:

"The Sultan had a servant called 'Omdat al-Dawla' who was the *Emir of the Matalibeen* and enormously rich and propertied. Matalibi is what they call the people who dig for buried treasure in the graves of Egypt. From the Maghreb (Morocco) and the lands of Egypt and Syria come people who endure many hardships and spend a lot of (their own) money in those graves and rock piles. Many a time buried treasure is discovered and often much outlay is made without anything being found. They say that in those places the wealth of the pharaohs is buried. Whenever anyone does find something, one fifth is given to the Sultan and the rest belongs to the finder. At any rate the Sultan dispatched this 'Omdat al-Dawla' to that province with great pomp and circumstance, outfitting him with all the trappings of kings, such as canopies, pavilions, and so on. When he reached Aleppo he waged war and was killed. He had so much wealth that it took two months for it to be transferred from his treasury to the Sultan's."

During the Fatimid Caliphate, the supervision of treasure hunters developed into a guild with its head known as *Naqeeb al-Mutalibeen* ("Chairman of the Guild"). The Egyptian historian Al-Maqrizi regarded the death of one such chairman, Abu al-Hassan Ali ibn Ibrahim al-Nursi, in 1010 as an important event in his annals. Treasure hunters from Egypt, North Africa and Greater Syria were encouraged to search for hidden treasures at their own expense under the government's supervision. Treasure hunting was also a hobby for some, such as Sheikh Muhammad ibn Mubarak al-Athari ("The Antiquarian"), also known as "Keeper of the Relics of the Prophet", whose death in 1403 was noted by Ibn Qadi Shuhba.

With the establishment of treasure hunting as a new industry, many treasure hunting manuals and guide books were written by experienced treasure hunters and alchemists which became best sellers in the medieval Arab world. They were used by treasure hunters as sources to utilize in their search for treasure. Abd al-Latif al-Baghdadi in the 12th century notes that poorer treasure hunters were often sponsored by rich businessmen to go on archeological expeditions. In some cases, an expedition could turn out to be fraud, with the treasure hunter dissappearing with large amounts of money extracted from sponsors. This fraudulent practice continues to the present day, with rich businessmen in Egypt still being deceived by local treasure hunters.

A number of stories within the *One Thousand and One Nights* (*Arabian Nights*) deal with lost ancient technologies, advanced ancient civilizations that went astray, and catastrophes which overwhelmed them. "The City of Brass" features a group of travellers on an archaeological expedition across the Sahara to find an ancient lost city and attempt to recover a brass vessel that Solomon once used to trap a jinn, and, along the way, encounter a mummified queen, petrified inhabitants, life-like humanoid robots and automata, seductive marionettes dancing without strings, and a brass horseman robot who directs the party towards the ancient city. "The City of Brass" can be considered an early example of proto-science fiction.

Archeological Methodology

Abu al-Hassan al-Hamadani of Yemen (d. 945) developed an early archeological methodology in his encyclopedic work *Al-Iklil*, which covers the archeology and history of South Arabia, including the pre-Islamic period, though only the eighth volume of his work has survived. The archeological method he employed can be summarized as follows:

- "observing and describing the site;"
- "excavating and recording of finds with exact provenance, descriptions and measurements;"
- "using knowledge of ancient writings to read Himyarite inscriptions;"
- "analysing the finds in light of religious and historical texts and oral history."

Al-Idrisi (d. 1251), an Egyptian historian, described a more elaborate archeological methodology in his book *Anwar,* a book on Egyptology which mainly focused on the Egyptian pyramids. The archeological methods described in his book include:

- "reasons for the study of the importance of the pyramids;"
- "description of the route to the site;"
- "description of the pyramids and their inscriptions;"
- "measuring, and checking previous measurements;"
- "analysis of the form of the pyramid and reasons for building, with a critical review of literature (more than 22 authorities quoted) on the subject;"
- "study of sediments as an indication of the flood level;"
- "chemical analysis of clay in building material, by studying its mineral content in order to check place of origin;"
- "regular visits to the site to see it in different conditions, and to recheck measurements;"
- "noting stones reused at Jeremias Monastery, Saqqara as evidence of earlier dates, an observation confirmed by modern research."

It was also a widespread practice among medieval Muslim archeologists to give the exact pronunciations of the names of places, people and things according to local tradition, which has led to many ancient place names being preserved in the Arabic language. For example, the name for the land of Punt was preserved in Arabic as *Punta,* as recorded in the book of geography by Ibn Sa'id al-Maghribi (d. 1286). Medieval Arabic treasure hunter manuals often gave remarkable advice on locating and identifying ancient tombs. One such manual advised its readers to "look out for areas where the earth is covered by broken pottery as an indication of ancient tombs." Another manual entitled *Ghayat al-Ma'rib* indicated that "the presence of bones of saluki dogs was a certain sign of royal tombs", which has been attested in Egyptian royal burials.

The Egyptologist Abd al-Latif al-Baghdadi established another important aspect of archeological methodology, which was to "search unopened tombs to answer specific questions", which he did during his quest to investigate the absence of camel, donkey and horse burials, after having questioned the local people who could not give him a convincing answer. This question has partly been resolved in modern times with the hypothesis that domestication of the horse was not introduced to the Near East until the Indo-Iranians invaded from Central Asia. As a physician, al-Baghdadi examined hundreds of ancient Egyptian mummies in order to resolve medical and anatomical questions.

He also demonstrated another important archeological methdology, which is the ethno-historical approach where contemporary practices are observed and traced back to the past. He often obtained information both from the educated urban population and from local peasants in the countryside. Geography in medieval Islam also played an important role in Arabic archeological methdology, with historians and geographers such as Estakhri, Ibn Hawqal and Al-Muqaddasi accompanying their accounts of Egypt with national maps displaying details of its landscape. This high regard for regional maps was uncommon in Europe until the late Middle Ages. The study of Egyptology began in Arab Egypt from the 9th century. Ja'far ibn Muhammad Abu Ma'shar al-Balkhi (787-886) divided the history of pre-Islamic ancient Egypt into the pre-flood and post-flood periods, in reference to Noah's flood.

He dated the flood to 3,671 years before Hijra (approximately 3100 BC), coinciding with the founding of the First dynasty of Egypt. Said Al-Andalusi (1029-1168) treated the history of Egypt as part of the universal history of all humanity. He and other Muslim historians linked

Egypt and Sudan to the history of the Arabs through a common ancestry. They linked ancient Egypt to Muslim history through Hajar (Hagar), the wife of Ibrahim (Abraham) and mother of Ismail (Ishmael), the patriarch of the Arabs, thus making Hajar the mother of the Arabs; and through Maria al-Qibtiyya, one of Muhammad's wives. Muhammad himself often praised Egypt, its produce, and its people, and according to this tradition, the Copts had kinship with the Arabs and enjoyed a close relationship with the new Islamic government after the Muslim conquest of Egypt from the Byzantines. According to a hadith narrated by by Ibn Zahira, Muhammad stated:

"You are going to enter Egypt a land where *qirat* (money unit) is used. Be extremely good to them as they have with us close ties and marriage relationships."

The Qur'an (Sura 2:127) credits Abrahim and Ishmael as the builders of the Kaaba, the most holy place of Islam, while the 9th century writer Al-Kindi (Alkindus) refers to Egyptian craftsmen rebuilding it. According to other hadiths attributed to Muhammad, he stated the following regarding Egypt:

"When you enter Egypt after my death, recruit many soldiers from among the Egyptians because they are the best soldiers on earth, as they and their wives are permanently on duty until the Day of Resurrection."

"Be good to the Copts of Egypt; you shall take them over, but they shall be your instrument and help."

"Egypt has the best soil on earth and its people are the most generous of all people."

"Blessing (*al-baraka*) was divided into ten parts, nine for Egypt and one part for the other lands. This will be always manifest (*baraka*) in Egypt more than in all other lands."

"Be Righteous to Allah about the Copts."

Muslim geographers and historians such as Ibn Abd-el-Hakem (d. 871) and Muhammad al-Idrisi (1100-1166) explained that it was Muhammad's praise for Egypt that inspired them to write about Egypt's monuments, history, knowledge and practice. In order to study Egyptian history, early Muslim historians drew on the study of native Egyptian culture; the critical examination of Egyptian oral traditions; discourses with Coptic monks; ancient Demotic, Greek and Latin literature; ethnographic and geographical studies; and the remains of Egyptian antiquities.

The first known attempts at deciphering Egyptian hieroglyphs were made by made by Muslim historians in medieval Egypt during the 9th and 10th centuries. By then, hieroglyphs had long been forgotten in Egypt, and were replaced by the Coptic and Arabic alphabets. Dhul-Nun al-Misri and Ibn Wahshiyya (who was attempting to uncover the secrets of alchemy) were the first historians to be able to at least partly decipher what was written in the ancient Egyptian hieroglyphs, by relating them to the contemporary Coptic language used by Coptic priests in their time.

Abd-al Latif al-Baghdadi, a teacher at Cairo's Al-Azhar University in the 13th century, wrote detailed descriptions on ancient Egyptian monuments. The Arabic manuscript of his *Account of Egypt* was discovered in 1665 by Edward Pococke the orientalist, and preserved in the Bodleian Library. He then published the Arabic manuscript in the 1680s. His son, Edward Pococke the Younger, translated the work into Latin, though he was only able to publish less than half of his work. Thomas Hunt attempted to publish Pococke's complete translation in 1746, though his attempt was unsuccessful. Pococke's complete Latin translation was eventually published by Professor Joseph White of Oxford in 1800. The work was then translated into French, with valuable notes, by Silvestre de Sacy in 1810. The 15th-century Egyptian historian Al-Maqrizi also wrote detailed accounts of Egyptian antiquities, and described Egyptian history from the pre-dynastic period up until the Islamic period of his time.

The Egyptian Muslim historian Mourtadi wrote an Arabic book on ancient Egyptian monuments, which was later published in France and Britain in the 17th century. An Arabic manuscript of Ibn Wahshiyya's book on Egyptology, in which he deciphered a number of Egyptian hieroglyphs, was later read by Athanasius Kircher in the 17th century, and then translated and published in English by Joseph Hammer in 1806 as *Ancient Alphabets and Hieroglyphic Characters Explained; with an Account of the Egyptian Priests, their Classes, Initiation, and Sacrifices in the Arabic Language by Ahmad Bin Abubekr Bin Wahishih*, 16 years before Jean-François Champollion's complete decipherment of Egyptian hieroglyphs.

Indology

Until the 10th century, history most often meant political and military history, but this was not so with Persian historian Biruni (973-1048). In his *Kitab fi Tahqiq ma l'il-Hind* (*Researches on India*), he did not record political and military history in any detail, but wrote more on India's cultural, scientific, social and religious history. Biruni is considered the father of Indology for his detailed studies on Indian history and anthropology.

Paleography

Abu al-Hassan al-Hamadani of Yemen (d. 945), who wrote the encyclopedic work, *Al-Iklil*, on the archeology and history of South Arabia, also wrote the earliest known manual on the subject of paleography. This subject not introduced in Europe until Bernard de Montfaucon wrote *Palaeographia graeca* in 1708. Al-Hamadani wrote the following reason for writing his paleography manual:

"Most of the disagreement among people with regard to

Himyarite inscriptions centres on the variations in form of the character [of its alphabet]. A character or letter may have four or five forms, while the person who reads it is familiar with only one form. Since, as a result, mistakes have crept in, we have decided to record underneath each letter in the alphabet various forms of its Himyarite equivalent."

Al-Saghani (d. 990) wrote some of the earliest comments on the history of science. These included the following comparison between the "ancients" (including the ancient Babylonians, Egyptians, Greeks and Indians) and the "modern scholars" (the Muslim scientists of his time):

"The ancients distinguished themselves through their chance discovery of basic principles and the invention of ideas. The modern scholars, on the other hand, distinguish themselves through the invention of a multitude of scientific details, the simplification of difficult (problems), the combination of scattered (information), and the explanation of (material which already exists in) coherent (form). The ancients came to their particular achievements by virtue of their priority in time, and not on account of any natural qualification and intelligence. Yet, how many things escaped them which then became the original inventions of modern scholars, and how much did the former leave for the latter to do."

In psychology, Islamic medicine stressed the need for individual understanding of their mental health. The first psychiatric hospitals and insane asylums were built in the Islamic world as early as the 8th century. The first psychiatric hospitals were built by Arab Muslims in Baghdad in 705, Fes in the early 8th century, and Cairo in 800. Other famous psychiatric hospitals were built in Damascus and Aleppo in 1270. Unlike medieval Christian physicians who relied on demonological explanations for mental illness, medieval Muslim physicians relied mostly on clinical psychiatry and clinical observations on mentally ill patients. They made significant advances to psychiatry and were the first to provide psychotherapy and moral treatment for mentally ill patients, in addition to other new forms of treatment such as baths, drug medication, music therapy and occupational therapy.

The concepts of mental health and "mental hygiene" were introduced by the Muslim physician Ahmed ibn Sahl al-Balkhi (850-934). In his *Masalih al-Abdan wa al-Anfus* (*Sustenance for Body and Soul*), he was the first to successfully discuss diseases related to both the body and the mind, and argued that "if the *nafs* [psyche] gets sick, the body may also find no joy in life and may eventually develop a physical illness."

Najab ud-din Muhammad (10th century) described a number of mental diseases in detail. He made many careful observations of mentally ill patients and compiled them in a book which "made up the most complete classification of mental diseases theretofore known." The mental illnesses first described by Najab include agitated depression, neurosis, priapism and sexual impotence (*Nafkhae Malikholia*), psychosis (*Kutrib*), and mania (*Dual-Kulb*). Symptoms resembling schizophrenia were also reported in later Arabic medical literature.

Ahmed ibn Sahl al-Balkhi was a pioneer of psychotherapy, psychophysiology and psychosomatic medicine. He recognized that the body and the soul can be healthy or sick, or "balanced or imbalanced", and that mental illness can have both psychological and/or physiological causes. He wrote that imbalance of the body can result in fever, headaches and other physical illnesses, while imbalance of the soul can result in anger, anxiety, sadness and other mental symptoms. He recognized two types of depression: one caused by known reasons such as loss or failure, which can be treated psychologically; and the other caused by unknown reasons possibly caused by physiological reasons, which can be treated through physical medicine.

Muhammad ibn Zakarîya Râzi (Rhazes) and al-Balkhi were the first known physicians to study psychotherapy. Razi was a Persian and Zoroasterian who adopted Islam only in name. He had a disdain for Islam. Razi in particular made significant advances in psychiatry in his landmark texts *El-Mansuri* and *Al-Hawi* in the 10th century, which presented definitions, symptoms and treatments for problems related to mental health and mental illness. He also ran the psychiatric ward of a Baghdad hospital. Such institutions could not exist in Europe at the time because of fear of demonic possessions.

In al-Andalus, Abu al-Qasim (Abulcasis), the father of modern surgery, developed material and technical designs which are still used in neurosurgery. Ibn Zuhr (Avenzoar) gave the first accurate descriptions on neurological disorders, including meningitis, intracranial thrombophlebitis, and mediastinal germ cell tumors, and made contributions to modern neuropharmacology. Averroes suggested the existence of Parkinson's disease and attributed photoreceptor properties to the retina. Maimonides wrote about neuropsychiatric disorders and described rabies and belladonna intoxication.

Ibn al-Haytham is considered by some to be the founder of experimental psychology and psychophysics, for his pioneering work on the psychology of visual perception in the *Book of Optics*. In Book III of the *Book of Optics*, Ibn al-Haytham was the first scientist to argue that vision occurs in the brain, rather than the eyes. He pointed out that personal experience has an effect on what people see and how they see, and that vision and perception are subjective. Along with al-Kindi and Ibn al-Haytham, al-Biruni was also a pioneer of experimental psychology, as he was the first to empirically describe the concept of reaction time:

"Not only is every sensation attended by a corresponding change localized in the senseorgan, which demands a certain time, but also, between the stimulation of the organ and consciousness of the perception an interval of time must elapse, corresponding to the transmission of stimulus for some distance along the nerves."

Avicenna was a pioneer of psychophysiology and psychosomatic medicine. He recognized 'physiological psychology' in the treatment of illnesses involving emotions, and developed a system for associating changes in the pulse rate with inner feelings, which is seen as an anticipation of the word association test attributed to Carl Jung. Avicenna was also a pioneer of neuropsychiatry. He first described numerous neuropsychiatric conditions, including hallucination, insomnia, mania, nightmare, melancholia, dementia, epilepsy, paralysis, stroke, vertigo and tremor.

The earliest works on social psychology and animal psychology were written by al-Jahiz (766–868), an AfroArab scholar who wrote a number of works dealing with the social organization of ants and with animal communication and psychology. Al-Farabi's *Social Psychology* and *Model City* were also some of the first treatises to deal with social psychology. Al Farabi's parents were both Persian/Iranian. His family was forced to adopt Islam. His thinking and writings were intrinsically derived from his Persian heritage.

His name is based on the name of the Farab River in Iran. He stated that "an isolated individual could not achieve all the perfections by himself, without the aid of other individuals." He wrote that it is the "innate disposition of every man to join another human being or other men in the labor he ought to perform." He concluded that in order to "achieve what he can of that perfection, every man needs to stay in the neighborhood of others and associate with them." Al-Farabi's treatise *Meanings of the Intellect* dealt with music therapy, where he discussed the therapeutic effects of music on the soul.

Early Social Changes under Islam

Many social changes took place under Islam between 610 and 661, including the period of Muhammad's mission and the rule of his four immediate successors who established the Rashidun Caliphate. According to William Montgomery Watt, for Muhammad, religion was not a private and individual matter but rather "the total response of his personality to the total situation in which he found himself. He was responding [not only]... to the religious and intellectual aspects of the situation but also the economic, social, and political pressures to which contemporary Mecca was subject."

Bernard Lewis says that there are two important political traditions in Islam - one that views Muhammad as a statesman in Medina, and another that views him as a rebel in Mecca. He sees Islam itself as a type of revolution that greatly changed the societies into which the new religion was brought. Historians generally agree that Islamic social reforms in areas such as social security, family structure, slavery and the rights of women and ethnic minorities improved on what was present in existing Arab society. For example, according to Lewis, Islam "from the first denounced aristocratic privilege, rejected hierarchy, and adopted a formula of the career open to the talents."

Advent of Islam

Bernard Lewis believes that the advent of Islam was a revolution which only partially succeeded due to tensions between the new religion and very old societies that the Muslims conquered. He thinks that one such area of tension was a consequence of what he sees as the egalitarian nature of Islamic doctrine. Islam from the first denounced aristocratic privilege, rejected hierarchy, and adopted a formula of the career open to the talents. Lewis however notes that the equality in Islam was restricted to free adult male Muslims, but even that "represented a very considerable advance on the practice of both the Greco-Roman and the ancient Iranian world."

Bernard Lewis writes about the significance of Muhammad's achievements:

"He had achieved a great deal. To the pagan peoples of western Arabia he had brought a new religion which, with its monotheism and its ethical doctrines, stood on an incomparably higher level than the paganism it replaced. He had provided that religion with a revelation which was to become in the centuries to follow the guide to thought and count of countless millions of Believers. But he had done more than that; he had established a community and a well organized and armed state, the power and prestige of which made it a dominant factor in Arabia."

Constitution of Medina

The Constitution of Medina, also known as the *Charter of Medina*, was drafted by the Prophet Muhammad in 622. It constituted a formal agreement between Muhammad and all of the significant tribes and families of Yathrib (later known as Medina), including Muslims, Jews, and pagans. The document was drawn up with the explicit concern of bringing to an end the bitter inter tribal fighting between the clans of the Aws (Aus) and Khazraj within Medina. To this effect it instituted a number of rights and responsibilities for the Muslim, Jewish, and pagan communities of Medina bringing them within the fold of one communitythe Ummah.

The precise dating of the Constitution of Medina remains debated but generally scholars agree it was written shortly after the hijra (622). It effectively established the first Islamic state. The Constitution established: the security of the community, religious freedoms, the role of Medina as a haram or sacred place (barring all violence and weapons), the security of women, stable tribal relations within Medina, a tax system for supporting the community in time of conflict, parameters for exogenous political alliances, a system for granting protection of individuals, a judicial system for resolving disputes, and also regulated the paying of blood-wite (the payment between families or tribes for the slaying of an individual in lieu of lex talionis).

Social Reforms

Muhammad preached against what he saw as the social evils of his day, *Encyclopedia of world history* states.

Practices

John Esposito sees Muhammad as a reformer who condemned practices of the pagan Arabs such as female infanticide, exploitation of the poor, usury, murder, false contracts, fornication, adultery, and theft. He states that Muhammad's "insistence that each person was personally accountable not to tribal customary law but to an overriding divine law shook the very foundations of Arabian society... Muhammad proclaimed a sweeping program of religious and social reform that affected religious belief and practices, business contracts and practices, male-female and family relations". Esposito holds that the Qur'an's reforms consist of "regulations or moral guidance that limit or redefine rather than prohibit or replace existing practices." He cites slavery and women's status as two examples.

According to some scholars, Muhammad's condemnation of infanticide was the key aspect of his attempts to raise the status of women. Regarding the prevalence of this practice, we know it was "common enough among the pre-Islamic Arabs to be assigned a specific term, *wad*" A much cited verse the Qur'anthat addresses this practice is: "When the sun shall be darkened, when the stars shall be thrown down, when the mountains shall be set moving, when the pregnant camels shall be neglected, when the savage beasts shall be mustered, when the seas shall be set boiling, when the souls shall be coupled, *when the buried infant shall be asked for what sin she was slain,* when the scrolls shall be unrolled..."

Social Security

William Montgomery Watt states that Muhammad was both a social and moral reformer. He asserts that Muhammad created a "new system of social security and a new family structure, both of which were a vast improvement on what went before. By taking what was best in the morality of the nomad and adapting it for settled communities, he established a religious and social framework for the life of many races of men." In pre-Islamic Arabia, upon capture, those captives not executed, were made to beg for their subsistence. During his life, Muhammad changed this custom and made it the responsibility of the Islamic government to provide food and clothing, on a reasonable basis, to captives, regardless of their religion. If the prisoners were in the custody of a person, then the responsibility was on the individual.

Slavery

The Qur'an makes numerous references to slavery, regulating but thereby also implicitly accepting this already existing institution. Lewis states that Islam brought two major changes to ancient slavery which were to have far-reaching consequences. "One of these was the presumption of freedom; the other, the ban on the enslavement of free persons except in strictly defined circumstances," Lewis continues. The position of the Arabian slave was "enormously improved": the Arabian slave "was now no longer merely a chattel but was also a human being with a certain religious and hence a social status and with certain quasilegal rights." Lewis states that in Muslim lands slaves had a certain legal status and had obligations as well as rights to the slave owner, an improvement over slavery in the ancient world. Due to these reforms the practice of slavery in the Islamic empire represented a "vast improvement on that inherited from antiquity, from Rome, and from Byzantium."

Although there are many common features between the institutions of slavery in the Qur'anand that of neighboring cultures, however the Qur'anic institution had some unique new features. According to Jonathan Brockopp, professor of History and Religious Studies, the idea of using alms for the manumission of slaves appears to be unique to the Qur'ân (assuming the traditional interpretation of verses and Qur'an). Similarly, the practice of freeing slaves in atonement for certain sins appears to be introduced by the Qur'an (but compare Exod 21:26-7). Brockopp adds that: "Other cultures limit a master's right to harm a slave but few exhort masters to treat their slaves kindly, and the placement of slaves in the same category as other weak members of society who deserve protection is unknown outside the Qur'ân. The unique contribution of the Qur'ân, then, is to be found in its emphasis on the place of slaves in society and society's responsibility toward the slave, perhaps the most progressive legislation on slavery in its time."

Muhammad highly recommended the freeing of slaves as a charitable act. The freeing of slaves was recommended both for the expiation of sins and as an act of simple benevolence. It exhorted masters to either free their slaves or allow slaves to earn or purchase their own freedom through manumission contracts.

Women's Rights

To evaluate the effect of Islam on the status of women, many writers have discussed the status of women in pre-Islamic Arabia, and their findings have been mixed. Some writers have argued that women before Islam were more liberated drawing most often on the first marriage of Muhammad and that of Muhammad's parents, but also on other points such as worship of female idols at Mecca. Other writers, on the contrary, have argued that women's status in pre-Islamic Arabia was poor, citing practices of female infanticide, unlimited polygyny, patrilineal marriage and others. Valentine M. Moghadam analyzes the situation of women from a Marxist theoretical framework and argues that the position of women are mostly influenced by the extent of urbanization, industrialization, poletarization and political ploys of the state managers rather than culture or intrinsic properties of Islam; Islam, Moghadam argues, is neither more nor less patriarchal than other world religions especially Hinduism, Christianity and Judaism.

Majid Khadduri writes that under the Arabian preIslamic law of status, women had virtually no rights. Islamic law, however, provided women with a number of rights. John Esposito states that the reforms affected marriage, divorce, and inheritance. Women were not accorded with such legal status in other cultures, including the West, until centuries later. *The Oxford Dictionary of Islam* states that the general improvement of the status of Arab women included prohibition of female infanticide, and recognizing women's full personhood. Gerhard Endress states: "The social system ... builds up a new system of marriage, family and inheritance; this system treated women as an individual too and guaranteed social security to her as well as to her children. Legally controlled polygamy was an important advance on the various loosely defined arrangements which had previously been both possible and current; it was only by this provision (backed up by severe punishment for adultery), that the family, the core of any sedentary society could be placed on a firm footing."

Marriage

Under the Arabian pre-Islamic law, no limitations were set on men's rights to marry or to obtain a divorce. Islamic law, however, restricted polygamy. The institution of marriage, characterized by unquestioned male superiority in the pre-Islamic law of status, was redefined and changed into one in which the woman was somewhat of an interested partner. 'For example, the dowry, previously regarded as a bride-price paid to the father, became a nuptial gift retained by the wife as part of her personal property' Under Islamic law, marriage was no longer viewed as a "status" but rather as a "contract". The essential elements of the marriage contract were now an offer by the man, an acceptance by the woman, and the performance of such conditions as the payment of dowry. The woman's consent was imperative. Furthermore, the offer and acceptance had to be made in the presence of at least two witnesses.

Inheritance and Wealth

'Women were given inheritance rights in a patriarchal society that had previously restricted inheritance to male relatives.' Annemarie Schimmel states that "Compared to the pre-Islamic position of women, Islamic legislation meant an enormous progress; the woman has the right, at least according to the letter of the law, to administer the wealth she has brought into the family or has earned by her own work" According to the Oxford Dictionary of Islam, Women were also granted the right to live in the matrimonial home and receive financial maintenance during marriage and a waiting period following the death and divorce.

The Status of Women

Watt states that Islam is still, in many ways, a man's religion. However, he states that Muhammad, in the historical context of his time, can be seen as a figure who testified on behalf of women's rights and improved things considerably. Watt explains the historical context surrounding women's rights at the time of Muhammad: "It appears that in some parts of Arabia, notably in Mecca, a matrilineal system was in the process of being replaced by a patrilineal one at the time of Muhammad. Growing prosperity caused by a shifting of trade routes was accompanied by a growth in individualism. Men were amassing considerable personal wealth and wanted to be sure that this would be inherited by their own actual sons, and not simply by an extended family of their sisters' sons.

This led to deterioration in the rights of women. At the time Islam began, the conditions of women were terrible - they had no right to own property, were supposed to be the property of the man, and if the man died everything went to his sons."

Muhammad, however, by "instituting rights of property ownership, inheritance, education and divorce gave women certain basic safeguards." "In the earliest centuries of Islam, the position of women was not bad at all. Only over the course of centuries was she increasingly confined to the house and was forced to veil herself." The Quran and Muhammad's example were more favorable to the security and status of women than history and later Muslim practice might suggest. For example, the Qur'an does not require women to wear veils; rather, it was a social habit picked up with the expansion of Islam. In fact, since it was impractical for working women to wear veils, "A veiled woman silently announced that her husband was rich enough to keep her idle."

Haddad and Esposito state that 'although Islam is often criticized for the low status it has ascribed to women; many scholars believe that it was primarily the interpretation of jurists, local traditions, and social trends which brought about a decline in the status of Muslim women. In this view Muhammad granted women rights and privileges in the sphere of family life, marriage, education, and economic endeavors, rights that help improve women's status in society.' However, 'the Arab Bedouins were dedicated to custom and tradition and resisted changes brought by the new religion.' Haddad and Esposito state that in this view 'the inequality of Muslim women happened because of the preexisting habits of the people among whom Islam took root. The economics of these early Muslim societies were not favorable to comfortable life for women. More important, during Islam's second and third centuries the interpretation of the Qur'an was in the hands of deeply conservative scholars, whose decisions are not easy to challenge today. The Qur'an is more favorable to women than is generally realized. In principle, except for a verse or two, the Qur'an grants women equality. For example, Eve was not the delayed product of Adam's rib (as in the tradition for Christians and Jews); the two were born from a single soul. It was Adam, not Eve, who let the devil convince them to eat the forbidden fruit. Muslim women are instructed to be modest in their dress, but only in general terms. Men are also told to be modest. Many Muslims believe the veiling and seclusion are later male inventions, social habits picked up with the conquest of the Byzantine and Persian Empires.'

Children

The Qur'an rejected the pre-Islamic idea of children as their fathers' property and abolished the pre-Islamic custom of adoption. A. Giladi holds that Quran's rejection of the idea of Children as their fathers' property was a Judaeo-Christian influence and was a response to the challenge of structural changes in tribal society. The Quran also replaced the pre-Islamic custom of adoption (assimilation of an adopted Child into another family in a legal sense) by the recommendation that "believers treat children of unknown origin as their brothers in the faith and clients. Adoption was viewed "as a lie, as an artificial tie between adults and children, devoid of any real emotional relationship, as a cause of confusion where lineage was concerned and thus a possible source of problems regarding marriage between members of the same family and regarding inheritance."

Sociological Reforms

Sociologist Robert Bellah (*Beyond belief*) argues that Islam in its seventh-century origins was, for its time and place, "remarkably modern...in the high degree of commitment, involvement, and participation expected from the rank-and-file members of the community." This because, he argues, that Islam emphasized on the equality of all Muslims. Leadership positions were open to all. However, there were restraints on the early Muslim community that kept it from exemplifying these principles, primarily from the "stagnant localisms" of tribe and kinship. Dale Eickelman writes that Bellah suggests "the early Islamic community placed a particular value on individuals, as opposed to collective or group responsibility." The Islamic idea of community (that of *umma*), established by Muhammad, is flexible in social, religious, and political terms and includes a diversity of Muslims who share a general sense of common cause and consensus concerning beliefs and individual and communal actions.

Moral Reforms

Muslims believe that Muhammad, like other prophets in Islam, was sent by God to remind human beings of their moral responsibility, and challenge those ideas in society which opposed submission to God. According to Kelsay, this challenge was directed against five main characteristics of pre-Islamic Arabia:

1. The division of Arabs into varying tribes (based upon blood and kinship). This categorization was confronted by the ideal of a unified community based upon Islamic piety, an "*umma;*"
2. The acceptance of the worship of a multitude of deities besides Allah - a view challenged by strict Islamic monotheism, which dictates that Allah has no partner in worship nor any equal;
3. The trait of *muruwwa* (manliness), which Islam discouraged, instead emphasizing on the traits of humility and piety;
4. The focus on achieving fame or establishing a legacy, which was replaced by the concept that mankind would be called to account before God on the day of resurrection;

5. The reverence of and compliance with ancestral traditions, a practice challenged by Islam — which instead assigned primacy to submitting to God and following revelation.

These changes lay in the reorientation of society as regards to identity, world view, and the hierarchy of values. From the viewpoint of subsequent generations, this caused a great transformation in the society and moral order of life in the Arabian Peninsula. For Muhammad, although pre-Islamic Arabia exemplified "heedlessness," it was not entirely without merit. Muhammad approved and exhorted certain aspects of the Arab pre-Islamic tradition, such as the care for one's near kin, for widows, orphans, and others in need and for the establishment of justice. However, these values would be re-ordered in importance and placed in the context of strict monotheism. Although Muhammad's preaching produced a "radical change in moral values based on the sanctions of the new religion, and fear of God and of the Last Judgment", the pre-Islamic tribal practices of the Arabs by no means completely died out.

Economic Reforms

Michael Bonner writes on poverty and economics in the Qur'an that the Qur'an provided a blueprint for a new order in society, in which the poor would be treated more fairly than before. This "economy of poverty" prevailed in Islamic theory and practice up until the 13th and 14th centuries. At its heart was a notion of property circulated and purified, in part, through charity, which illustrates a distinctively Islamic way of conceptualizing charity, generosity, and poverty markedly different from "the Christian notion of perennial reciprocity between rich and poor and the ideal of charity as an expression of community love." The Qur'an prohibits bad kind of circulation (riba, often understood as usury or interest) and asks for good circulation (zakat [legal alms giving]). Some of the recipients of charity appear only once in the Qur'an, and others—

such as orphans, parents, and beggars—reappear constantly. Most common is the triad of kinsfolk, poor, and travelers.

Unlike pre-Islamic Arabian society, the Qur'anic idea of economic circulation as a return of goods and obligations was for everyone, whether donors and recipients know each other or not, in which goods move and society does what it is supposed to do. The Qur'an's distinctive set of economic and social arrangements in which poverty and the poor have important roles show signs of newness. The *Qur'an* told that the guidance comes to a community that regulates its flow of money and goods in the right direction (from top down) and practices generosity as reciprocation for God's bounty. In a broad sense, the narrative underlying the *Qur'an* is that of a tribal society becoming urbanized.

Many scholars have characterized both the *Qur'an* and Islam as highly favorable to commerce and to the highly mobile type of society that emerged in the medieval Near East. Muslim tradition (both hadith and historiography) maintains that Muhammad did not permit the construction of any buildings in the market of Medina other than mere tents; nor did he permit any tax or rent to be taken there. This expression of a "free market"—involving the circulation of goods within a single space without payment of fees, taxes, or rent, without the construction of permanent buildings, and without any profiting on the part of the caliphal authority (indeed, of the Caliph himself)—was rooted in the term sadaqa, "voluntary alms." This coherent and highly appealing view of the economic universe had much to do with Islam's early and lasting success. Since the poor were at the heart of this economic universe, the teachings of the Qur'an on poverty had a considerable, even a transforming effect in Arabia, the Near East, and beyond.

Civil Reforms

Social welfare in Islam started in the form of the

construction and purchase of wells. Upon his hegira to Medina, Muhammad found only one well to be used. The Muslims bought that well and consequently it was used by the general public. After Muhammad's declaration that "water" was a better form of charity, many of his companions sponsored the digging of new wells. During the Caliphate, the Muslims repaired many of the aging wells in the lands they conquered. In addition to wells, the Muslims built many tanks and canals. Many canals were purchased, and new ones constructed.

While some canals were excluded for the use of monks (such as a spring purchased by Talha), and the needy, most canals were open to general public use. Some canals were constructed between settlements, such as the Saad canal that provided water to Anbar, and the Abi Musa Canal to providing water to Basra. During a famine, Umar ibn al-Khattab ordered the construction of a canal in Egypt to connect the Nile with the Red Sea. The purpose of the canal was to facilitate the transport of grain to Arabia through a sea-route, hitherto transported only by land. The canal was constructed within a year by Amr bin al Aas, and Abdus Salam Nadiv writes, Arabia was rid of famine for all the times to come."

Ecological Responsibility

Perhaps due to resource scarcity in most Islamic nations, there was an emphasis on limited (and some claim also sustainable) use of natural capital, i.e. producing land. Traditions of haram and hima and early urban planning were expressions of strong social obligations to stay within carrying capacity and to preserve the natural environment as an obligation of khalifa or "stewardship". Muhammad is considered a pioneer in environmentalism for his teachings on environmental preservation. His hadiths on agriculture and environmental philosophy were compiled in the "Book of Agriculture" of the *Sahih Bukhari*.

Political Changes

Arabia

Islam began in Arabia in the 7th century under the leadership of Muhammad, who eventually united many of the independent nomadic tribes of Arabia under Islamic law. There were also some Jewish and Christian tribes in Arabia. Some tension between Muhammad and the Jews of Medina soon arose and intensified. Muhammad accused the Jews of Medina of treason and expelled some of them from Medina and wiped out some others who he deemed to be traitors.

Middle East

The pre-Islamic Middle East was dominated by the Byzantine and Sassanian empires. The Roman-Persian Wars between the two had devastated the inhabitants, making the empires unpopular amongst the local tribes. The Byzantines persecuted Jews as well as Christians they deemed "heretic". During the early Islamic conquests, the Rashidun army, mostly led by Khalid ibn al-Walid and Amr ibn al-As, defeated both empires, making the Islamic state the dominant power in the region. Within only a decade, Muslims conquered Mesopotamia and Persia during the Islamic conquest of Persia and Roman Syria and Roman Egypt during the early Byzantine-Arab Wars.

According to Francis Edwards Peters:

The conquests destroyed little: what they did suppress were imperial rivalries and sectarian bloodletting among the newly subjected population. The Muslims tolerated Christianity, but they disestablished it; henceforward Christian life and liturgy, its endowments, politics and theology, would be a private and not a public affair. By an exquisite irony, Islam reduced the status of Christians to that which the Christians had earlier thrust upon the Jews, with one difference. The reduction in Christian status was merely judicial; it was unaccompanied by either systematic persecution or a blood lust, and generally, though not elsewhere and at all times, unmarred by vexatious behaviour.

The Islamic conquest lowered taxes, and provided greater local autonomy and religious freedom for Jews and as well as most of the Christian Churches in the conquered areas (such as Nestorians, Monophysites, Jacobites and Copts who were deemed heretic by Christian Orthodoxy). Bernard Lewis wrote:

Some even among the Christians of Syria and Egypt preferred the rule of Islam to that of Byzantines... The people of the conquered provinces did not confine themselves to simply accepting the new regime, but in some cases actively assisted in its establishment. In Palestine the Samaritans, according to tradition, gave such effective aid to the Arab invaders that they were for some time exempted from certain taxes, and there are many other reports in the early chronicles of local Jewish and Christian assistance.

Other Reforms

Islam reduced the devastating effect of blood feuds, which was common among Arabs, by encouraging compensation in money rather than blood. In case the aggrieved party insisted on blood, unlike the pre-Islamic Arab tradition in which any male relative could be slain, only the culprit himself could be executed. *The Cambridge History of Islam* states that the nomadic structure of pre-Islamic Arabia had the serious moral problem of the care of the poor and the unfortunate. "Not merely did the Qur'an urge men to show care and concern for the needy, but in its teaching about the Last day it asserted the existence of a sanction applicable to men as individuals in matters where their selfishness was no longer restrained by nomadic ideas of dishonour." Islam teaches support for the poor and the oppressed. In an effort to protect and help the poor and orphans, regular almsgiving — zakat — was made obligatory for Muslims. This regular alms-giving developed into a form of income tax to be used exclusively for welfare.

6

Islamic Revolution

In revolutions, even more than in other forms of political activity, there is an element of theater. This is evidenced by the almost universal use of such words as *drama, stage, scene, role,* even *actor,* in speaking of revolutionary events. Revolutionaries are, of course, conscious of this dramatic element. Some indeed, Karl Marx among them, have even used such unkind words as *farce* and *burlesque* to describe certain revolutionary activities. We do not hear these words applied to the revolution in Iran. Playwrights and actors alike are especially aware of their audiences, both present and future. This awareness affects revolutionaries as they write, direct, interpret, and perform their roles in the revolutionary drama. The theater of revolution is essentially participatory, requiring more than the usual rapport between actors and audience. It depends on knowledge and empathy on the part of the public, who are not just spectators. As in Greek tragedy, the Japanese No, the Turkish or Egyptian shadow play, the English Punch and Judy, and the American western, the audience must know, preferably know intimately, the essentials of the plot, the characters and roles of the good and evil figures, and the desired, indeed the inevitable, outcome.

The dramatist, the director, and the actors can appeal to a shared frame of reference, and, more important, of allusion, of memories: symbols that they can invoke to gain the interest, sympathy, and finally the enthusiastic participation of the audience. During the last two hundred years, the dominant models of successful revolution in most of the world have been those of France and Russia, and the most dramatically effective roles those of the Jacobins and the Bolsheviks. In the nineteenth and early twentieth centuries, many revolutionary leaders attempted, in the differing conditions of their own countries, to reenact the magnificent climax of the storming of the Bastille and the proclamation of the Republic. After 1917, many tried to act out the Bolshevik script, sometimes with the aid of a prompter, sometimes without. These models were most influential in societies that shared with France and Russia a common heritage of usable allusions and symbols, drawn from their European or Europe-derived culture, and from its ultimate sources in the Greco-Roman and Judeo-Christian traditions.

At a time when Europe was paramount in the world, they were also adopted by aspiring non-European revolutionaries, at first against their own "old regimes," later against their European imperial masters. There have been several movements called revolutionary in the lands of Islam in this century, starting with the Persian and Turkish constitutional revolutions in 1905 and 1908, followed by many others after the withdrawal of Britain and France and the collapse of the regimes to which they had transferred power. In the early years of the century, it was the French model that prevailed among Westernizing Middle Eastern elites, to be supplemented, in the interwar and postwar decades, by other examples drawn first from Eastern and then from Southern and Central Europe. Public life in Muslim countries was enriched—if that is the right word—with a new system of values and symbols, drawn from European thought and from the European past.

The Islamic revolution which won power in Iran in 1979 and continues to offer a major challenge to existing regimes in other Islamic lands uses none of these symbols. For the

Ayatollahs and those who respond to them, neither the Bible nor the Latin and Greek classics, neither Jacobins nor Bolsheviks, neither Paris nor Petrograd provide usable models or evocative symbols. This of course does not mean that they have none. Islam has its own scriptures and classics. Islamic history provides its own models of revolution; its own prescriptions on the theory and practice of dissent, disobedience, resistance, and revolt; its own memories of past revolutions, some ending in success, others, in the historic memory the more significant ones, ending in failure and martyrdom. It is against this background of Islamic action and ideas, memories and symbols that the Islamic revolution must be studied and may, just possibly, be understood. Two preliminary questions must be asked and answered. Is the Islamic revolution in Iran a real revolution as that word has been used in the Western world, where it was first coined and applied, and if so, why is it called Islamic; why apply, to a major political, social, and economic transformation, a religious label?

At one time the word *revolution* carried a connotation of profound and far-reaching change in the polity and perhaps also in the society, of some epoch-making upheaval in human affairs. It was in this sense that seventeenth century Englishmen spoke of the first true national revolution, that eighteenth-century Americans and Frenchmen and twentieth-century Russians and Chinese denoted the profound transformations that they brought to their countries. Since then, the word *revolution*, like most other things in our world, in our time, has undergone a process of continuous devaluation, and is nowadays used for all kinds of trivial changes and innovations. In the West, the term *revolution* is now most commonly used to denote some above-average variation in style of life, production methods, or marketing; elsewhere it serves to designate violent seizures of power of the kind that used to be called *coups d'état*. All too often, the "revolution"is accomplished by a squadron of tanks, the officers of which seize the office of the president or prime minister, the central telephone exchange, the telegraph office, and one or two other strategic points, and proclaim a new regime administered by a *soi-disant* revolutionary command council, otherwise described as a military junta.

The Islamic revolution in Iran is, in its way, as authentic a revolution as the French or the Russian. For better or for worse—which remains to be seen—what happened in Iran was a revolution in the classical sense, a mass movement with wide popular participation that resulted in a major shift in economic as well as political power, and that inaugurated, or, perhaps more accurately, continued, a process of vast social transformation. As with other revolutions, it was preceded by a long period of preparation in which the transfer of power was merely a stage, introduced by what went before and facilitating what came after. It arose from deep discontents; it was inspired by passionate beliefs and driven by ardent hopes. And it still has a long way to go before it works itself out, and before one can determine its nature and consequences. As in France under the Bourbons and Russia under the Romanovs, so also in Iran under the Pahlavis, a major process of change was already underway, and it had advanced to a point at which it required a change in political power in order to continue. And in the Iranian as in other revolutions, there was always the possibility that something might happen whereby the process of change was deflected, perverted, or even annulled. Some Iranians, arguing from very different premises, would claim that this has already happened. But there is still some way to go before us, or for that matter the Iranians themselves, can say what kind of revolution this is or in which direction it is going.

So much for "revolution." What about "Islamic"? Why an Islamic revolution? We do not speak of the Tupamaros and Montaneros and other picturesquely named groups in

Latin America as Christian revolutionaries, nor do we refer to the various upheavals that have taken place in Chris-tendom in the last few centuries as Christian revolutions. Why then Islamic revolution? The first and obvious answer is: that is how they themselves describe it, how the revolutionaries, both the actors and the theorists, perceive and present their aims and their achievements. And in a very important sense, the Islamic revolutionaries are historically right in so doing, in seeing the Islamic revolution as a reassertion of certain basic loyalties, a return to the mainstream of their own history. Revolutions move to different scripts, and their actors assume different roles. The French Revolution, with its ideological background in the eighteenth-century enlightenment, formulated its ideals as liberty, equality, fraternity.

The Russian Revolution, with a background of nineteenth-century socialism, expressed its ideal as a classless state to be achieved through the dictatorship of the proletariat. The Iranian revolution expresses itself in the language of Islam, that is to say, as a religious movement with a religious leadership, a religiously formulated critique of the old order, and religiously expressed plans for the new. Muslim revolutionaries look to the birth of Islam as their model, and see themselves as engaged in a struggle against paganism, oppression, and empire. When we in the Western world, nurtured in the Western tradition, use the words *Islam* and *Islamic,* we tend to assume that religion means the same for Muslims as it has meant in the Western world, even in medieval times: that is to say, a section or compartment of life reserved for certain matters, and separate, or at least separable, from other compartments of life designed to hold other matters. This is not so in the Islamic world. It was never so in the past, and the attempt in modern times to make it so may perhaps be seen in the longer perspective of history as an unnatural aberration that has come to an end in Iran and may also be ending in some other Islamic countries.

What then is the power, the attraction of Islam as a revolutionary appeal? This is a large and complex question, from which it may be useful to isolate a few points. The first is that in most Muslim countries Islam is still the basic criterion of group identity and loyalty. It is Islam that distinguishes between self and other, between in and out, between brother and stranger. We in the West have become accustomed to other criteria of classification: by nation, by country, and by various subdivisions of these. Both nation and country are of course old facts in the Islamic world, but as determinants of political loyalty they are modern and intrusive notions. Some countries—notably Turkey and Egypt—have become more or less accustomed to these notions. But there is a recurring tendency, in times of emergency, for Muslims to find their basic identity and loyalty in the religious community—that is to say, in an entity defined by Islam rather than by ethnic or territorial criteria.

A second, related, point is that Islam is still the most acceptable, indeed in times of crisis the only acceptable, basis for authority. Political authority, even in an authoritarian polity, requires some legitimacy. It can be maintained for a while by mere force, but not indefinitely, not over large areas for long periods. Power seeks legitimacy, and attains it more effectively, among Muslims, from Islam rather than from national or patriotic or even dynastic claims, still less from the Western notion of national or popular sovereignty. To Muslims Islam offers the most intelligible formulation of ideas, on the one hand of social norms and laws, on the other of new ideals and aspirations for the future. And finally, a practical matter, but one of considerable significance; Islam, as recent events have demonstrated again and again, provides the most effective system of symbols—one might say of slogans, though no derogatory sense is meant—for mobilizing public opinion, for arousing the people in defense of a regime that is perceived as possessing the necessary legitimacy, or against a regime that is perceived as lacking that legitimacy, in other words, as not being Islamic.

It was and is in Islamic terms that those who overthrew the Shah, murdered Anwar Sadat, seized the Great Mosque in Mecca, and now threaten the existing order in many Muslim countries justified their actions and appealed for popular support. It is by now a truism that in Islam there is no distinction between church and state. In Christendom the existence of two authorities goes back to the founder of Christianity, who enjoined his followers to render to Caesar that which is Caesar's and to God that which is God's. There are two powers: God and Caesar. They may be associated, they may be separated; they may be in harmony, they may be in conflict; one or the other may dominate; one may interfere, the other may protest, as we have learned recently. But always there are two: God and Caesar, Church and state. In classical Islam, that is to say in pre-Westernized Islam, there is no such distinction.

There were not two powers but one, and the question of separation did not therefore arise. This difference between the religions goes back to the very beginnings of Islam and to the career of its founder. Unlike Moses, Muhammad lived to enter and conquer his promised land. Unlike Jesus, he triumphed in his lifetime over his worldly enemies and established an Islamic state in Medina of which he was sovereign. As the Ayatollah Khomeini has reminded us, Muhammad exercised the normal functions of a head of state—he dispensed justice, he raised taxes, he promulgated laws, he made war, and he made peace. In other words, from the very beginning, in the sacred biography of its Prophet, in its earliest history enshrined in scripture and tradition, Islam as a religion has been associated with the exercise of power. Again to quote Khomeini: "Islam is politics or it is nothing." Its founder was judge, statesman, and general, as well as prophet. Church and state were not separable since they did not exist as different institutions or even as different concepts. These came, but much later and from elsewhere.

There are many different strands in the rich and varied traditional culture of Islam. There are in particular two political traditions, one of which might be called quietist, the other activist. The arguments in favor of both are based, as are most early Islamic arguments, on the Holy Book and on the actions and sayings of the Prophet. The quietist tradition obviously rests on the Prophet as sovereign, as judge and statesman. But before the Prophet became a head of state, he was a rebel. Before he traveled from Mecca to Medina, where he became sovereign, he was an opponent of the existing order. He led an opposition against the pagan oligarchy of Mecca and at a certain point went into exile and formed what in modern language might be called a "government in exile," with which finally he was able to return in triumph to his birthplace and establish the Islamic state in Mecca. The Prophet's departure from Mecca—the *hijra*—marks the starting point of the Muslim era. The struggles in adversity that preceded his exile, like the ultimate triumph that ended his career, are all part of the Islamic tradition, of the holy life of the Prophet.

Of these two traditions, that of the Prophet as sovereign is obviously far better known and far better documented, but the tradition of the Prophet as rebel is also old and deep-rooted, and it recurs throughout the centuries of Islamic history. The activist tradition has been stronger and more explicit among the Shi'a, but it is not exclusive to them, and there has been no lack of Shi'i quietists and Sunni dissidents in Islamic history. The Prophet as rebel has provided a sort of paradigm of revolution—opposition and rejection, withdrawal and departure, exile and return. Time and time again movements of opposition in Islamic history tried to repeat this pattern, a few of them successfully. The rebels who carried out the first great Islamic revolution in the eighth century went to Eastern Iran and from there they came to Iraq and founded the great Abbasid Caliphate in Baghdad. Another group of religiously inspired rebels, in the tenth century, went to

Yemen and then to North Africa and from there they conquered Egypt and established the great Fatimid Caliphate in Cairo. Khomeini went to Iraq, and thence to Neauphle le Château, outside Paris, and from there he returned to rule in Tehran.

Does all this mean that Islam is a theocracy? Different observers have answered both yes and no. Some Western observers, particularly of late, have described Islam as a theocratic system. Most Muslim writers reject this with indignation. In the terms in which they argue, both sides are right, depending on what is meant by theocracy. From the point of view of Muslim scholars, historians, theologians, and others, who reject the idea of Islam's being a theocracy, the meaning of the word is very clear. There is, as they rightly point out, no church in Islam. There is no priesthood in the sense of an ordination and a sacred office. There is no Vatican, no pope, no cardinals, no bishops, no church councils; there is no hierarchy such as exists in Christendom. Consequently, they argue, since theocracy means government by the church, rule by the priests, and since Islam has neither church nor priests, it follows that Islam is not, indeed cannot be, a theocracy. The opposing argument takes theocracy in a rather different sense. Proponents of this view concede that there is no priesthood in Islam in the sense of an ordained intermediary performing some sacred office between God and man, but they claim that there is a very important priesthood in a sociological sense.

It consists of a class of professional men of religion whose status is acquired by learning rather than by ordination and hierarchic rank, but who nevertheless functions in most respects as a clergy. And these men of religion, the theologians and the jurists (the two in Islam are intimately associated), represent God and God's law for most practical purposes, and therefore in a very real sense exercise authority, though not the ultimate political authority, which until the present regime in Iran has never been exercised by the professional men of religion. In this respect, the Iranian Mullahs are not, as they claim, restoring the order that existed in antiquity; they are creating something entirely new in Islamic doctrine or history. Islam is in principle, if not in practice, theocratic in another and deeper sense. Theocracy literally means the rule of God. And in this sense Islam has, in theory, always been a theocracy. In Rome, Caesar was God. In Christendom, God and Caesar coexist. In Islam, God is Caesar, in that he alone is the supreme head of state, the source of sovereignty and hence also of authority and of law. The state is God's state; the law is God's law. The army is God's army—and of course the enemy is God's enemy.

"The enemies of God" is an expression that is often heard nowadays in Iran, both in political polemics against enemies abroad and in criminal charges against enemies at home. To modern man, the idea that God not only has enemies, but needs human help in coping with them, may seem a little strange. But the notion of God's enemies is a very old one, with preclassical, classical, biblical, Islamic, and Iranian antecedents. It becomes much more intelligible in its modern context if we bear in mind the Islamic perception of God as the head of state. Those who exercise authority do so on behalf of God, in the same way and perhaps to the same extent as the prime minister of England exercises authority on behalf of the Queen and the president of the United States on behalf of the people. And since the state undoubtedly can have enemies, it follows that the enemies of the state are the enemies of God.

The larger question arises of the definition of the other, the outsider, the stranger. If the definition of self is by Islam, if the insider is the Muslim, it follows that the "other" is the non-Muslim, the unbeliever, the Kaffir. And this for most purposes is seen as the basic division of mankind. In classical usage, the difference between Muslim and unbeliever was one of creed and allegiance. The Iranian revolutionaries have given this ancient dichotomy a modern dimension, by linking it with another distinction drawn from the Koran, between the humbled and the haughty. In the religious and political language of present-day Iran, the humbled (one might also translate the Arabic word *mustad'af* as deprived, downtrodden) include even the non-Muslim oppressed, who benefit from a kind of Islam of grace. Similarly the haughty (in Arabic *mustakbir,* which in the Koran means something like hubristic) include even those, both at home and abroad, who profess the Islamic religion but do not accept the teachings and discipline of the revolution. They too are counted among the enemies of God, and against them there is a perpetual obligation of struggle (in Arabic *jihad,* usually inaccurately translated as "holy war"), until all mankind adopts the faith and obeys the law of Islam.

These enemies are perceived as falling into two basic categories: the external and the internal. The external enemy means the non-Islamic world, relations with which, in war and in truce, are elaborately regulated by Islamic Holy Law. But for the revolutionaries, it is the enemy within Islam that is their first and main concern. Since we are talking about religiously defined politics, a term that would most naturally occur to a Western observer is heresy. It would not be appropriate. Heresy is not an Islamic notion; there is not even an Islamic term corresponding to it. Heresy is a Christian term meaning a deviation, officially defined as such, from an officially defined orthodoxy. And since Islam has no councils or churches or hierarchy, there is no officially defined orthodoxy and there cannot therefore be any officially defined and condemned deviation from orthodoxy. What can happen is something much more serious and much more dangerous. If a Muslim deviates from Islam to the point where he is no longer regarded as a Muslim with the minimum of correct belief, he is something much worse than a heretic. He is an apostate. The process by which one is declared to be an apostate is called *takfir,* naming and denouncing a Kaffir, an unbeliever. This term is much used in religious movements nowadays, notably by the group responsible for the murder of Sadat.

The penalty for apostasy, in Islamic law, is death. Islam is conceived as a polity, not just as a religious community. It follows therefore that apostasy is treason. It is a withdrawal, a denial of allegiance as well as of religious belief and loyalty. Any sustained and principled opposition to the existing regime or order almost inevitably involves such a withdrawal. In fourteen centuries of Islamic history there have been many opposition movements within Islam. Almost all of them and certainly all those of any significance were religiously expressed. Opposition to the prevailing order, criticism of an existing regime, found expression in religious terms, just as the prevailing regime defined its authority and its legitimacy in religious terms. To confront a religious regime, one needed a religious challenge.

In a sense, the advent of Islam was itself a revolution, which after long struggles only partially succeeded. After the Islamic conquests of the seventh century, there was a continuing tension between the new religion and its message and the very old societies of the countries that the Muslims conquered. Islam came, not into a new world, like Chris-tendom in Europe, but to lands of ancient civilization and deep-rooted traditions. This tension between Islamic dynamism and the older forces of the river-valley societies continued through medieval into modern times. For example, Islamic doctrine is basically egalitarian. It is true that the equality of Islam is limited to free adult male Muslims, but even this represented a very considerable advance on the practice of both the Greco-Roman and the ancient Iranian world. Islam from the first denounced aristocratic privilege, rejected hierarchy, and adopted a formula of the career open to the talents.

Resistance to all this was, of course, very powerful. On the whole Islam triumphed only in certain limited spheres of social and family life. In most political and public matters it was overwhelmed by the more ancient traditions of the regions, which survived in an Islamic disguise, notably in the persistence of the autocratic, monarchical form of government. So we find through the centuries a recurring theme of revolt: a feeling that history had somehow taken a wrong turn; that Islam had been perverted; that the Islamic community was being ruled by non-Muslims, by bad Muslims, by renegade Muslims, by those who had betrayed the heritage of the Prophet and were leading the community as a whole into sin; and that therefore it was the duty of the Muslims to overthrow and replace such an evil regime. In time, this belief began to acquire a messianic character, and a whole cluster of traditions and practices developed, associated with the figure of the Mahdi, the divinely guided one who will come in God's good time, overthrow the kingdoms of evil, and establish the world of justice and divine law.

Normally this was to be accomplished by armed insurrection against the existing order. But armed insurrection was not always feasible and when it was not, according to the more extreme Shi'ites, it was permissible to have recourse to what we would nowadays call terrorist methods. At quite an early stage there were extremist and deviant Shi'ite groups who not only practiced terror but made a kind of sacrament of it. The most famous of course were the Assassins, the ones who took up the patent of the procedure that still bears their name. They flourished in Iran and from there spread to Syria. They were active in both countries roughly from the eleventh to the thirteenth centuries, and disposed, always by dramatic public assassination, of a fairly large number of people. Contrary to the popular belief in the West, the Assassins were not greatly concerned with the struggle against the Crusaders. Of their many victims very few were Crusaders, and the great majority was Muslim princes and dignitaries. Theirs was a revolutionary struggle against the Lords of Islam at that time. Their actions against crusading chiefs were minor and incidental.

A familiar feature of revolutions, such as the French and the Russian, is the tension, often conflict, between moderates and extremists—Girondins and Jacobins in the French Revolution, Mensheviks and Bolsheviks in the Russian, as well as numerous smaller splinter groups. Some historians have found similar differences in Islamic revolutions of the past; some observers have discerned them in the course of events in Iran. Certainly there has been no lack of such tensions and conflicts between rival groups, factions, and tendencies within the revolutionary camp. The distinction between moderates and extremists is, however, one derived from Western history, and may be somewhat misleading when applied to the Islamic revolution in Iran. A more accurate description, for this as for other previous Islamic revolutions, would present the conflict as one between pragmatists and ideologues. The latter are those who insist, against all difficulties and obstacles, on maintaining the pure doctrine of the revolution as taught by them. The former are those who, when they have gained power and become involved in the processes of government at home and abroad, find it necessary to make compromises.

Sometimes they go so far as to modify their revolutionary teachings; more often, they tacitly disregard them. This conflict, between those who reject and those who practice compromise, can be traced throughout Islamic history, from the venerated Companions of the Prophet—those who embraced Islam and joined him during his lifetime—to the henchmen of Khomeini. In times of revolution, it becomes particularly bitter. Each side has certain advantages. The ideologues have the better rhetoric, the stronger appeal, the greater popular support. The pragmatists are better equipped to deal with the practical problems of government, at home and abroad. Part of their pragmatism is to try to avoid an open clash with the ideologues. When they fail, and a clash occurs, they are usually defeated, since in a time of revolutionary change the ideologues are better placed to mobilize support. It is not easy to rouse the masses for such tasks as compromising with Iraq, mending fences with the United States, or slowing the pace of revolutionary change.

When pragmatists in office go too far, they are ruthlessly suppressed, and their careers end in exile, imprisonment, or death. At best, they fade out of public life and are rendered innocuous. Such have been the various fates of once prominent figures like the former foreign minister Sadeq Qotbzadah, who was executed; the former president Abolhasan Bani Sadr, who escaped to Paris; and the first prime minister of the revolutionary regime, Mehdi Bazargan, who, though alive and in Iran, has been excluded from power and reduced to insignificance. The ideologues rule, and since the practical problems remain, in time a new group of pragmatists emerges among the victorious ideologues, and the conflict is renewed, usually with the same result. The process continues until the revolutionary passion is spent, and a group of pragmatists survives, succeeds, and remains in power. Then the ways of government return to normal, and the ideologues return to the world of theory and preaching from which the revolution had enabled them, briefly, to emerge. It would seem that this stage has not yet been reached in Iran. In recent years it has become common practice to use the Western term *fundamentalist* to denote a wide range of militant Islamic movements, both radical and conservative.

The term has spread from English to other European languages, and of late—the ultimate irony—it has even been translated into Arabic and is used by secularized Muslims to describe their militant Islamic compatriots. Despite its common use, the term is inaccurate and misleading. *Fundamentalist* is a term originating in the United States in the early twentieth century, and used to refer to certain Protestant groups that asserted, against the growing influence of liberal theology and critical Bible studies, their belief in the literal divine origin and textual inerrancy of the Bible. The so-called Muslim fundamentalists are something quite different. In principle, all Muslims believe in the literal divine origin and textual inerrancy of the Koran. No one within Islam has ever asserted otherwise, and there is no liberal theology or critical Koran study against which a protest or reaction might be necessary. Where the socalled Muslim fundamentalist differs from other Muslims—and incidentally also from Christian fundamentalists—is in their scholasticism and their legalism.

The gravamen of their case against existing regimes and prevailing ideologies is the abandonment of the *Shari'a*, the systematized law of Islam, and the adoption of what they see as infidel laws and customs. In his denunciation of the misdeeds of the Shah, Khomeini laid special emphasis on the Western-style emancipation of women, and the sharing of political power with non-Muslims. Other proponents of re-Islamization, in Egypt and elsewhere, have made similar complaints. Their critique is not, however, limited to these issues, but covers the whole range of social and cultural modernization. Their declared purpose is to undo all the political, legal, and consequent social changes that have been introduced during the period of Westernization, and to restore the full panoply of the Islamic state and the Islamic holy law. Only when the neopagan apostates who rule in Islamic lands have been deposed, and their laws and institutions abrogated and annulled, will the true Islamic life become possible and the true mission of Islam be accomplished. For the most consequent of these radicals, the fight against foreign enemies is at this point a distraction. The true enemy is at home, and only when he has been conquered will the fight against the alien intruder become necessary and victory against him desirable. In Iran, according to the exponents of the Iranian revolution, the first stage has already been accomplished, and the second is under way. In other Islamic countries, the first task still remains.

The external enemy Iran now confronts is, for the present rulers of that country, defined by Islamic law and identified by Islamic history. In the classical and sanctified texts that determine their view of the world, mankind is divided into two parts: the House of Islam and the House of Unbelief, more commonly called the House of War. Historically, in the Muslim perception, the House of War par excellence has been Christendom, later called Europe, in modern times redefined as the West. To the east and south of the classical Islamic world there were only pagans, some of them, as in India and China, with high levels of material culture, but both essentially regional, and neither offering a serious challenge to Islam. Only in the West was there a major adversary—an alternative dispensation, expressed in a rival world civilization and a competing world power. This perception was reinforced by centuries of conflict—*jihad* and crusade, conquest and reconquest, the Muslim invasions of Europe and the European invasion of Islam. If the main rival was the Christian and Western world, the archenemy was whoever was seen as the leading power of that world—at different times the Byzantine and Holy Roman Emperors, the imperial powers of Europe, and now the United States of America, described, in the theologically colored language favored by Khomeini, as "the great Satan." This role came to the United States by inheritance and is retained by leadership, as the preeminent power of the West and the ultimate custodian of Western values.

With that leadership comes the inevitable price of hatred. The United States might escape this hatred by changing its civilization—hardly a serious proposition—or by relinquishing its leadership and relapsing, like former leaders, into relative insignificance and perceived harmlessness. There may be another way—when the Muslim leaders are persuaded that it is no longer the West or Christendom that is the main enemy and the main danger, but another creed and another power that offer a far greater threat to all that they cherish. Though recent events do not encourage such a perspective, some Muslim leaders have already begun to look in that direction. But most find it easier—and much safer—to direct their hostility against the West, the source of most of the changes that have come to the Islamic lands in modern times and, as they see it, have undermined and disrupted the Islamic way of life. In principle, the aim of the Islamic revolution, in Iran and eventually elsewhere, is to sweep away all the alien and infidel accretions that were imposed on Muslim lands and peoples in the era of alien dominance and influence, and to restore the true Islamic order as it existed in the days of the Prophet and his companions. An examination of the record however, in Iran and elsewhere, reveals that the rejection of Europe and its offerings is by no means as comprehensive and as undiscriminating as the propaganda might indicate, and that some of the importations from the lands of unbelief are still very welcome.

Some of these are obvious. The Islamic revolution in Iran was the first truly modern revolution of the electronic age. Khomeini was the first charismatic orator who sent his oratory to millions of his compatriots at home on cassettes; he was the first revolutionary leader in exile who directed his followers at home by telephone, thanks to the direct dialing that the Shah had introduced in Iran and that was available to him in France (though not in Iraq). Needless to say, in the long war in which they have been engaged with Iraq, the Iranian revolutionary leaders have made the fullest use of such weapons as the West and its imitators are willing to supply—guns, rockets, tanks, and planes on the one hand, radio, television, and the printing press on the other. There is another respect in which the Islamic revolutionaries in Iran have, alas, borrowed from Europe. While their symbols and allusions are Islamic rather than European, the leaders and practitioners of the revolution have found their models of style and method in European history. The summary trial and execution of great numbers of ideologically defined enemies; the driving into exile of hundreds of thousands of men and women; the large-scale confiscation of private property; the mixture of repression and subversion, of violence and indoctrination that accompanied the consolidation of power—all this owes far more to the examples of Robespierre and Stalin than to those of Muhammad and Ali.

These methods are deeply un-Islamic; they are, however, thoroughly revolutionary. But that is not all. In addition to the necessary technology of warfare and propaganda, there were other innovations that at first sight would appear to be neither Islamic nor necessary. The Islamic Republic of Iran has a written constitution and an elected parliament, in which lively debates take place. None of these things existed in the Islamic past, and there has been no serious attempt to argue that they did. While Western-inspired laws have been abrogated and replaced by the *Shari'a,* Western-style legal procedures remain, and there are courts and lawyers to administer them. These too are not insignificant remnants of the age of European influence. There has been no loss of interest—if anything rather an increase—in the study of foreign languages, and the books to which knowledge of foreign language gives access.

What then, in Islamic ideology, is the revolution about? What are the grievances that have aroused such passionate anger, and that call so urgently for remedy? A study of revolutionary writings and speeches reveals two main theses. One of these themes might be called religious in the narrower, Western sense of the word—that is to say, relating to belief, ritual, and observance. While no one, apart from a few Marxists and they at peril of their lives, has openly challenged Muslim beliefs, there has been a growing laxness among educated classes, particularly those who have received some measure of Western or Westernized education. Even more offensive—since Muslims have always been more concerned with practice than with belief—is the laxness in Muslim observance, and in respect for the basic norms of the Muslim way of life. In many Muslim cities, forbidden food and drinks are freely available and openly consumed, to the scandal of the believers, while the cinema and the television screen bring indecency and immorality into both the public place and the private home.

Linked with this is the second theme, the polemic—itself a borrowing from the West—against consumerism and the cult of worldly goods, and the championing of the poor and oppressed against their rich and powerful oppressors. There had always been rich and poor in the Islamic world, and the difference between them was accepted and in a sense sanctified by Islamic law, which recognizes private wealth, regulates inheritance, and prescribes charity. But Westernization made the gap between rich and poor both greater and more visible. It also—through a rapidly rising rate of natural increase—made the poor much more numerous. Western commerce and industry created vast new opportunities for both enrichment and expenditure; the Western press and television have made the poor, as never before, conscious of their own poverty and of the wealth of their neighbors. In the past, rich and poor had basically worn the same kind of clothes, eaten the same kind of food, lived the same kind of life, and been held together by a complex web of loyalties and obligations. In the modern age, a Westernized elite and an un-Westernized populace live in different worlds, and the loyalties that once held them together have been broken or discredited. Such disparities did much to provoke and exacerbate the alienation and anger that destroyed the head of state in Egypt, and the entire regime in Iran.

Like the French and the Russian in their time, the Iranian revolutionaries play to international as well as domestic audiences, and their revolution exercises a powerful fascination over other peoples outside Iran, in other countries within the same culture, within the same universe of discourse. The appeal was naturally strongest among Shi'i populations, as in South Lebanon and some of the Gulf States, and weakest among their immediate Sunni neighbors. It was and remains very strong in the greater part of the Muslim world, where Shi'ism is virtually unknown. In these, the sectarian difference is unimportant; Khomeini can be seen not as a Shi'ite or a Persian but as an Islamic revolutionary leader. Like the Western radicals who, in their day, responded with almost messianic enthusiasm to the events in Paris and Petrograd, events "that shook the world," so did millions of young and not so young men and women all over the world of Islam, from West Africa to Indonesia, from the Sudan to Sarajevo and Kossovo in Yugoslavia, and, more recently, among the millions of Muslim immigrants and guest workers in Western Europe. Sarajevo is a particularly striking case.

Though its population is predominantly Muslim, Sarajevo is a European city in a country that had by then been under communist rule for thirty-five years. Nevertheless, the appeal of the Iranian revolution was so strong that the Yugoslav papers reported trials of young men in Sarajevo accused of plotting to overthrow the regime and establish an Islamic republic in Bosnia. If that could happen in Sarajevo, one wonders what might be happening among the sixty million Muslims in the Soviet Union, far closer to Iran, in both geography and culture, than those of Yugoslavia. The parallel is again very close between what happened in the Islamic world in our day and what happened in Europe and beyond following the Russian and French Revolutions—the same upsurge of emotion, the same uplifting of hearts, the same boundless hopes, the same willingness to excuse and condone all kinds of horrors, and the same questions. Where next? Who could have predicted in 1795 or in 1925 the further development of the French or Russian revolutions and the careers of Napoleon or Stalin? I shall not attempt it for Iran. Only this much can be said: that what is in progress is producing vast, deep, and irreversible changes that the forces that are causing these changes are not yet spent and that their destination is still unknown.

Muslim Agricultural Revolution

The Islamic Golden Age from the 8th century to the 13th century witnessed a fundamental transformation in agriculture known as the Arab Agricultural Revolution, Medieval Green Revolution, or Muslim Agricultural Revolution. The global economy established by Arab and other Muslim traders across the Old World, enabled the diffusion of many crops and farming techniques among different parts of the Islamic world, as well as the adaptation of crops and techniques from and to regions beyond the Islamic world. Crops from Africa such as sorghum, crops from China such as citrus fruits, and numerous crops from India such as mangos, rice, cotton and sugar cane, were distributed throughout Islamic lands, which previously had not grown these crops. Some writers have referred to the diffusion of numerous crops during this period as the Globalization of crops. These introductions, along with an increased mechanization of agriculture, led to major changes in economy, population distribution, vegetation cover, agricultural production and income, population levels, urban growth, the distribution of the labour force, linked industries, cooking, diet and clothing in the Islamic world.

Age of Discovery

The earliest forms of globalization began emerging during the Islamic Empire and the Islamic Golden Age, when the knowledge, trade and economies from many previously isolated regions and civilizations began integrating due to contacts with Muslim explorers, sailors, scholars, traders, and travelers. Some have called this period the "Pax Islamica" or "Afro-Asiatic age of discovery", in reference to the Jewish (known as Radhanites), Sogdian and Muslim Southwest Asian and North African traders and explorers who travelled most of the Old World, and established an early global economy across most of Asia and Africa and much of Europe, with their trade networks extending from the Atlantic Ocean and Mediterranean Sea in the west to the Indian Ocean and China Sea in the east. This helped establish the Islamic Empire (including the Rashidun, Umayyad, Abbasid and Fatimid caliphates) as the world's leading extensive economic power throughout the 7th-13th centuries. Several contemporary medieval Arabic reports also suggest that Muslim explorers from al-Andalus and the Maghreb may have travelled in expeditions across the Atlantic Ocean, possibly even to the Americas, between the 9th and 14th centuries.

Agricultural Innovations

Muslims widely practiced cash cropping and the modern crop rotation system where land was cropped four or more times in a two-year period. Winter crops were followed by summer ones, and in some cases there was in between. In areas where plants of shorter growing season were used, such as spinach and eggplants, the land could be cropped three or more times a year. In parts of Yemen, wheat yielded two harvests a year on the same land, as did rice in Iraq. Muslims developed a scientific approach based on three major elements; sophisticated systems of crop rotation, highly developed irrigation techniques, and the introduction of a large variety of crops which were studied and catalogued according to the season, type of land and amount of water they require. Numerous encyclopaedias on farming and botany were produced, with highly accurate precision and details.

Advanced Agricultural Systems

As early as the 9th century, an essentially modern agricultural system became central to economic life and organization in the Arab caliphates, replacing the largely export driven Roman model. Cities of the Near East, North Africa, and Moorish Spain were supported by elaborate agricultural systems which included extensive irrigation based on knowledge of hydraulic and hydrostatic principles, some of which were continued from Roman times. In later centuries, Persian Muslims began to function as a conduit, transmitting cultural elements, including advanced agricultural techniques, into Turkic lands and western India. The Muslims introduced what was to become an agricultural revolution based on four key areas:

- Development of a sophisticated system of irrigation using machines such as norias, water mills, water raising machines, dams and reservoirs. With such technology they managed to greatly expand the exploitable land area.
- The adoption of a scientific approach to farming enabled them to improve farming techniques derived from the collection and collation of relevant information throughout the whole of the known world. Farming manuals were produced in every corner of the Muslim world detailing where, when and how to plant and grow various crops. Advanced scientific techniques allowed leaders like Ibn al-Baitar to introduce new crops and breeds and strains of livestock into areas where they were previously unknown.
- Incentives based on a new approach to land ownership and labourers' rights, combining the recognition of private ownership and the rewarding of cultivators with a harvest share commensurate with their efforts. Their counterparts in Europe struggled under a feudal system in which they were almost slaves (serfs) with little hope of improving their lot by hard work.
- The introduction of new crops transforming private farming into a new global industry exported everywhere, including Europe, where farming was mostly restricted to wheat strains obtained much earlier via central Asia. Spain received what she in turn transmitted to the rest of Europe; many agricultural and fruit-growing processes, together with many new plants, fruit and vegetables. These new crops included sugar cane, rice, citrus fruit, apricots, cotton, artichokes,

aubergines, and saffron. Others, previously known, were further developed. Muslims also brought to those country lemons, oranges, cotton, almonds, figs and sub-tropical crops such as bananas and sugar cane. Several were later exported from Spanish coastal areas to the Spanish colonies in the New World. Also transmitted via Muslim influence, a silk industry flourished, flax was cultivated and linen exported, and esparto grass, which grew wild in the more arid parts, was collected and turned into various articles.

Economic and Social Reforms

The caliphate understood that incentives were needed to increase productivity and wealth, thus enhancing tax revenues. Hence, they introduced a social transformation through the changed ownership of land, where any individual of any gender or any ethnic or religious background had the right to buy, sell, mortgage and inherit land for farming or any other purposes. They also introduced the signing of a contract for every major financial transaction concerning agriculture, industry, commerce, and employment. Copies of the contract were usually kept by both parties involved. The two types of economic systems that prompted agricultural development in the Islamic world were either politicallydriven, by the conscious decisions of the central authority to develop underexploited lands; or market-driven, involving the spread of advice, education, and free seeds, and the introduction of high value crops or animals to areas where they were previously unknown.

These led to increased subsistence, a high level of economic security that ensured wealth for all citizens, and a higher quality of life due to the introduction of artichokes, spinach, aubergines, carrots, sugar cane, and various exotic plants; vegetables being available all year round without the need to dry them for winter; citrus and olive plantations becoming a common sight, market gardens and orchards springing up in every Muslim city; intense cropping and the technique of intensive irrigation agriculture with land fertility replacement; a major increase in animal husbandry; higher quality of wool and other clothing materials; and the introduction of selective breeding of animals from different parts of the Old World resulting in improved horse stocks and the best load-carrying camels. The average life expectancy in the lands under Islamic rule also experienced an increase, due to the Agricultural Revolution as well as improved medical care.

In contrast to the average lifespan in the ancient Greco-Roman world (22-28 years), the average lifespan in the early Islamic Caliphate was more than 35 years. The average lifespans of the Islamic scholarly class in particular was much higher: 84.3 years in 10th-11th century Iraq and Persia, 72.8 years in the 11th century Middle East, 69-75 years in 11th century Islamic Spain, 75 years in 12th century Persia, and 59-72 years in 13th century Persia. The Islamic Empire also experienced a growth in literacy, having the highest literacy rate of the middle Ages, comparable to Athens' literacy in Classical Antiquity but on a larger scale.

Sugar Industry

During the Muslim Agricultural Revolution, sugar production was refined and transformed into a large-scale industry by the Arabs. The Arabs and Berbers diffused sugar throughout the Arab Empire from the 8th century.

Other Innovations

Many other agricultural innovations were introduced by Muslim farmers and engineers, such as new forms of land tenure, improvements in irrigation, a variety of sophisticated irrigation methods, the introduction of fertilizers and widespread artificial irrigation systems, the develop-ment of gravityflow irrigation systems from rivers and springs, the first uses of noria and chain pumps for irrigation purposes, the establishment of the sugar cane industry in the Mediterranean and experimentation in sugar cultivation, numerous advances in industrial milling and water-raising machines, and many other improvements and innovations.

Agricultural Sciences

During the Muslim Agricultural Revolution, Muslim scientists laid the foundations of agricultural science, which included significant advances in the fields of agronomy, astronomy, botany, earth science, environmental philosophy, and environmental science. In particular, the experimental scientific method was introduced into the field in the 13th century by the Andalusian-Arab botanist Abu al-Abbas al-Nabati, the teacher of Ibn al-Baitar. Al-Nabati introduced empirical techniques in the testing, description and identification of numerous materia medica, and he separated unverified reports from those supported by actual tests and observations.

The earliest known work dedicated to the study of agriculture was Ibn Wahshiyya's *Nabatean Agriculture,* which also dealt with the related field of botany and was also an early cookbook. The early Arab lexicographs were the first known works to separate the two disciplines of agriculture and botany, though both were considered part of the medical sciences due to agriculture's primary role being to feed and botany's primary role being to heal. The agri-cultural sciences were known by the Arabic term *filaha,* which had a dual meaning, to both care for the Earth and to take care of plants. Many of the early Islamic authors on botany were often philologists, due to their role in the translation of ancient scientific texts. This was also the case with early Arabic zoology, like with al-Jahiz for example. Al-Asma'i was the earliest known Arab biologist, botanist and zoologist; his works include the *Book of Distinction, Book of the Wild Animals, Book of the Horse,* and *Book of the Sheep.*

Agronomy

Muslim agriculturists demonstrated advanced agronomic, agrotechnical and economic knowledge in areas such as meteorology, climatology, hydrology, soil occupation, and the economy and management of agricultural enterprises. They also demonstrated agricultural knowledge in areas such as pedology, agricultural ecology, irrigation, preparation of soil, planting, spreading of manure, killing herbs, sowing, cutting trees, grafting, pruning vine], prophylaxis, phytotherapy, the care and improvement of microbiological cultures and plants, and the harvest and storage of crops.

Ibn Wahshiyya's *Nabatean Agriculture* was an early Arabic work on agronomy and agriculture. The following eight chapters of the book are dedicated to water in the context of agriculture:

1. Research of water and related technical knowledge
2. Digging wells and increasing their flow using proven artifices and techniques
3. The drilling of wells
4. Artifices used to increase water in a well
5. Making water rise up a very deep well
6. Augmenting the quantity of water in wells and sources
7. Modifying and improving the taste of water
8. "On the difference in nature and action of the water according to its position" close of far away "with regard to the ecliptic"

The *Nabatean Agriculture* then goes on to discuss a number of other complex issues on agriculture, including the management of an agricultural enterprise and the duties of the owner regarding his enterprise and workers; the official (*wakil*) in charge of the management of the enterprise, his obligation towards the farmer]s, and applying the instructions he receives from his boss; the weather forecasting of atmospheric changes and signs from the planetary astral alterations; signs of rain based on observation of the lunar phases, nature of thunder and lightning, direction of sunrise, behaviour of certain plants and animals, and weather forecasts based on the movement of winds; the recognition of plant tissue cultures which succeed in certain years; a list of work to be done in each month of year; the position of the moon relative to the Earth; the required knowledge of a farmer and the owner of an agricultural enterprise; pollenized air and winds; and formation of winds and vapours.

Other agricultural topics discussed in the *Nabatean Agriculture* include the causes of the corruption of plants and of torrential rain; the nature of soils and their different flavours; the manure; how to get rid of bad herbs and how to cut plants which need to be cut; and a number of other agricultural topics. In 12th century al-Andalus, Ibn al-'Awwam al-Ishbili wrote the *Kitab al-Filaha* which synthe-sized his own agricultural knowledge with that of the *Naba-tean Agriculture* and his other Arabic predecessors. This work also described 585 microbiological cultures, 55 of which concern fruit trees. This work was influential in Europe after it was translated into Spanish by Banqueri in Madrid in 1801 and into French by Clement-Mullet in Paris in 1864.

Astronomy and Meteorology

Another innovation during this period was the application of astronomy to agriculture and botany. As weather forecasting predictions and the measurement of time and the onset of seasons became more precise and reliable, farmers became informed of these advances and often employed them in agriculture. They also benefited from the compilation of calendars with information on when to plant each type of crop, when to graft trees, when and how to fertilize crops, when to harvest, and what to eat and what to avoid at each time of year. These advances made it possible for farmers to plan the growth of each of their crops for specific markets and at specific times of the year. Parts of al-Dinawari's *Book of Plants* deal with the applications of astronomy and meteorology to agriculture. It describes the astronomical and meteorological character of the sky, the planets and constellations, the sun and moon, the lunar phases indicating seasons and rain, the *anwa* (heavenly bodies of rain), and atmospheric phenomena such as winds, thunder, lightning, snow, floods, valleys, rivers, lakes, wells and other sources of water.

Botany

Muslims developed a scientific approach to botany and agriculture based on three major elements: sophisticated systems of crop rotation, highly developed irrigation techniques, and the introduction of a large variety of crops which were studied and catalogued according to the season, type of land and amount of water they require. Numerous encyclopaedias on botany were produced, with highly accurate precision and details. The 9th century botanist al-Dinawari is considered the founder of Arabic botany. He wrote a botanical encyclopedia entitled *Kitab al-Nabat* (*Book of Plants*), which consisted of six volumes. Only the third and fifth volumes have survived, though the sixth volume has partly been reconstructed based on citations from later works. In the surviving portions of his works, 637 plants are described from the letters *sin* to *ya*. He also discusses plant evolution from its birth to its death, describing the phases of plant growth and the production of flowers and fruit.

In the early 13th century, Ibn al-Baitar published the *Kitab al-Jami fi al-Adwiya al-Mufrada*, which is considered one of the greatest botanical compilations and pharmaceutical encyclopedias, and was a botanical authority for centuries. It contains details on at least 1,400 different plants, foods, and drugs, 300 of which were his own original discoveries. The *Kitab al-Jami fi al-Adwiya al-Mufrada* was also influential in Europe after it was translated into Latin in 1758, where it was being used up until the early 19th century.

Earth Science

Muslim scientists made a number of contributions to the earth sciences. Alkindus introduced experimentation into the Earth sciences. Parts of al-Dinawari's *Book of Plants* deals with the Earth sciences in the context of agriculture. He considers the Earth, stone and sands, and describes different types of ground, indicating which types are more convenient for plants and the qualities and properties of good ground. Biruni is considered the father of geodesy for his important contributions to the field, along with his significant contributions to geography and geology.

Among his writings on geology, Biruni wrote the following on the geology of India:

"But if you see the soil of India with your own eyes and meditate on its nature, if you consider the rounded stones found in earth however deeply you dig, stones that are huge near the mountains and where the rivers have a violent current: stones that are of smaller size at a greater distance from the mountains and where the streams flow more slowly: stones that appear pulverised in the shape of sand where the streams begin to stagnate near their mouths and near the sea - if you consider all this you can scarcely help thinking that India was once a sea, which by degrees has been filled up by the alluvium of the streams."

"Important contributions to geodesy and geography were also made by al-Biruni. He introduced techniques to measure the earth and distances on it using triangulation. He found the radius of the earth to be 6339.6 km, a value not obtained in the West until the 16th century. His *Masudic canon* contains a table giving the coordinates of six hundred places, almost all of which he had direct knowledge." In geology, Avicenna hypothesized on two causes of mountains in *The Book of Healing*. In cartography, the Piri

Reis map drawn by the Ottoman cartographer Piri Reis in 1513, was one of the earliest world maps to include the Americas, and perhaps the first to include Antarctica. His map of the world was considered the most accurate in the 16th century.

Environmental Philosophy

Perhaps due to resource scarcity in most Islamic nations, there was an emphasis on limited (and some claim also sustainable) use of natural capital, i.e. producing land. Traditions of haram and hima and early urban planning were expressions of strong social obligations to stay within carrying capacity and to preserve the natural environment as an obligation of khalifa or "stewardship". Muhammad is considered a pioneer of environmentalism for his teachings on environmental preservation. His hadiths on agriculture and environmental philosophy were compiled in the "Book of Agriculture" of the *Sahih Bukhari*, which included the following saying:

"There is none amongst the believers who plants a tree, or sows a seed, and then a bird, or a person, or an animal eats thereof, but it is regarded as having given a charitable gift [for which there is great recompense]."

Several such statements concerning the environment are also found in the Qur'an, such as the following:

"And there is no animal in the earth or bird that flies with its two wings, but that they are communities like you."

Environmental Science

The earliest known treatises dealing with environmentalism and environmental science, especially pollution, were Arabic medical treatises written by al-Kindi, Qusta ibn Luqa, al-Razi, Ibn Al-Jazzar, al-Tamimi, al-Masihi, Avicenna, Ali ibn Ridwan, Ibn Jumay, Isaac Israeli ben Solomon, Abd-el-latif, Ibn al-Quff, and Ibn al-Nafis. Their works covered a number of subjects related to pollution such as air pollution, water pollution, soil contamination, municipal solid waste mishandling, and environmental impact assessments of certain localities. Cordoba, al-Andalus also had the first waste containers and waste disposal facilities for litter collection.

Zoology

In the zoology field of biology, Muslim biologists developed theories on evolution and natural selection which were widely taught in medieval Islamic schools. John William Draper, a contemporary of Charles Darwin, considered the "Mohammedan theory of evolution" to be developed "much farther than we are disposed to do, extending them even to inorganic or mineral things." According to al-Khazini, ideas on evolution were widespread among "common people" in the Islamic world by the 12th century. The first Muslim biologist to develop a theory on evolution was al-Jahiz (781-869). He wrote on the effects of the environment on the likelihood of an animal to survive, and he first described the struggle for existence and an early form of natural selection. Al-Jahiz was also the first to discuss food chains, and was also an early adherent of environmental determinism, arguing that the environment can determine the physical characteristics of the inhabitants of a certain community and that the origins of different human skin colors are the result of the environment.

Ibn al-Haytham wrote a book in which he argued for evolutionism (although not natural selection), and numerous other Islamic scholars and scientists, such as Ibn Miskawayh, the Brethren of Purity, al-Khazini, Abû Rayhân al-Bîrûnî, Nasir al-Din Tusi, and Ibn Khaldun, discussed and developed these ideas. Translated into Latin, these works began to appear in the West after the Renaissance and appear to have had an impact on Western science. Ibn Miskawayh's *al-Fawz al-Asghar* and the Brethren of Purity's *Encyclopedia of the Brethren of Purity* (*The Epistles of Ikhwan al-Safa*) expressed evolutionary ideas on how species evolved from matter, into vapor, and then water, then minerals, then plants, then animals, then apes, and then humans. These works were known in Europe and likely had an influence on Darwinism.

Capitalist Market Economy

Capitalism developed much earlier in Islamic regions than in the Occident. Subhi Y. Labib argues the reason for this was the growing trade economy of the Muslim world, and security from Barbarian invasions. The first market economy and earliest forms of merchant capitalism took root between the 8th–12th centuries in the Caliphate, which are referred to as "Islamic capitalism". A vigorous monetary economy was created on the basis of the expanding levels of circulation of a stable high-value currency (the dinar) and the integration of monetary areas that were previously independent. Innovative new business techniques and forms of business organisation were introduced by economists, merchants and traders during this time. Such innovations included the earliest trading companies, big businesses, contracts, bills of exchange, long-distance international trade, the first forms of partnership (*mufawada*) such as limited partnerships (*mudaraba*), and the earliest forms of credit, debt, profit, loss, capital (*al-mal*), capital accumulation (*nama al-mal*), circulating capital, capital expenditure, revenue, cheques, promissory notes, trusts and charitable trusts, startup companies, savings accounts, transactional accounts, pawning, loaning, exchange rates, bankers, money changers, ledgers, deposits, assignments, the double-entry bookkeeping system, and lawsuits.

Organizational enterprises similar to corporations' independent from the state also existed in the medieval Islamic world, while the agency and aval institutions was also introduced. Many of these early capitalist concepts were adopted and further advanced in medieval Europe from the 13th century onwards. The systems of contract relied upon by merchants was very effective. Merchants would buy and sell on commission, with money loaned to them by wealthy investors, or a joint investment of several merchants, who were often Muslim, Christian and Jewish. Recently, a collection of documents was found in an Egyptian synagogue shedding a very detailed and human light on the life of medieval Middle Eastern merchants. Business partnerships would be made for many commercial ventures, and bonds of kinship enabled trade networks to form over huge distances.

Crops

Hundreds of crops were diffused throughout the Islamic world and beyond as a result of the Muslim Agricultural Revolution, some of which include artichokes, bananas, coconut palms, colocasia, cotton, eggplants, hard wheat, lemons, limes, mangos, plantains, rice, sorghum, sour oranges, spinach, sugar cane, and watermelons, among hundreds of other crops.

Industrial Growth

Muslim engineers in the Islamic world were responsible for numerous innovative industrial uses of hydropower, early industrial uses of tidal power, wind power, and fossil fuels such as petroleum, and the earliest large factory complexes (*tiraz* in Arabic). The industrial uses of watermills in the Islamic world date back to the 7th century, while horizontal-wheeled and vertical-wheeled water mills were both in widespread use since at least the 9th century. A variety of industrial mills were first invented in the Islamic world, including fulling mills, gristmills, hullers, paper mills, sawmills, shipmills, stamp mills, steel mills, sugar mills, tide mills, and windmills.

By the 11th century, every pro-vince throughout the Islamic world had these industrial mills in operation, from al-Andalus and North Africa to the Middle East and Central Asia. Muslim engineers also invented crankshafts and water turbines, first employed gears in mills and water-raising machines, and pioneered the use of dams as a source of water power, used to provide additional power to watermills and water-raising machines.

Such advances made it possible for many industrial tasks that were previously driven by manual labour in ancient times to be mechanized and driven by machinery instead in the medieval Islamic world. The transfer of these technologies to medieval Europe later laid the foundations for the Industrial Revolution in 18th century Europe. Many industries were generated due to the Muslim Agricultural Revolution, including the earliest industries for agribusiness, astronomical instruments, ceramics, chemicals, distillation technologies, clocks, glass, mechanical hydropowered and wind powered machinery, matting, mosaics, [Pulp and paper industry | pulp and paper, perfumery, petroleum, pharmaceuticals, rope-making, shipping, shipbuilding, silk, sugar, textiles, weapons, and the mining of minerals such as sulfur, ammonia, lead and iron].

The first large factory complexes (*tiraz*) were built for many of these industries. Knowledge of these industries was later transmitted to medieval Europe, especially during the Latin translations of the 12th century, as well as before and after. For example, the first glass factories in Europe were founded in the 11th century by Egyptian craftsmen in Greece. The agricultural and handicraft industries also experienced high levels of growth during this period.

Industrial Milling

Muslim engineers pioneered two solutions to achieve the maximum output from a water mill. The first solution was to mount them to piers of bridges to take advantage of the increased flow. The second solution was the shipmill, a unique type of water mill powered by water wheels mounted on the sides of ships moored in midstream. This was first employed along the Tigris and Euphrates rivers in 10th century Iraq, where large shipmills made of teak and iron could produce 10 tons of flour from corn every day for the granary in Baghdad. Industrial water mills were also employed in the first large factory complexes built in al-Andalus between the 11th and 13th centuries.

Windmills were first built in Sistan, Afghanistan, from the 7th century. These were vertical axle windmills, which had long vertical driveshafts with rectangle shaped blades. The first windmill was built by the Rashidun caliph Umar (634–44). Made of six to twelve sails covered in reed matting or cloth material, these windmills were used to grind corn and draw up water, and were used in the gristmilling and sugarcane industries. After paper was introduced into the Islamic world by Chinese prisoners following the Battle of Talas, Muslims made significant improvements to paper-making and built the first paper mills in Baghdad, Iraq, as early as 794. Papermaking was transformed from an art into a major industry as a result. The first fulling mills were later invented in the 10th century, followed by the first stamp mills and steel mills in the 11th century.

The first gristmills were invented by Muslim engineers in the Islamic world, and were used for grinding corn and other seeds to produce meals, and many other industrial uses such as fulling cloth, husking rice, papermaking, pulping sugarcane, and crushing metallic ores before extraction. Gristmills in the Islamic world were often made from both watermills and windmills. In order to adapt water wheels for gristmilling purposes, cams were used for raising and releasing trip hammers to fall on a material. The first water turbine, which had water wheels with curved blades onto which water flow was directed axially, was also first invented in the Islamic world, and was described in a 9th century Arabic text for use in a watermill.

Labour Force

The labour force in the caliphate were employed from diverse ethnic and religious backgrounds, while both men and women were involved in diverse occupations and economic activities. Women were employed in a wide range of commercial activities and diverse occupations in the primary sector (as farmers for example), secondary sector (as construction workers, dyers, spinners, etc.) and tertiary sector (as investors, doctors, nurses, presidents of guilds, brokers, peddlers, lenders, scholars, etc.). Muslim women also held a monopoly over certain branches of the textile industry, the largest and most specialized and market-oriented industry at the time, in occupations such as spinning, dying, and embroidery. In comparison, female property rights and wage labour were relatively uncommon in Europe until the Industrial Revolution in the 18th and 19th centuries.

The division of labour was diverse and had been evolving over the centuries. During the 8th–11th centuries, there were on average 63 unique occupations in the primary sector of economic activity (extractive), 697 unique occupations in the secondary sector (manufacturing), and 736 unique occupations in the tertiary sector (service). By the 12th century, the number of unique occupations in the primary sector and secondary sector decreased to 35 and 679 respectively, while the number of unique occupations in the tertiary sector increased to 1,175. These changes in the division of labour reflect the increased mechanization and use of machinery to replace manual labour and the increased standard of living and quality of life of most citizens in the Caliphate.

An economic transition occurred during this period, due to the diversity of the service sector being far greater than any other previous or contemporary society, and the high degree of economic integration between the labour force and the economy. Islamic society also experienced a change in attitude towards manual labour. In previous civilizations such as ancient Greece and in contemporary civilizations such as early medieval Europe, intellectuals saw manual labour in a negative light and looked down on them with contempt. This resulted in technological stagnation as they did not see the need for machinery to replace manual labour. In the Islamic world, however, manual labour was seen in a far more positive light, as intellectuals such as the Brethren of Purity likened them to a participant in the act of creation, while Ibn Khaldun alluded to the benefits of manual labour to the progress of society.

Mechanical Technology

Noria and chain pump (saqiya) machines became more widespread during the Muslim Agricultural Revolution, when Muslim engineers made a number of improvements to the device. These include the first uses of noria and chain pumps for irrigation purposes, and the invention of the flywheel mechanism, used to smooth out the delivery of power from a driving device to a driven machine, which was first invented by Ibn Bassal (fl. 1038–75) of al-Andalus, who pioneered the use of the flywheel in the saqiya and noria. In 1206, al-Jazari invented a variety of machines for raising water, which were the most efficient in his time, as well as water wheels with cams on their axle used to operate automata. He invented the crankshaft and connecting rod, and employed them in a crank-connecting rod system for two of these water-raising machines. His invention of the crankshaft is considered the most important single mechanical invention after the wheel, as it transforms continuous rotary motion into a linear reciprocating motion, and is central to modern machinery such as the steam engine and the internal combustion engine.

Urbanization

There was a significant increase in urbanization during this period, due to numerous scientific advances in fields such as agriculture, hygiene, sanitation, astronomy, medicine and engineering. This also resulted in a rising middle class population. As urbanization increased, Muslim cities grew unregulated, resulting in narrow winding city streets and neighborhoods separated by different ethnic backgrounds and religious affiliations. These qualities proved efficient for transporting goods to and from major commercial centers while preserving the privacy valued by Islamic family life. Suburbs lay just outside the walled city, from wealthy residential communities, to working class semi-slums. City garbage dumps were located far from the city, as were clearly defined cemeteries which were often homes for criminals. A place of prayer was found just near one of the main gates, for religious festivals and public executions. Similarly, Military Training grounds were found near a main gate.

While varying in appearance due to climate and prior local traditions, Islamic cities were almost always dominated by a merchant middle class. Some peoples' loyalty towards their neighborhood was very strong, reflecting ethnicity and religion, while a sense of citizenship was at times uncommon (but not in every case). The extended family provided the foundation for social programs, business deals, and negotiations with authorities. Part of this economic and social unit was often the tenants of a wealthy landlord. State power normally focused on Dar al Imara, the governor's office in the citadel. These fortresses towered high above the city built on thousands of years of human settlement. The primary function of the city governor was to provide for defence and to maintain legal order. This system would be responsible for a mixture of autocracy and autonomy within the city. Each neighborhood, and many of the large tenement blocks, elected a representative to deal with urban authorities.

These neighborhoods were also expected to organize their young men into a militia providing for protection of their own neighborhoods, and as aid to the professional armies defending the city as a whole. The head of the family was given the position of authority in his household, although a qadi, or judge was able to negotiate and resolve differences in issues of disagreements within families and between them. The two senior representatives of municipal authority were the qadi and the muhtasib, who held the responsibilities of many issues, including quality of water, maintenance of city streets, containing outbreaks of disease, supervising the markets, and a prompt burial of the dead. Another aspect of Islamic urban life was waqf, a religious charity directly dealing with the qadi and religious leaders. Through donations, the waqf owned many of the public baths and factories, using the revenue to fund education, and to provide irrigation for orchards outside the city. Following expansion, this system was introduced into Eastern Europe by Ottoman Turks.

While religious foundations of all faiths were tax exempt in the Muslim world, civilians paid their taxes to the urban authorities, soldiers to the superior officer, and landowners to the state treasury. Taxes were also levied on an unmarried man until he was wed. Instead of zakat, the mandatory charity required of Muslims, non-Muslims were required to pay the jizya, a discriminatory religious tax, imposed on Christians and Jews. During the Muslim Conquests of the 7th and 8th centuries conquered populations were given the three choices of converting to Islam, paying the jizya, or dying by the sword. Animals brought to the city for slaughter were restricted to areas outside the city, as were any other industries seen as unclean. The more valuable a good was, the closer its market was to the center of town. Because of this, booksellers and goldsmiths clustered around the main mosque at the heart of the city.

Civil Engineering

Many dams, acequia and qanat water supply systems, and "Tribunal of Waters" irrigation systems, were built during the Islamic Golden Age and are still in use today in the Islamic world and in formerly Islamic regions of Europe such as Sicily and the Iberian Peninsula, particularly in the Andalusia, Aragon] and Valencia provinces of Spain. The Arabic systems of irrigation and water distribution were later adopted in the Canary Islands and Americas due to the Spanish and are still used in places like Texas, Mexico, Peru, and Chile. Muslim cities also had advanced domestic water systems with sewers, public baths, drinking fountains, piped drinking water supplies, and widespread private and public toilet and bathing facilities. By the 10th century, Cordoba had 700 mosques, 60,000 palaces, and 70 libraries, the largest of which had 600,000 books, while as many as 60,000 treatises, poems, polemics and compilations were published each year in al-Andalus.

The library of Cairo had more than 100,000 books, while the library of Tripoli is said to have had as many as three million books. The number of important and original Arabic works on science that have survived is much larger than the combined total of Greek and Latin works on science. Islamic cities also had an early public health care service. "The extraordinary provision of public bath-houses, complex sanitary systems of drainage (more extensive even than the famous Roman infrastructures), fresh water supplies, and the large and sophisticated urban hospitals, all contributed to the general health of the population."

Timeline of Science and Engineering in the Islamic World

This timeline of science and engineering in the Islamic world covers both the classical Islamic Golden Age (usually dated from the 7th to 16th centuries) and the post-classical period (after the 16th century). From the 19th century onwards, the advances by Muslim scientists and engineers occurred both within and outside of the Islamic world. All year dates are given according to the Gregorian calendar except where noted.

Islamic economics in the World

Islamic economics in practice, or economic policies supported by self-identified Islamic groups, has varied throughout its long history.

Traditional Islamic concepts having to do with economics included

- *Zakat* - the "taxing of certain goods, such as harvest, with an eye to allocating these taxes to expenditures that are also explicitly defined, such as aid to the needy."
- *Gharar* - "the interdiction of chance ... that is, of the presence of any element of uncertainty, in a contract (which excludes not only insurance but also the lending of money without participation in the risks)"
- *Riba* - "referred to as usury"

These concepts, like others in Islamic law and jurisprudence, came from the "prescriptions, anecdotes, examples, and words of the Prophet, all gathered together and systematized by commentators according to an inductive, casuistic method." Sometimes other sources such as al-urf, (the custom), al-aql (reason) or al-ijma (consensus of the jurists) were employed. In addition, Islamic law has developed areas of law that correspond to secular laws of contracts and torts.

7

Reforms under Islam and Ethics

Early Islamic Economics

Some argue early Islamic theory and practice formed a "coherent" economic system with "a blueprint for a new order in society, in which all participants would be treated more fairly". Michael Bonner, for example, has written that an "economy of poverty" prevailed in Islam until the 13th and 14th centuries. Under this system God's guidance made sure the flow of money and goods was "purified" by being channeled from those who had much of it to those who had little by encouraging zakat (charity) and discouraging riba (usury/interest) on loans. Bonner maintains the prophet also helped poor traders by allowing only tents, not permanent buildings in the market of Medina, and not charging fees and rents there.

Corporate Social Responsibility in Commerce

Social responsibility and corporate social responsibility in commerce was stressed in Islamic sociology. The development of Islamic banks and Islamic economics was a side effect of this sociology: usury was rather severely restrained, no interest rate was allowed, and investors were not permitted to escape the consequences of any failed venture — all financing was equity financing (*Musharaka*). In not letting borrowers bear all the risk/cost of a failure, an extreme disparity of outcomes between "partners" is thus avoided. Ultimately this serves a social harmony purpose. Muslims also could not and cannot (in shariah) finance any dealings in forbidden goods or activities, such as wine, pork, gambling, etc. Thus ethical investing is the only acceptable investing, and moral purchasing is encouraged.

Legal Institutions

Hawala Agency

The *Hawala*, an early informal value transfer system, has its origins in classical Islamic law, and is mentioned in texts of Islamic jurisprudence as early as the 8th century. *Hawala* itself later influenced the development of the agency in common law and in civil laws such as the *aval* in French law and the *avallo* in Italian law. The words *aval* and *avallo* were themselves derived from *Hawala*. The transfer of debt, which was "not permissible under Roman law but became widely practiced in medieval Europe, especially in commercial transactions", was due to the large extent of the "trade conducted by the Italian cities with the Muslim world in the Middle Ages."

The agency was also "an institution unknown to Roman law" as no "individual could conclude a binding contract on behalf of another as his agent." In Roman law, the "contractor himself was considered the party to the contract and it took a second contract between the person who acted on behalf of a principal and the latter in order to transfer the rights and the obligations deriving from the contract to him." On the other hand, Islamic law and the later common law "had no difficulty in accepting agency as one of its institutions in the field of contracts and of obligations in general."

Waqf Trust

The *waqf* in Islamic law, which developed in the medieval

Islamic world from the 7th to 9th centuries, bears a notable resemblance to the English trust law. Every *waqf* was required to have a *waqif* (founder), *mutawillis* (trustee), *qadi* (judge) and beneficiaries. Under both a *waqf* and a trust, "property is reserved, and its usufruct appropriated, for the benefit of specific individuals, or for a general charitable purpose; the corpus becomes inalienable; estates for life in favor of successive beneficiaries can be created" and "without regard to the law of inheritance or the rights of the heirs; and continuity is secured by the successive appointment of trustees or *mutawillis*."

The only significant distinction between the Islamic *waqf* and English trust was "the express or implied reversion of the *waqf* to charitable purposes when its specific object has ceased to exist", though this difference only applied to the *waqf ahli* (Islamic family trust) rather than the *waqf khairi* (devoted to a charitable purpose from its inception). Another difference was the English vesting of "legal estate" over the trust property in the trustee, though the "trustee was still bound to administer that property for the benefit of the beneficiaries." In this sense, the "role of the English trustee therefore does not differ significantly from that of the *mutawalli*."

The trust law developed in England at the time of the Crusades, during the 12th and 13th centuries, was introduced by Crusaders who may have been influenced by the *waqf* institutions they came across in the Middle East. After the Islamic waqf law and madrassah foundations were firmly established by the 10th century, the number of Bimaristan hospitals multiplied throughout throughout Islamic lands. In the 11th century, every Islamic city had at least several hospitals. The waqf trust institutions funded the hospitals for various expenses, including the wages of doctors, ophthalmologists, surgeons, chemists, pharmacists, domestics and all other staff, the purchase of foods and remedies; hospital equipment such as beds, mattresses, bowls and perfumes; and repairs to buildings. The waqf trusts also funded medical schools, and their revenues covered various expenses such as their maintenance and the payment of teachers and students.

Classical Muslim Commerce

During the Islamic Golden Age, guilds were formed though officially unrecognized by the medieval Islamic city. However, trades were recognized and supervised by officials of the city. Each trade developed its own identity, whose members would attend the same mosque, and serve together in the militia. Technology and industry in Islamic civilization were highly developed. Distillation techniques supported a flourishing perfume industry, while chemical ceramic glazes were developed constantly to compete with ceramics imported from China. A scientific approach to metallurgy made it easier to adopt and improve steel technologies from India and China. Primary exports included manufactured luxuries, such as wood carving, metal and glass, textiles, and ceramics.

The systems of contract relied upon by merchants was very effective. Merchants would buy and sell on commission, with money loaned to them by wealthy investors, or a joint investment of several merchants, who were often Muslim, Christian and Jewish. Recently, a collection of documents was found in an Egyptian synagogue shedding a very detailed and human light on the life of medieval Middle Eastern merchants. Business partnerships would be made for many commercial ventures, and bonds of kinship enabled trade networks to form over huge distances. Networks developed during this time enabled a world in which money could be promised by a bank in Baghdad and cashed in Spain, creating the cheque system of today.

Each time items passed through one of the cities along this extraordinary network, the city imposed a tax, resulting in high prices once the items reached their final destinations. These innovations made by Muslims and Jews laid the foundations for the modern economic system. Transport was simple, yet highly effective. Each city had an area outside its gates where pack animals were assembled; found in the cities' markets were large secure warehouses; while accommodations were provided for merchants in cities and along trade routes by a sort of medieval motel. The concepts of welfare and pension were introduced in early Islamic law as forms of *Zakat* (charity), one of the Five Pillars of Islam, since the time of the Abbasid caliph Al-Mansur in the 8th century.

The taxes (including *Zakat* and *Jizya*) collected in the treasury of an Islamic government was used to provide income for the needy, including the poor, elderly, orphans, widows, and the disabled. According to the Islamic jurist Al-Ghazali (Algazel, 1058-1111), the government was also expected to store up food supplies in every region in case a disaster or famine occurs. The Caliphate was thus one of the earliest welfare states, particularly the Abbasid Caliphate.

Age of Discovery

The Islamic Empire significantly contributed to globalization during the Islamic Golden Age, when the knowledge, trade and economies from many previously isolated regions and civilizations began integrating due to contacts with Muslim explorers, sailors, scholars, traders, and travelers. Some have called this period the "Pax Islamica" or "Afro-Asiatic age of discovery", in reference to the Muslim South-west Asian and North African traders and explorers who travelled most of the Old World, and established an early global economy across most of Asia and Africa and much of Europe, with their trade networks extending from the Atlantic Ocean and Mediterranean Sea in the west to the Indian Ocean and China Sea in the east.

This helped establish the Islamic Empire (including the Rashidun, Umayyad, Abbasid and Fatimid caliphates) as the world's leading extensive economic power throughout the 7th-13th centuries. Several contemporary medieval Arabic reports also suggest that Muslim explorers from al-Andalus and the Maghreb may have travelled in expeditions across the Atlantic Ocean between the 9th and 14th centuries. Arabic silver *dirham* coins were being circulated throughout the Afro-Eurasian landmass, as far as subSaharan Africa in the south and northern Europe in the north, often in exchange for goods and slaves. In England, for example, the Anglo-Saxon king Offa of Mercia (r. 757-796) had coins minted with the Shahadah in Arabic. These factors helped establish the Arab Empire (including the Rashidun, Umayyad, Abbasid and Fatimid caliphates) as the world's leading extensive economic power throughout the 7th–13th centuries.

Agricultural Revolution

During the Muslim Agricultural Revolution, the Caliphate understood that real incentives were needed to increase productivity and wealth, thus enhancing tax revenues, hence they introduced a social transformation through the changed ownership of land, where any individual of any gender or any ethnic or religious background had the right to buy, sell, mortgage and inherit land for farming or any other purposes. They also introduced the signing of a contract for every major financial transaction concerning agriculture, industry, commerce, and employment. Copies of the contract were usually kept by both parties involved. The two types of economic systems that prompted agricultural development in the Islamic world were either politically-driven, by the conscious decisions of the central authority to develop underexploited lands; or market-driven, involving the spread of advice, education, and free seeds, and the introduction of high value crops or animals to areas where they were previously unknown.

These led to increased subsistence, a high level of economic security that ensured wealth for all citizens, and a higher quality of life due to the introduction of artichokes, spinach, aubergines, carrots, sugar cane, and various exotic plants; vegetables being available all year round without the need to dry them for winter; citrus and olive plantations becoming a common sight, market gardens and orchards springing up in every Muslim city; intense cropping and the technique of intensive irrigation agriculture with land fertility replacement; a major increase in animal husbandry; higher quality of wool and other clothing materials; and the introduction of selective breeding of animals from different parts of the Old World resulting in improved horse stocks and the best load-carrying camels.

The Islamic Empire experienced a growth in literacy, having the highest literacy rate of the middle Ages, comparable to Athens' literacy in Classical Antiquity but on a larger scale. The average life expectancy in the lands under Islamic rule also experienced an increase, due to the Agricultural Revolution as well as improved medical care. In contrast to the average lifespan in the ancient Greco-Roman world (22-28 years), the average lifespan in the early Islamic Caliphate was more than 35 years. The average lifespans of the Islamic scholarly class in particular was much higher: 84.3 years in 10th-11th century Iraq and Persia, 72.8 years in the 11th century Middle East, 69-75 years in 11th century Islamic Spain, 75 years in 12th century Persia, and 59-72 years in 13th century Persia.

Classical Islamic Economic Thought

To some degree, the early Muslims based their economic analyses on the Qu'ran (such as opposition to *riba*, meaning usury or interest), and from Sunnah, the sayings and doings of Muhammad.

Early Islamic Economic Thinkers

Al-Ghazali (1058–1111) classified economics as one of the sciences connected with religion, along with metaphysics, ethics, and psychology. Authors have noted, however, that this connection has not caused early Muslim economic thought to remain static. Persian philosopher Nasir al-Din al-Tusi (1201-1274) presents an early definition of economics (what he calls hekmat-e-madani, the science of city life) in discourse three of his *Ethics*:

"The study of universal laws governing the public interest (welfare?) in so far as they are directed, through cooperation, toward the optimal (perfection)."

Many scholars trace the history of economic thought through the Muslim world, which was in a Golden Age from the 8th to 13th century and whose philosophy continued the work of the Greek and Hellenistic thinkers and came to influence Aquinas when Europe "rediscovered" Greek philosophy through Arabic translation. A common theme among these scholars was the praise of economic activity and even self-interested accumulation of wealth. Persian leader Shams al-Mo'ali Abol-hasan Ghaboos ibn Wushmgir (Qabus) (died 1012) advises his son in the work *Qabus nama*:

"My son, do not be indifferent to the acquisition of wealth. Assure yourself that everything you acquire shall be the best quality and is likely to give you pleasure."

Persian philosopher Ibn Miskawayh (b. 1030) notes:

"The creditor desires the well-being of the debtor in order to get his money back rather than because of his love for him. The debtor, on the other hand, does not take great interest in the creditor."

This view is in conflict with an idea Joseph Schumpeter called the great gap. The great gap thesis comes out of Schumpeter's 1954 *History of Economic Analysis* which discusses a break in economic thought during the five hundred year period between the decline of the Greco-Roman civilizations and the work of Thomas Aquinas (1225-1274). However in 1964, Joseph Spengler's "Economic Thought of Islam: Ibn Khaldun" appeared in the journal *Comparative Studies in Society and History* and took a large step in bringing early Muslim scholars to the attention of the contemporary West.

The influence of earlier Greek and Hellenistic thought on the Muslim world began largely with Abbasid caliph al-Ma'mun, who sponsored the translation of Greek texts into Arabic in the 9th century by Syrian Christians in Baghdad. But already by that time numerous Muslim scholars had written on economic issues, and early Muslim leaders had shown sophisticated attempts to enforce fiscal and monetary financing, use deficit financing, use taxes to encourage production, the use of credit instruments for banking, including rudimentary savings and checking accounts, and contract law.

Among the earliest Muslim economic thinkers was Abu Yusuf (731-798), a student of the founder of the Hanafi Sunni School of Islamic thought, Abu Hanifah. Abu Yusuf was chief jurist for Abbasid Caliph Harun al-Rashid, for whom he wrote the *Book of Taxation* (*Kitab al-Kharaj*). This book outlined Abu Yusuf's ideas on taxation, public finance, and agricultural production. He discussed proportional tax on produce instead of fixed taxes on property as being superior as an incentive to bring more land into cultivation. He also advocated forgiving tax policies which favor the producer and a centralized tax administration to reduce corruption. Abu Yusuf favored the use of tax revenues for socioeconomic infrastructure, and included discussion of various types of taxes, including sales tax, death taxes, and import tariffs.

Early discussion of the benefits of division of labour are included in the writings of Qabus, al-Ghazali, al-Farabi (873–950), Ibn Sina (Avicenna) (980–1037), Ibn Miskawayh, Nasir al-Din al-Tusi (1201–74), Ibn Khaldun (1332-1406), and Asaad Davani (b. 1444). Among them, the discussions included division of labor within house-holds, societies, factories, and among nations. Farabi notes that each society lacks at least some necessary resources, and thus an optimal society can only be achieved where domestic, regional, and international trade occur, and that such trade can be beneficial to all parties involved. Ghazali was also noted for his subtle understanding of monetary theory and formulation of another version of Gresham's Law.

The power of supply and demand was understood to some extent by various early Muslim scholars as well. Ibn Taymiyyah illustrates:

"If desire for goods increases while its availability decreases, its price rises. On the other hand, if availability of the good increases and the desire for it decreases, the price comes down."

Ghazali suggests an early version of price inelasticity of demand for certain goods, and he and Ibn Miskawayh discuss equilibrium prices. Other important Muslim scholars who wrote about economics include al-Mawardi (1075–1158), Ibn Taimiyah (1263–1328), and al-Maqrizi.

Riba

The common view of *riba* (usury) among classical jurists of Islamic law and economics during the Islamic Golden Age was that it is only *riba* and therefore unlawful to apply interest to money *exnatura sua*—exclusively gold and silver currencies—but that it is not *riba* and is therefore acceptable to apply interest to *fiat* money—currencies made up of other materials such as paper or base metals—to an extent. The definition of *riba* in classical Islamic jurisprudence was "surplus value without counterpart."

When "currencies of base metal were first introduced in the Islamic world, no jurist ever thought that paying a debt in a higher number of units of this *fiat* money was *riba*" as they were concerned with the real value of money rather than the numerical value. For example, it was acceptable for a loan of 1000 gold dinars to be paid back as 1050 dinars of equal aggregate weight. The rationale behind *riba* according to classical Islamic jurists was "to ensure equivlency in real value" and that the "numerical value was immaterial." Thus an interest rate that did not exceed the rate of inflation was not *riba* according to classical Islamic jurists.

Ibn Khaldun

Perhaps the most well known Islamic scholar who wrote about economics was Ibn Khaldun of Tunisia (1332–1406), who is considered a father of modern economics. Ibn Khaldun wrote on economic and political theory in the introduction, or *Muqaddimah* (*Prolegomena*), of his *History of the World* (*Kitab al-Ibar*). In the book, he discussed what he called *asabiyya* (social cohesion), which he sourced as the cause of some civilizations becoming great and others not. Ibn Khaldun felt that many social forces are cyclic, although there can be sudden sharp turns that break the pattern. His idea about the benefits of the division of labor also relate to *asabiyya*, the greater the social cohesion, the more complex the successful division may be, the greater the economic growth. He noted that growth and development positively stimulates both supply and demand, and that the forces of supply and demand are what determines the prices of goods.

He also noted macroeconomic forces of population growth, human capital development, and technological developments effects on development. In fact, Ibn Khaldun thought that population growth was directly a function of wealth. Although he understood that money served as a standard of value, a medium of exchange, and a preserver of value, he did not realize that the value of gold and silver changed based on the forces of supply and demand. He also introduced the concept known as the Khaldun-Laffer Curve (the relationship between tax rates and tax revenue increases as tax rates increase for a while, but then the increases in tax rates begins to cause a decrease in tax revenues as the taxes impose too great a cost to producers in the economy).

Ibn Khaldun used a dialectic approach to describe the sociological implications of tax choices, which is now of course part of economics:

"In the early stages of the state, taxes are light in their incidence, but fetch in large revenue...As time passes and kings succeed each other, they lose their tribal habits in favor of more civilized ones. Their needs and exigencies grow...owing to the luxury in which they have been brought up. Hence they impose fresh taxes on their subjects...and sharply raise the rate of old taxes to increase their yield...But the effects on business of this rise in taxation make themselves felt. For business men are soon discouraged by the comparison of their profits with the burden of their taxes...Consequently production falls off, and with it the yield of taxation."

This analysis anticipates the modern economic concept known as the Laffer Curve. Ibn Khaldun also introduced the labor theory of value. He described labor as the source of value, necessary for all earnings and capital accumulation, obvious in the case of craft. He argued that even if earning "results from something other than a craft, the value of the resulting profit and acquired (capital) must (also) include the value of the labor by which it was obtained. Without labor, it would not have been acquired."

His theory of *asabiyyah* has often been compared to modern Keynesian economics, with Ibn Khaldun's theory clearly containing the concept of the multiplier. A crucial difference, however, is that whereas for John Maynard Keynes it is the middle class's greater propensity to save that is to blame for economic depression, for Ibn Khaldun it is the governmental propensity to save at times when investment opportunities do not take up the slack which leads to aggregate demand.

Another modern economic theory anticipated by Ibn Khaldun is supply-side economics. He "argued that high taxes were often a factor in causing empires to collapse, with the result that lower revenue was collected from high rates." He wrote:

"It should be known that at the beginning of the dynasty, taxation yields large revenue from small assessments. At the end of the dynasty, taxation yields small revenue from large assessments."

Post-Colonial Era

During the modern post-colonial era, as Western ideas, including Western economics, began to influence the Muslim world, some Muslim writers sought to produce an Islamic discipline of economics. Because Islam is "not merely a spiritual formula but a complete system of life in all its walks", it logically followed that Islam also had its own economic system unique from and superior to non-Islamic systems. To date, however, there has been no agreement as to the methodological definition and scope of Islamic Economics.

In the 1960s and 70s Shia Islamic thinkers worked to develop a unique Islamic economic philosophy with "its own answers to contemporary economic problems." Several works were particularly influential,

- *Eslam va Malekiyyat* (Islam and Property) by Mahmud Taleqani (1951),
- *Iqtisaduna* (Our Economics) by Mohammad Baqir al-Sadr (1961) and
- *Eqtesad-e Towhidi* (The Economics of Divine Harmony) by Abolhassan Banisadr (1978)
- *Some Interpretations of Property Rights, Capital and Labor from Islamic Perspective* by Habibullah Peyman (1979).

Al-Sadr in particular has been described as having "almost single-handedly developed the notion of Islamic economics."

In their writings Sadr and the other Shia authors "sought to depict Islam as a religion committed to social justice, the equitable distribution of wealth, and the cause of the deprived classes," with doctrines "acceptable to Islamic jurists", while refuting existing non-Islamic theories of capitalism and Marxism. This version of Islamic economics, which influenced the Iranian Revolution, called for public ownership of land and of large "industrial enterprises," while private economic activity continued "within reasonable limits." These ideas helped shape the large public sector and public subsidy policies of the Iranian Islamic revolution.

In the 1980s and 1990s, as the Iranian revolution failed to reach the per capita income level achieved by the regime it overthrew, and Communist states and socialist parties in the non-Muslim world turned away from socialism, Muslim interest shifted away from government ownership and regulation. In Iran, it is reported that "*eqtesad-e Eslami* (meaning both Islamic economics and economy) ... once a revolutionary shibboleth, is indubitably absent in all official documents and the media. It disapperared from Iranian political discourse about 15 years ago [1990]."

But in other parts of the Muslim world the term lived on, shifting form to the less ambitious goal of interest-free banking. Some Muslim bankers and religious leaders suggested ways to integrate Islamic law on usage of money with modern concepts of ethical investing. In banking this was done through the use of sales transactions (focusing on the fixed rate return modes) to achieve similar results to interest. This has been criticised by some western writers as a means of covering conventional banking with an Islamic facade.

Traditional Approach

While most Muslims believe Islamic law is perfect by virtue of its being revealed by God, Islamic law on economic issues was/is not "economics" in the sense of a systematic study of production, distribution, and consumption of goods and services.

Contemporary Economics

In modern times, economic policies of the 1979 Islamic Revolution in predominately Shia Iran were heavily statist with a very large public sector, and official rhetoric celebrating revolution and the rights of the dispossessed, although this tendency has faded over time. In Sudan, the policies of the National Islamic Front party dominated regime in the 1990s have been the reverse, employing economic liberalism and accepting "market forces in the formulation of state policies." In Algeria, Jordan, Egypt, and Pakistan, Islamist parties have supported populist policies, showing a "marked reluctance to adopt austerity policies and decreased subsidies."

In 2008, at least $500 billion in assets around the world were managed in accordance with Sharia, or Islamic law, and the sector was growing at more than 10% per year. Islamic finance seeks to promote social justice by banning exploitative practices. In reality, this boils down to a set of prohibitions—on paying interest, on gambling with derivatives and options, and on investing in firms that make pornography or pork. Another form of modern finance that originated from the Muslim world is microcredit and microfinance. It began in Bangladesh with Grameen Bank, founded by Muhammad Yunus, recipient of the 2006 Nobel Peace Prize.

8

Qur'an, Science and Ethics

The relation between Qur'an and science is strongly affirmed in Islamic thought. Almost all sources, classical and modern, agree that the Qur'an condones, even encourages, the acquisition of science and scientific knowledge. The contemporary Islamic discourse on the Qur'an and science abounds with assertions of the relationship between the two. This presumed relationship is construed in a variety of ways, the most common of which are the efforts to prove the divine nature of the Qur'an through modern science. The belief that Qur'an had prophesied scientific theories and discoveries - known as Ijaz al-Qur'an - has become a strong and widespread belief in the contemporary Islamic world. Alleged prophecies are often provided to show a connection between the Qur'an and miracles, and to support the belief of divine origin for the Qur'an.

Science-Related Prophecies

According to Qur'an; natural phenomena comprises a large portion of the divine signs; nature itself praises God, and God proclaims that he will show humankind his signs on the furthest horizons we well as deep within themselves:

"A time is fixed for every prophecy; you will come to know in time".

Islamic scholar Zaghloul El-Naggar thinks that this verse refers to the scientific signs in the Qur'an that would be discovered by the world in modern time, centuries after the revelation. The scientific signs claimed to be in the Qur'an exist in different subjects, including creation, astronomy, the animal and vegetables kingdom, and human reproduction. Some of those claimed prophecies are:

- The Qur'an contains a number of verses pertaining to some biological specificities regarding human reproduction and development. According to Keith L. Moore (professor emeritus of anatomy at the University of Toronto, and son of a Protestant clergyman) the scientific meaning of certain surahs in the Qur'an has become clear only recently. Moore has concluded that God revealed the Qur'an to Muhammad, and has disseminated this view in many lectures, panel discussions and articles.
- The Qur'an referenced the heavens and earth as originally being an integrated mass before God split them *"Have not those who disbelieve known that the heavens and the earth were of one piece, then We parted them"*, which has been interpreted by some as being "nothing short of a condensed version of the Big bang theory".
- The Qur'an talked about cosmic orbital motion: *"It is not for the sun to overtake the moon, nor doth the night outstrip the day. They float each in an orbit"* at a period of time when the common belief was that earth was flat and stationary. The notion of a spherical earth was by no means new at the time the Qur'an was written, however. Around 330 BC, Aristotle provided observational evidence for the spherical Earth. Furthermore, around 10 BC, the Greek geographer Strabo cited various phenomena observed at sea as suggesting that the Earth was spherical.

The most famous proponent of this argument is perhaps Maurice Bucaille, a French physician and author of the popular book *The Bible, The Quran and Science.* Maurice Bucaille asserts in his book that "he could not find a single error in the Qur'an", and that the Qur'an does "not contain a single statement which is assailable from a modern scientific point of view", which led him to believe that no human author in the seventh century could have written "facts" which "today are shown to be keeping with modern scientific knowledge". Bucaille's opinion did not gain scientific consensus on the matter. The search for Qur'anic references to and prophecies of modern scientific discoveries has become a "popular trend" in some Muslim societies; as a manifestation of the popularity of the scientific miracles belief, the Muslim World League at Mecca formed a committee named Committee on the Scientific Miracles of the Qur'anand the Sunna to investigate the relation between Qur'an and science, headed by Zaghloul El-Naggar.

According to some recent studies of the relationship between science education and religion, one of the ways in which science education in strongly Islamic societies is impacted by religiosity is when "acceptable" scientific discoveries can be found to have been anticipated or "identified" by the Qur'an, with consequent implications for what is taught and not taught.

Scientific Exegesis of the Qur'an

Scientific exegesis of the Qur'an is the assumption that all sorts of findings of the modern natural sciences have been anticipated in the Qur'an and that many unambiguous references to them can be discovered in its verses. Many Islamic authors, classical and modern, believe that all the sciences were contained in the Qur'an. The practise of *tafsir 'ilmi*, or scientific exegesis, which was "almost forgotten, has been revived in modern times; the classical attempt to incorporate all streams of human knowledge into the Qur'an has been updated with a special focus on the natural sciences.

This method of scientific interpretation did not find

general approval among Muslim authors. Many classical Muslim commentators and scientists, notably al-Biruni, assigned to the Qur'an a separate and autonomous realm of its own and held that the Qur'an "does not interfere in the business of science nor does it infringes on the realm of science." These medieval scholars argued for the possibility of multiple scientific explanations of the natural phenomena, and refused to subordinate the Qur'an to an everchanging science.

Author Rotraud Wielandt summarizes the arguments of the modern Muslim commentators such as Mahmud Shaltut and Sayyid Qutb who reject a scientific method of interpretation of the Qur'an as follows:

1. It is lexicographically untenable, since it falsely attributes modern meanings to the quranic vocabulary.
2. It neglects the contexts of words or phrases within the quranic text, and also the occasions of revelation where these are transmitted.
3. It ignores the fact that, for the Quran to be comprehensible for its first audience, the words of the Qur'anhad to conform to the language and the intellectual horizon of the ancient Arabs at the Prophet's time — an argument already used by the Andalusian Mâlikite scholar al-Shâmibî (d. 790/1388) against the scientific exegesis of his time.
4. It does not take notice of the fact that scientific knowledge and scientific theories are always incomplete and provisory by their very nature; therefore, the derivation of scientific knowledge and scientific theories in Qur'-ânic verses is actually tantamount to limiting the validity of these verses to the time for which the results of the science in question are accepted.
5. Most importantly, it fails to comprehend that the Qur'an is not a scientific book, but a religious one designed to guide human beings by imparting to them a creed and a set of moral values.

In defense of their efforts the exegetes use two verses in the Qur'an: one that states "*and We have sent down to thee the Book explaining all things*" and another which says "*We have neglected nothing in the Book*". The classical objection to these verses being used as a basis for intensive *tafsir 'ilmi* is that the "Book" mentioned in these verses is not the Qur'an itself, but a "well-preserved tablet" in heaven, of which the earthly Qur'an is a reflection.

Creationism

The Qur'an is insistent that Allah is the sole creator of all things; the universe and humans. Qur'an does not assert that God created the universe at some definable point in the past. As opposed to deism or to certain readings of Newtonian physics, God continues to sustain the creation during every moment of its existence. And in fact the Qur'an is deeply impressed with the ongoing order of nature and summons all humankind to share in its admiration and to learn from it:

Your Guardian-Lord is Allah, Who created the heavens and the earth in six days, and is firmly established on the throne (of authority): He draweth the night as a veil o'er the day, each seeking the other in rapid succession: He created the sun, the moon, and the stars, (all) governed by laws under His command. Is it not His to create and to govern? Blessed be Allah, the Cherisher and Sustainer of the worlds! God's purpose in the creation of the universe was focused on humanity. This is manifest, for example, in the fact that the universe is admirably designed to provide for human needs and wants. The Qur'an offers its own version of cosmic anthropic principle.

Universal Creation

Qur'an contains many verses describing the universe creation; God created heavens and earth in six days, the heavens and earth were completed in two days, and in four days God furnished the creation of the earth with mountains, rivers and fruit-gardens. Heavens and earth formed from an integrated disk-shaped mass which had to be split, the seven heavens were created from smoke, forming layers, one above the other. God and angels inhabit the seventh heaven. The lowest heaven is adorned with lights, the sun and the moon (which follow a regular path), the stars and the constellations of the zodiac.

Human Creation

According to Qur'an, Adam is the first human being and the father of humankind. First Adam was created from clay, God himself formed the material of which Adam is made and breathed his spirit into him, and then Eve was created from Adam, the Qur'an does not report when she was created. Subsequently all humankind was created from clay. Today, some modern Muslim commentators have decided that, since the Qur'an makes no mention of the evolution of one species to another kind of species, the Darwinian theory of evolution is contrary to the teachings of the Qur'an. An apt verse that summarizes the process of human creation is:

"From the (earth) did We create you, and into it shall We return you, and from it shall We bring you out once again"

Embryology

In Qur'an reference is made to fetal development and growth, explanations of these verses express the view that "sperm" and "safe lodging" refer to sperm within the female uterus. Prior to fertilization, sperm bind to the zona pellucida or outer covering of the ovum. Following such lines of interpretation, *clot* could be a reference to this, i.e. to sperm clinging to the ovum. However, *clot* is also interpreted by some exegetes as *blood clot* and taken to refer to "something that clings" to the uterus. For those modern commentators who then extrapolate this interpretation scientifically, the *blood clot* could be taken to represent the fertilized ovum or early embryo implanting itself in the endometrium or uterine lining. Some modern interpreters combine these verses with, seeing in the reference to the "three veils of darkness" a reflection of the three anatomical layers that protect the fetus – the abdominal wall, the uterus wall and amniotic sac.

It is widely recognized that the Qur'an and hadith contain a number of verses pertaining to human reproduction and development. In his book *A History of Embryology,* Professor Joseph Needham describes some of the embryological passages in the Qur'an, verses. For the past 100 years this verse has been translated to describe the second stage of the embryo being a "clot of blood", but it has been argued that the word "alaqa", prior to one hundred years ago, and during the prophet Muhammad's lifetime, the definition of this word "alaqa" and the context in which it was used was "that which clings". Dr. Keith L. Moore, who is most known for his textbooks on the subjects of anatomy and human embryology, had to say of the Qur'an and Muhammad, "It is clear to me that these statements (of the Qur'an about human development) must have come to Muhammad from God, because almost all of this knowledge was not discovered until many centuries later.

This proves to me that Muhammad must have been a messenger of God", then he was asked does this mean you believe that the Qur'an is the word of God? He replied "I found no difficulty in accepting this as a seventh century echo of Aristotle and Ayurveda." According to Dr. Moore, professor emeritus of Anatomy at the University of Toronto, the scientific meaning of certain surahs in the Quran has become clear only recently. An example cited by him is verse. However when asked in a 2002 if he would be willing to be interviewed about Qur'anic scientific miracles, Moore declined saying, "it's been 10 or 11 years since I was involved in the Quran."

The Story of Civilization

The Story of Civilization by Will and Ariel Durant is an eleven-volume set of books. It was written over a lifetime, and it totals two million words across nearly 10,000 pages. The series is incomplete: in the first book of the series (*Our Oriental Heritage,* which covers the history of the East through 1933), Mr. Durant stated that he wanted to include the history of the West through the early 20th century. However, the series ends with *The Age of Napoleon* since the Durants died before any additional volumes could be completed. The first six volumes of *The Story of Civilization* are credited to Will Durant, with Ariel receiving recognition in the acknowledgements.

The Story of Civilization has been criticized by some for simplifications, rash judgments colored by personal convictions, and story-telling, and described as a careless dabbling in historical scholarship. Professor J. H. Plumb's opinion on the series was that "historical truth... can rarely be achieved outside the professional world [of historians]." The counter to such criticism is that Durant's purpose in writing the series was not to create a definitive scholarly production but to make a large amount of information accessible and comprehensible to the educated public in the form of a comprehensive "composite history." Given the massive undertaking in creating these 11 volumes over 50 years, errors and incompleteness have occurred; yet for an attempt as large in breadth of time and scope as this, there are no similar works to compare.

As Durant says in the preface to his first work, *Our Oriental Heritage*:

I wish to tell as much as I can, in as little space as I can, of the contributions that genius and labor have made to the cultural heritage of mankind - to chronicle and contemplate, in their causes, character and effects, the advances of invention, the varieties of economic organization, the experiments in government, the aspirations of religion, the mutations of morals and manners, the masterpieces of literature, the development of science, the wisdom of philosophy, and the achievements of art. I do not need to be told how absurd this enterprise is, nor how immodest is its very conception ... Nevertheless I have dreamed that despite the many errors inevitable in this undertaking, it may be of some use to those upon whom the passion for philosophy has laid the compulsion to try to see things whole, to pursue perspective, unity and time, as well as to seek them through science in space. ... Like philosophy, such a venture [as the creation of these 11 volumes] has no rational excuse, and is at best but a brave stupidity; but let us hopes that, like philosophy, it will always lure some rash spirits into its fatal depths.

The Impact of Translations of Muslim Sciences on the West

Although translations of Islamic science were undertaken in Barcelona, Tarazon, Segovia, Leon, Pamplona, Toulouse, Beziers, Narbonne and Marseille, the chief centre of translation remained: Toledo. Re-conquered by the Christians in 1085, after being almost four centuries (702-1085) in Muslim hands, Toledo, the ancient Visigoth capital, soon became the ideal place from where Muslim science was to be transferred north. It was in Toledo that possibly the greatest translation effort in the history of science took place. Throughout the early stages of the 12th century Toledo was the focal point, which attracted every single minded scholar and translator of the Christian West. D'Alverny explains how:

"Following the steps of the Christian armies, students from all countries rushed to Spain to lay hands on the treasures of science piling in the 'armaria' of the Infidels," D'Alverny

The Translators

Scholars from all Christian lands rushed to that place to translate Muslim science, and thus start the scientific awakening of Europe. Many of course were Spaniards: John of Seville, Hugh of Santalla, and those working under the patronage of King Alfonso; another translator was Herman from Dalmatia; two came from Flanders, Rudolph of Bruges and Henry Bate; many from southern France: Armengaud son of Blaise, Jacob Anatoli, Moses ibn Tibbon, Jacob ben Mahir, and from Italy: Plato of Tivoli, Gerard of Cremona, Aristippus of Catania, Salio of Padua, John of Brescia.

From the British Isles will arrive Robert of Chester, Daniel of Morley, M. Scot, and possibly Adelard (of Bath), and others, including the intermediaries who helped transfer Islamic science from Arabic into Latin or local languages.

Amongst such translators the most prolific of all was the Italian Gerard of Cremona, who translated about 87 works amongst which included the Toledan tables of al-Zarqali Canones Arzachelis and Jabir ibn Aflah's Islah al-Majisti (correction of the Almagest of Ptolemy.) His other translations include The Banu Musa's Liber trium fratrum, Al-Khwarizmi's: De jebra et elmucabala, Abu Kamil: Liber qui secundum Arabes vocatur algebra et almucabala,-Abu'l Qasim Al-Zahrawi: Liber Azaragui de cirurgia (treatise on surgery), Al-Farabi: De scientiis,-Al-Kindi'sworks on physics and mechanics: De aspectibus; followed by De umbris et de diversitate aspecturm, Ibn al-Haytham's work on physics: De crepusculis et nubium ascensionibus, Al-Kindi's : De gradibus medicinarum (on medicine).

Amongst the translations made by the Jew turned Christian, John of Seville, are Al-Battani's Treatise on astronomy and other works; Thabit ibn Qura: De imaginibus astronomicis; Maslama ibn Ahmed al Majriti: De astrolabio; Al-Farabi: Ihsa al-Ulum; Abu Ma'shar: Al-Madkhal ila 'ilm ahkam al-nujum; Al-Ghazali: Maqasid Al-Falasifa; Al-Farghani: Kitab fi harakat al-Samawiya wa jawami' ilm al-nujum...

It is not necessary to list all the translations since they can be found in greater detail, together with their successive editions, and a vast bibliography relating to them in G. Sarton's Introduction.

Medical Sciences

Every science was affected by the translation movement. The list and variety of seminal Muslim medical works that were translated at Toledo and used for inspiration is endless. Campbell, and by far the best work on the subject by Leclerc remain very good sources of reference for any curious mind on this matter.

Just to mention briefly here, that it was a Tunisian born named Constantine, who introduced modern medicine into Europe through the southern Italian town of Salerno making it the first medical centre of Europe from which medical learning radiated north to Padua, Montpellier etc. Constantine had, indeed, carried with him vast amount of knowledge from Qayrawan northwards to Europe, following which arose 'a generation of prominent medical teachers.' Constantine's best known translation is that of Ali Abbas al-Majusti's Kitab al-Malaki, known under the Pantegni.

One does not need to dwell here on the many translations and editions up to the 18th century of the works of Ibn Sina and Al-Razi, and other medical works by Ibn Zuhr, Ibn Rushd, etc. However it must be stressed that the Muslims pioneered and had an early impact in the sphere of mental health. It was in fact the direct contribution of Al-Razi, who set up an exclusive ward for the mentally ill in Baghdad. And it was the Muslims, who, as Syed explains, 'brought a refreshing spirit of dispassionate clarity into psychiatry.' And as they were free from 'the demonological theories' which were sweeping over the Christian world, they could make clear cut clinical observations about such diseases.

Surgery

Modern surgery owes about everything to Al-Zahrawi. Al-Zahrawi's chapter on surgery from Kitab al-Tasrif is 'particularly outstanding' due to the frequent illustration of instruments and 'its pervading sense of personal experience.' Most of the instruments were devised and made by al-Zahrawi himself and their introduction and use was a major breakthrough at the time, and had a lasting influence. His surgical techniques were also revolutionary, and Smith gives very good illustrations of them. For calculus in the urethra, for instance, Al-Zahrawi introduced the technique of using a fine drill inserted through the urinary passage. In the case of tonsillectomies, whilst he held the tongue by a tongue depressor, he removed the swollen tonsil holding it by a hook, and then removed it with a scissor like instrument with transverse blades, which cut the gland, whilst holding it for removal from the throat. Al-Zahrawi also described how to connect sound teeth to those that were loose by gold or silver wire.

In gynaecology, his work, alongside that of other pioneering Muslim surgeons, included instructions on training midwives to perform unusual deliveries, ways of extracting dead foetuses, the removal of the afterbirth, the design and introduction of vaginal dilators, the description of forceps, and the use of caesarean methods. The surgical part of Al-tasrif was translated into Latin by Gerard of Cremona, and various editions were published at Venice in 1497, at Basel in 1541 and Oxford in 1778, and for centuries, it remained the manual of surgery in all early medical universities such as Salerno and Montpellier, whilst the illustrations of his instruments laid the foundations for surgery in Europe. Muslim surgeons also, as Smith observes, displayed a sensible and humane reluctance to undertake the riskiest and most painful operations, and were also aware of the discomfort they inflicted on patients. This could be seen as a decisive breakthrough in the relationship between the surgeon and the patient.

Pharmacy

The Muslim influence on pharmacy is similarly considerable. Levey gives a very good account of such influence. According to him, many influential Latin works of the 'Renaissance' and thereafter are just compilations and slightly altered works of previous Muslim treatises. Belonging to such recessions is Johannes of St Awand's Expositio Supra Nicolai Antidotarium written in 1250 and published in Venice in 1495, 1599 and 1602. Conciliator and De Venenorum remediis by Albano (professor in Padua from 1306 to 1316), while extensive extracts from Ibn Rushd and Al Maradini were repeatedly printed over the years.

An important work on pharmacy in the modern sense, Levey maintains, is greatly influenced by the works of Ibn Sinna, Ibn Sarabiyun (known in Latin as Serapion), Al-Zahrawi and Ibn Masawaih (al-Maradini) in form and content was written by Saladin of Ascolo, a well known physician of the 15th century, and called Compendium aromatariorum. Divided into seven parts, this work follows exactly Muslim categorisation of subjects: examination of the pharmacist, the qualities desired for the pharmacist, substitute drugs, care of simple and compound drugs, etc. Another work that also greatly influenced European pharmacopoeias using material from Muslim treatises on simple 'drug' substitutes, preservation of drugs, lists of little known drugs, etc, was that by Ludovico dal Pozzo Toscanelli, a physician of Florence who was authorised to do so by the Florentine College of Physicians, and from which compendium various editions were made.

Pharmacopoeias in German, French, English and Spanish also showed Muslim influence, whilst a later edition of the London Dispensatory, in the late 17th century, in its list of botanicals, minerals, simple / compound drugs for external and internal uses, oils, pills, cataplasms, etc, reflects the extent of Muslim influence. Most Muslim material was in fact used until late in the nineteenth century, and Levey concludes that there is much to be learned yet from their early drug treatises.

Chemistry

In chemistry, the works of Jabir and Al-Razi set the foundations to the modern science. Jabir, known as Geber in Latin, described the preparation of many chemical substances: sulphide of mercury, oxides, arsenics etc. He made applications that led to major industrial transformations, including the refining of metals, dyeing of clothes (crucial for the textile industry some centuries later), the use of manganese in glass making (to become another fundamental industry in Europe,) use of pyrites, and gave an exact description of processes such as calcination, crystallisation, solution, sublimation and reduction.

Al-Razi's work is wary of using the mystical and even occult elements which affect so much of Jabir's and his predecessors' works. His Secret of Secrets, in Latin Liber secretorum bubacaris, describes the chemical processes and experiments conducted by him, and which can be identified as equivalent to modern processes ranging from distillation to calcination, crystallization etc. Al-Razi also divided substances into animal, vegetable, and mineral; the mineral substances include mercury, gold, silver, pyrites, glass etc: vegetable substances were mainly used by physicians; whilst animal substances divided into hair, blood, milk, eggs, bile etc. Al-Razi was also a practical chemist giving laboratory work pre-eminence over theoretical observations. Hill points out that Al-Razi's 'Book of Secrets' `foreshadows a laboratory manual' and deals with substances, equipment and processes. Al-Razi's laboratory includes many items still in use today: crucible; decensory; cucurbit or retort for distillation (qar) and the head of a still with a delivery tube (ambiq, Latin alembic); various types of furnace or stove etc.

Some of Al-Razi's revolutionary experiments, derived from his 'Secret of Secrets', include ways of smelting metals, the sublimation of mercury, the preparation of caustic soda, the use of the mercury ammonium chloride solution as a dissolving reagent, and the preparation of glycerine from olive oil. Al-Razi's lead in careful experimentation and observations demonstrated, as Holmyard put it:

> *"That a by-product of alchemy was a steadily increasing body of reliable chemical knowledge, a trend which Al-Razi did most to establish and for which he deserves the gratitude of succeeding generations"* - Holmyard

Still on chemistry, Hill also notes that works by many Muslim chemists included recipes for products that had industrial or military uses. He points out that the discovery of inorganic acids was of crucial importance for the history of chemistry. These acids were produced during chemical experiments but became valuable agents for industrial applications.

Optics

In optics, the works of the Muslims set up the foundations for all that was to follow. Excellent extracts can be found in Lindberg's study of the Islamic impact on Latin optics in Rashed's Encyclopaedia. The Islamic role is highlighted by their demolition of the previous Greek erroneous assumptions of optical theory. Hunain ibn Ishaq, first, followed by al-Kindi, criticised the Greek theory a critique outlined by Lindberg. It was, however, Ibn al-Haytham who revolutionised the whole science, determining by experimentation many optical phenomena. Ibn al-Haytham's achievements, as summarised by Lindberg, show that he did not just explain the principal facts of visual perception but also managed to establish the intromission theory of vision beyond all doubt and dispute for good.

He 'fundamentally' altered the aims and scope of the optical theory, and also managed to integrate into his theory anatomical and physiological claims of the medical theory. Thus, as Lindberg concludes, he was able 'to draw together the mathematical, physical and medical traditions into a single comprehensive theory.... He created a new optical tradition and established the aims and criteria of optics which would prevail, though not without rivals, until Kepler and beyond.' Further achievements of Ibn al-Haytham include developing precision instrumentalisation, expounding for the first time the use of the camera obscura, and writing treatises on the halo and rainbow. Hill states, 'unquestionably, the most important work on physics to reach the West in medieval times was Kitab al-Manazir.' The influence of this work, with its intromission theory of vision and its completely new methodology had a profound impression on others, particularly Roger Bacon and Witelo.

7th Century

- 610 - 632 [empiricism, theology] The Qur'an, which was revealed during this time, emphasized the use of empirical observation and reason. It has been claimed that the Qur'an also contains knowledge that was far ahead of its time.
- 610 - 632 [astrology] several hadiths attributed to Muhammad show that he was generally opposed to astrology as well as superstition in general. An example of this is when an eclipse occurred during his son Ibrahim ibn Muhammad's death, and rumours began spreading about this being God's personal condolence. Muhammad is said to have replied: "*An eclipse is a phenomenon of nature. It is foolish to attribute such things to the death or birth of a human being.*"
- 610 - 632 [medicine] Muhammad is reported to have made the following statements on early Islamic medicine: "*There is no disease that Allah has created, except that He also has created its treatment*"; "*Make use*

of medical treatment, for Allah has not made a disease without appointing a remedy for it, with the exception of one disease, namely old age"; "Allah has sent down both the disease and the cure, and He has appointed a cure for every disease, so treat yourselves medically"; "The one who sent down the disease sent down the remedy." The belief that there is a cure for every disease encouraged Muslims at the time to seek out a remedy for every disease known to them.

- 610 - 632 [medicine, pathology] Early ideas on contagion can be traced back to several hadiths attributed to Muhammad, who is said to have understood the contagious nature of leprosy, mange, and sexually transmitted disease. These early ideas on contagion arose from the generally sympathetic attitude of Muslim physicians towards lepers (who were often seen in a negative light in other ancient and medieval societies) which can be traced back through hadiths attributed to Muhammad and to the following advice given in the Qur'an: *"There is no fault in the blind, and there is no fault in the lame, and there is no fault in the sick."*
- 622 [calendar] Islamic calendar developed by Muhammad.
- 634 - 644 [technology] Windmill invented in Afghanistan during the time of the Rashidun caliph, Umar.
- 650 - 704 [alchemy] Calid (Khalid ibn Yazid), an Umayyad prince, was the first Muslim alchemist, and he translated the literature on Egyptian alchemy into the Arabic language.

8th Century

- 8th century - [ceramics, pottery] Lustreware is invented in Iraq by Islamic potters.
- 700s - [ceramics, pottery] From the eighth to eighteenth centuries, the use of glazed ceramics was prevalent in Islamic art, usually assuming the form of elaborate pottery. Tin-opacified glazing was one of the earliest

new technologies developed by the Islamic potters. The first Islamic opaque glazes can be found as blue-painted ware in Basra, dating to around the 8th century.

- 700s - [ceramics, glass, industry, pottery] The first industrial factory complex for Islamic pottery and glass production is built in Ar-Raqqah, Syria. Extensive experimentation is carried out at the complex, which is two kilometres in length, and a variety of innovative high-purity glass is developed there. Two other similar complexes are also built, and nearly three hundred new chemical recipes for glass are produced at all three sites.
- 702 - 765 - [chemistry] Ja'far al-Sadiq, refuted Aristotle's theory of the four classical elements and theorized that each one is *made up of different chemical elements: "I wonder how a man like Aristotle could say that in the world there are only four elements - Earth, Water, Fire, and Air. The Earth is not an element. It contains many elements. Each metal, which is in the earth, is an element."* Al-Sadiq also developed a *particle theory, which he described as follows: "The universe was born out of a tiny particle, which had two opposite poles. That particle produced an atom. In this way matter came into being. Then the matter diversified. This diversification was caused by the density or rarity of the atoms."* Al-Sadiq also wrote a theory on the opacity and transparency of materials. He stated that materials which are solid and absorbent are opaque, and materials which are solid and repellent are more or le
- 715 - 815 - [chemistry] Geber (Jabir ibn Hayyan), a Muslim chemist, is "considered by many to be the father of chemistry", for introducing the experimental scientific method for chemistry, as well as laboratory apparatus such as the alembic, still and retort, and chemical processes such as pure distillation, liquefaction, crystallisation, purification, oxidisation, evaporation and filtration. He also invented more than twenty types of

laboratory apparatus. His collection of works (known as the *Jabirian corpus*) include *The elaboration of the Grand Elixir, The chest of wisdom* in which he introduces nitric acid, *Kitab al-Istitmam* (later translated to Latin as *Summa Perfectionis*), and many others.

- 715 - 815 - [alchemy] Geber, also a Muslim alchemist, introduces theories on the transmutation of metals, the philosopher's stone, and *Takwin,* the artificial creation of life in the laboratory. He also further developed the five classical elements into seven elements by adding two metals: sulfur ('the stone which burns' that characterized the principle of combustibility) and mercury (which contained the idealized principle of metallic properties) as 'elements'.
- 715 - 815 - [chemical substances] In contrast to the ancients ("the only acid known to the ancients was vinegar"), Jabir was the first to produce a number of other acids: mineral acids such as nitric acid, sulfuric acid and hydrochloric acid, uric acid, acetic acid, citric acid, tartaric acid andaqua regia. Several chemical elements were also first discovered by Geber: arsenic, antimony and bismuth. Geber was also the first to classify sulfur and mercury as 'elements'. He also discovered a number of other chemical substances.
- 715 - 815 - [crystallography] Crystallization is invented by Geber.
- 715 - 815 - [glass] Geber wrote on adding colour to glass by adding small quantities of metallic oxides to the glass, such as manganese dioxide (magnesia).
- 715 - 815 - [chemical technology, glass] In the *Book of the Hidden Pearl,* Geber scientifically described 46 original recipes for producing coloured glass, in addition to 12 recipes inserted by al-Marrakishi in a later edition of the book; the first recipes for the manufacture of artificial pearls and for the purification of pearls that were discoloured from the sea or from grease; the first

recipes for the dying and artificial colouring of gemstones and pearls; the first recipes for the manufacture of glue from cheese; and invented plated mail for use in armours (*jawasin*), and first described the production of high quality coloured glass cut into artificial gem-stones.

- 715 - 815 - [chemistry] Destructive distillation is developed by Arabic chemists. [dubious – discuss]
- 740 - 828 - [animal husbandry, botany, zoology] Al-Asma'i was the earliest Arab biologist, botanist and zoologist; his works include the *Book of Distinction*, *Book of the Wild Animals*, *Book of the Horse*, and *Book of the Sheep*.
- 751 - [technology] Papermaking is introduced to the Islamic world from Chinese prisoners after the Battle of Talas.
- 754 - [medicine, pharmacy] The first pharmacy and drugstores are opened in Baghdad. The first apothecary shops are also opened in the Islamic world.
- 763 - 809 - [library] The House of Wisdom is founded by the Abbasid caliph Harun al-Rashid.
- 763 - 809 - [medicine] "The first free public hospital was opened in Baghdad during the Caliphate of Haroon-ar-Rashid." These "Bimaristans" were hospitals in the modern sense, an establishment where the ill were welcomed and cared for by qualified staff. In this way, Muslim physicians were the first to make a distinction between a hospital and other different forms of healing temples, sleep temples, hospices, assylums, lazarets and leper-houses, all of which in ancient times were more concerned with isolating the sick and the mad from society "rather than to offer them any way to a true cure." The medieval Bimaristan hospitals are thus considered "the first hospitals" in the modern sense of the word.
- 763 - 800 - [medicine, psychiatry, psychology] The first psychiatric hospitals and insane asylums are built by the Muslim Arabs in Baghdad and then Fes.

- 764 - 800 - [petroleum, civil engineering] The streets of the newly constructed Baghdad are paved with tar, derived from petroleum, coming from natural oil fields in the region, through the process of destructive distillation.
- 770 - [astronomy, mathematics] An Indian astronomer visits the court of Caliph Al-Mansur, and brings with him the *Surya Siddhanta* and the works of Aryabhata and Brahmagupta.
- 777 - [astronomy, mathematics] Muhammad al-Fazari and Yaqûb ibn Târiq translate the *Surya Siddhanta* and *Brahmasphutasiddhanta*, and compile them as the *Zij al-Sindhind*, the first Zij treatise.
- 794 - [industry, technology] The first paper mills are created in Baghdad, marking the beginning of the paper industry.
- c. 796 - [astronomical instruments] The first person credited for building the brass astrolabe in the Islamic world is reportedly Muhammad al-Fazari.
- Late 700s - early 800s - [musical science] Mansour Zalzal of Kufa. Musician (luth) and composer of the Abbasid era. Contributed musical scales that were later named after him (the Mansouri scale) and introduced positions (intervals) within scales such as the *wasatizalzal* that was equidistant from the *alwasati alqadima* and *wasati al-fors*. Made improvements on the design of the luth instrument and designed the Luth. Teacher of Is-haq al-Mawsili.
- 700 - 900 - [legal science] Charitable trust first developed in Islamic law as the *Waqf*.

9th Century

- 721 - 900 - [chemistry] Chemical processes first described by Muslim chemists include: assation (or roasting), cocotion (or digestion), ceration, lavage, solution, mixture, and fixation. Arab chemists were the first to produce purified water, through water puri-fication and distillation, used for water supply systems and for long journeys across deserts where the supplies were uncertain. Petrol is also first produced by Muslim chemists.

- 721 - 925 - [chemical technology] In his *Secretum secretorum* (Latinized title), Muhammad ibn Zakarîya Râzi (Rhazes) described the following tools that were invented by him and his Muslim predecessors (Calid, Geber and Al-Kindi) for melting substances (*li-tadhwib*): hearth (*kur*), bellows (*minfakh aw ziqq*), crucible (*bawtaqa*), the *but bar but* (in Arabic) or *botus barbatus* (in Latin), tongs (*masik aq kalbatan*), scissors (*miqta*), hammer (*mukassir*), file (*mibrad*).
- 721 - 925 - [chemical technology] Muhammad ibn Zakarîya Râzi described the following tools that were invented by him and his Muslim predecessors for the preparation of drugs (*li-tadbir al-aqaqir*): cucurbit and still with evacuation tube (*qar aq anbiq dhu-khatm*), receiving matras (*qabila*), blind still (without evacuation tube) (*al-anbiq al-ama*), aludel (*al-uthal*), goblets (*qadah*), flasks (*qarura* or *quwarir*), rosewater flasks (*ma wariyya*), cauldron (*marjal aw tanjir*), earthenware pots varnished on the inside with their lids (*qudur aq tanjir*), water bath or sand bath (*qadr*), oven (*al-tannur* in Arabic, *athanor* in Latin), small cylindirical oven for heating aludel (*mustawqid*), funnels, sieves, filters, etc.
- 721 - 925 - [chemical substances] Muhammad ibn Zakarîya Râzi wrote that he and his Muslim predecessors (Calid, Geber and al-Kindi) invented the following derivative and artificial chemical substances: lead(II) oxide (PbO), red lead (Pb3O4), tin(II) oxide (*Isfidaj*), copper acetate (*Zaniar*), copper(II) oxide (CuO), lead sulfide, zinc oxide, bismuth oxide, antimony oxide, iron rust, iron acetate, *Daws* (a contituent of steel), cinnabar (HgS), arsenic trioxide (As2O3), alkali (*al-Qili*), sodium hydroxide (caustic

soda), and *Qalimiya* (anything that separates from metals during their purification).

- 721 - 925 - [chemical substances] Muhammad ibn Zakarîya Râzi classified the natural chemical substances that were discovered by him and his Muslim predecessors (mainly Calid, Geber, al-Kindi and al-Tamimi) as follows: Four spirits (mercury, sal ammoniac, arsenic, sulfur), eight fusible metals (gold, silver, copper, iron, tin, lead, mercury), rhirteen stones (*mar-qashisha, maghnisiya, daws* (a constituent of iron and steel), *tutiya*, lapis lazuli, malachite green, turquoise, hematite, arsenic oxide, lead sulfide, *talq* (mica and asbestos), gypsum, glass), six vitriols (black vitriol, alum, *qalqand, qalqadis, qalqatar, suri*), seven borates (borax, bread borax, natron, nitrate, sodium nitrate, potassium nitrate, sodium borate), and thirteen salts (lead(II) acetate (sweet), magnesium sulfate (bitter), *andarani* salt, *tabarzad*, potassium nitrate, naphthenate, black salt (Indian), salt of egg, alkali (*al-qali*), salt of urine, calcium hydroxide (slaked lime), salt of oak ashes, natron).
- 780 - 850 - [astronomical instruments] Muhammad ibn Mûsâ al-Khwârizmî (Algorismi) invents the quadrant, mural instrument, sine quadran, horary quadrant, and alhidade.
- 789 - 857 - [cosmetics, cuisine, fashion, hygiene] Ziryab ("Blackbird") opens a beauty parlour or "cosmetology school" for women near Alcázar, Al-Andalus, where he introduces a "shorter, shaped cut, with bangs on the forehead and the ears uncovered." He also taught "the shaping of eyebrows and the use of chemical depilatories for removing body hair", and he introduced new perfumes and cosmetics. Ziryab is also known to have invented early toothpaste, which he popularized throughout Islamic Spain. The exact ingredients of this toothpaste are not currently known,

but it was reported to have been both "functional and pleasant to taste." He also invented under-arm deodorants and "new short hairstyles leaving the neck, ears and eyebrows free," as well as shaving for men. He also introduced the three-course meal, insisting that meals should be served in three separate courses consisting of soup, the main course, and dessert.

- 800 - [medicine, psychiatry, psychology] The first psychiatric hospital and insane asylum in Egypt is built by Muslim physicians in Cairo.
- 800 - 868 - [biology, language, linguistics, zoology] 'Amr ibn Bahr al-Jahiz wrote a number of works on zoology, Arabic grammar, rhetoric, and lexicography. His most famous work is the *Book of Animals,* in which he was the first to discuss food chains, and was an early adherent of environmental determinism, arguing that the environment can determine the physical characteristics of the inhabitants of a certain community and that the origins of different human skin colors is the result of the environment. He was also the first to describe the struggle for existence and an early theory on evolution by natural selection.
- 800 - 873 - [technology] The Banû Mûsâ brothers write the *Book of Ingenious Devices,* in which they describe their following inventions: valve, float valve, feedback controller, float chamber, automatic control, Automatic flute player, Programmable machine, Trick drinking vessels, gas mask, grab, clamshell grab, fail-safe system, hurricane lamp, self-feeding oil lamp, self-trimming oil lamp, mechanical musical instrument, and Hydropowered organ.
- 800s - [education] The first universities in the modern sense, namely institutions of higher education and research which issue academic degrees at all levels (bachelor, master and doctorate), were medieval madrasahs known as *Jami'ah* founded in the 9th century. The first universities in Europe were influenced in many ways by the madrasahs in Islamic Spain and

the Emirate of Sicily at the time and in the Middle East during the Crusades. The Islamic scholarly system of *fatwa* and *ijma,* meaning opinion and consensus respectively, formed the basis of the "scholarly system the West has practised in university scholarship from the middle Ages down to the present day."

- 800s - [chemistry, petroleum] Oil fields first appear in Baku, Azerbaijan, and generate commercial activities and industry. These oil fields, where oil wells are dug to get the *Naft* (naphta, or crude petroleum), are described by geographer Masudi in the 10th century and by Marco Polo in the 13th century, who described the output of those wells as hundreds of shiploads.
- 800s - [education, legal science] Madrasahs were the first law schools, and it is likely that the "law schools known as Inns of Court in England" may have been derived from the madrasahs which taught Islamic law and jurisprudence.
- 800s - [legal science, education] The origins of the doctorate dates back to the *ijazat attadris wa 'l-ifta'* ("license to teach and issue legal opinions") in the medieval Islamic legal education system, which was equivalent to the Doctor of Laws qualification and was developed during the 9th century after the formation of the *Madh'hab* legal schools. To obtain a doctorate, a student "had to study in a guild school of law, usually four years for the basic undergraduate course" and ten or more years for a post-graduate course. The "doctorate was obtained after an oral examination to determine the originality of the candidate's theses," and to test the student's "ability to defend them against all objections, in disputations set up for the purpose" which were scholarly exercises practiced throughout the student's "career as a graduate student ot law." After students completed their post-graduate education, they were awarded doctorates giving them the status of *faqih*

(meaning "master of law"), *mufti* (meaning "professor of legal opinions") and *mudarris* (meaning "teacher"), which were later translated into Latin as *magister*, *professor* and *doctor* respectively.

- 800s - [ceramics, pottery] Another significant contribution of Islamic pottery was the development of stonepaste ceramics, originating from 9th century Iraq.
- 800s - [chemistry] The first oil fields and oil wells are created in Baku, Azerbaijan, in order to produce naphtha. Coffee was also invented by Khalid in Ethiopia.
- 800s - [milling technology] The water turbine is invented by Muslim engineers in the Islamic world.
- 800s - [astronomical instruments] Muslim astronomers invent the universal sundial and universal horary dial in Baghdad. The first navigational astrolabe was also invented in the medieval Islamic world, and employed the use of a polar projection system.
- 800 - 873 - [chemistry, environment, medicine, philosophy, physics] Ibn Ishaq Al-Kindi (Latinized, *Alkindus*) contributed to early Islamic philosophy, Islamic physics, optics, Islamic medicine, Islamic mathematics, cryptography, and metallurgy. He worked at the House of Wisdom which was set up in 810. He introduces quantification into medicine in his *De Gradibus*, and he is the first to isolate ethanol (alcohol) as a pure compound.
- 810 - 888 - [aviation, glass, medicine, technology] Abbas Ibn Firnas "was a polymath: a physician, a rather bad poet, the first to make glass from stones (quartz), a student of music, and inventor of some sort of metronome." He contributed to the mechanics of flight, planetarium, and artificial crystals, and he made the earliest recorded attempt at controlled flight. He also designed a water clock, devised means of manufacturing colorless glass, developed a chain of rings that could be used to display the motions of the

planets and stars, and developed a process for cutting rock crystal. Another one of his inventions was an artificial weather simulation room, in which spectators saw stars and clouds, and were astonished by artificial thunder and lightning due to mechanisms hidden in the basement. He also describes corrective lens and clear colourless high-purity glass, and invents silica glass and fused quartz glass.

- 813 - 833 - [library] A large number of ancient Greek, Sanskrit and Pahlavi texts on mathematics and astronomy are translated into Arabic at Baghdad's House of Wisdom (*Bayt al-Hikma*) during Al-Ma'mun's time.
- 813 - 833 - [education, medicine] The first medical schools are founded in Baghdad during Al-Ma'mun's time. These also became the first medical universities, where academic degrees and diplomas (*ijazah*) were issued to those students who were qualified to be practising doctors of medicine.
- 820 - [mathematics] Muhammad ibn Mûsâ al-Khwârizmî (Persian name: Arabicized name *al-Khwarizmi*, Latinized name *Algorithm*) wrote the *Hisab al-jabr w'al-muqabala* (*Calculus of resolution and juxtaposition*), more briefly referred to as *al-jabr*, or algebra. "Algebra was a unifying theory which allowed rational numbers, irrational numbers, geometrical magnitudes, etc., to all is treated as "algebraic objects". It gave mathematics a whole new development path so much broader in concept to that which had existed before, and provided a vehicle for future development of the subject. Another important aspect of the introduction of algebraic ideas was that it allowed mathematics to be applied to itself in a way which had not happened before." As Rashed writes: "Al-Khwarizmi's successors undertook a systematic application of arithmetic to algebra, algebra to arithmetic, both to trigonometry, algebra to the

Euclidean theory of numbers, algebra to geometry, and geometry to algebra. This was how the creation of polynomial algebra, combinatorial analysis, and numerical analysis, the numerical solution of equations, the new elementary theory of numbers, and the geometric construction of equations arose."

- 820 - [mathematics] Al-Mahani (full name Abu Abdollah Muhammad ibn Isa Mahani - in Arabic Al-Mahani). Conceived the idea of reducing geometrical problems such as duplicating the cube to problems in algebra.
- 828 - 896 [agriculture, astronomy, biology, botany, Earth sciences, meteorology] Al-Dinawari, the founder of Arabic botany, writes the *Book of Plants*, which describes at least 637 plants; discusses plant evolution from its birth to its death, describing the phases of plant growth and the production of flowers and fruit. He also deals with the applications of Islamic astronomy and meteorology to agriculture: he describes the astronomical and meteorological character of the sky, the planets and constellations, the sun and moon, the lunar phases indicating seasons and rain, the *anwa* (heavenly bodies of rain), and atmospheric phenomena such as winds, thunder, lightning, snow, floods, valleys, rivers, lakes, wells and other sources of water. He also deals with the Earth sciences in the context of agriculture: he considers the Earth, stone and sands, and describes different types of ground, indicating which types are more convenient for plants and the qualities and properties of good ground.
- 836 - 901 [anatomy; astronomy; mathematics; mechanics] Thabit Ibn Qurra (Latinized, Thebit) studied at Baghdad's House of Wisdom under the Banu Musa brothers. He made many contributions to mathematics, particularly in geometry and number theory. He discovered the theorem by which pairs of amicable numbers can be found; i.e., two numbers such

that each is the sum of the proper divisors of the other. Later, al-Baghdadi (b. 980) and al-Haytham (born 965) developed variants of the theorem.

- 838 - 870 - Tabari (full name: Ali ibn Sahl Rabban Al-Tabari). Medicine, Mathematics, Calligraphy, Literature.
- mid-800s - [chemistry] Al-Kindi writes on the distillation of wine as that of rose water and gives 107 recipes for perfumes, in his book *Kitab Kimia al-'otoor wa al-tas'eedat* (*Book of the chemistry of perfumes and distillations*).
- 850/858 - 929 - [astronomy - mathematics] Al-Battani (Albatenius) writes works on astronomy and trigonometry. He is mentioned twenty-three times in Copernicus' work *De revolutionibus orbium celestium (On the Revolution of Heavenly Spheres).*
- 850 - 930 [mathematics] born Abu Kamil of Egypt (full name, Abu Kamil Shuja ibn Aslam ibn Muhammad ibn Shuja) Forms an important link in the development of algebra between al-Khwarizmi and al-Karaji. Despite not using symbols, but writing powers of x in words, he had begun to understand what we would write in symbols as $x^n \cdot x^m = x^{m+n}$.
- 852 - [aviation, flight] Abbas Ibn Firnas (Armen Firman) made the first successful parachute fall using a huge wing-like cloak to break his fall, near Córdoba, Spain.
- 859 - [education] The University of Al Karaouine in Fes, Morocco, is recognized by the Guinness Book of World Records as the oldest academic degree-granting university in the world with its founding in 859 by the princess Fatima al-Fihri.
- ca. 860 - [astronomy, engineering] Al-Farghani (*Algraganus*) contributes to Islamic astronomy and civil engineering.
- 861 [architecture, engineering] The first Nilometer is built in Egypt. Its construction was ordered by the

Abbasid Caliph Al-Mutawakkil.

- 864 - 930 - [chemistry, medicine] Al-Razi (Rhazes) wrote on *Naft* (naphta or petroleum) and its distillates in his book *Kitab sirr al-asrar* (*Book of the secret of secrets*). When choosing a site to build Baghdad's hospital, he hung pieces of fresh meat in different parts of the city. The location where the meat took the longest to rot was the one he chose for building the hospital. He advocated that patients not be told their real condition so that fear or despair does not affect the healing process. He wrote the earliest descriptions on alkali, caustic soda, glycerine, and he first described the modern formula for soap and invented the soap bar. He also gave descriptions of equipment, processes and methods in his book *Kıtab al-Asrar* (*Book of Secrets*) in 925, and he was the first to clearly describe and differentiate between measles and smallpox. He was also a pioneer of chemotherapy and antiseptics.
- 870 - 950 - Al-Farabi (Al-Pharabius) contributes to early Islamic philosophy, early Muslim sociology, and logic in Islamic philosophy, political science, and musical science.
- 875 - [aviation, flight] Abbas Ibn Firnas made the first recorded attempt at controlled flight employing a glider.
- 889 - [navigation] Khashkhash Ibn Saeed Ibn Aswad made the earliest known attempt to cross the Atlantic Ocean. According to Abu al-Hasan 'Alî al-Mas'ûdî's *The fields of gold and the mines of jewels*, Khashkhash Ibn Saeed Ibn Aswad, from Delba (Palos de la Frontera) crossed the Atlantic Ocean in 889 and returned with a shipload of valuable treasures.

10th Century

- 800 - 1000 [technology] The first wind powered gristmills and sugar refineries appear in Afghanistan, Pakistan and Iran. The first geared gristmills and the on/off switch are also invented by Muslim engineers. Other inventions from the Islamic world include the paned window, street lamp, Mercury escapement mechanism, bridge dam and Milling dam in Iran, diversion dam in Iraq, and litter collection, waste containers and Waste disposal in Al-Andalus.

- 800 - 1000 [drinking industry] Soft drinks, sherbets and syrup are invented in the Islamic world.
- 800 - 1000 The first public library and lending library are built in the Islamic world. The library catalog is also invented in Islamic libraries.
- 800 - 1300 [environmental science] The earliest known treatises dealing with environmentalism and environmental science, especially pollution, were Arabic medical treatises written by al-Kindi, Qusta ibn Luqa, al-Razi, Ibn Al-Jazzar, al-Tamimi, al-Masihi, Avicenna, Ali ibn Ridwan, Ibn Jumay, Isaac Israeli ben Solomon, Abd-el-latif, Ibn al-Quff, and Ibn al-Nafis. Their works covered a number of subjects related to pollution such as air pollution, water pollution, soil contamination, municipal solid waste mishandling, and environmental impact assessments of certain localities. Cordoba, al-Andalus also had the first waste containers and waste disposal facilities for litter collection.
- 800 - 1300 [medicine, urology] In sexual health, Muslim physicians and pharmacists identified the issues of sexual dysfunction and erectile dysfunction, and they were the first to prescribe medication for the treatment of these problems. They developed several methods of therapy for this issue, including the single drug method where a drug is prescribed, and a "combination method of either a drug or food." These drugs were also occasionally used for recreational drug use to improve male sexuality in general by those who did not suffer from sexual dysfunctions. Most of these drugs were oral medication, though a few patients were

also treated through topical and transurethral means. Sexual dysfunctions were being treated with tested drugs in the Islamic world since the 9th century until the 16th century by a number of Muslim physicians and pharmacists, including Ibn Al-Jazzar, Al-Razi, Thabit bin Qurra, Avicenna (*The Canon of Medicine*), Averroes, Ibn al-Baitar, and Ibn al-Nafis (*The Comprehensive Book on Medicine*).

- 865 - 925 [chemistry, medicine] Muhammad ibn Zakarîya Râzi (Rhazes), in his *Doubts about Galen,* was the first to prove both Aristotle's theory of classical elements and Galen's theory of humorism wrong using an experimental method. He carried out an experiment which would upset these theories by inserting a liquid with a different temperature into a body resulting in an increase or decrease of bodily heat, which resembled the temperature of that particular fluid. Al-Razi noted particularly that a warm drink would heat up the body to a degree much higher than its own natural temperature, thus the drink would trigger a response from the body, rather than transferring only its own warmth or coldness to it. Al-Razi's chemical experiments further suggested other qualities of matter, such as "oiliness" and "sulfurousness", or inflammability and salinity, which were not readily explained by the traditional fire, water, earth and air division of elements.
- 858 - 1048 [astronomical instruments] The first reference to an "observation tube" is found in the work of Al-Battani, and the first exact description of the observation tube was given by al-Biruni, in a section of his work that is "dedicated to verifying the presence of the new crescent on the horizon." Though these early observation tubes did not have lenses, they "enabled an observer to focus on a part of the sky by eliminating light interference." These observation tubes were later adopted in Latin-speaking Europe, where they influenced the development of the telescope.

- 865 - 925 [chemical technology] Kerosene was produced from the distillation of petroleum and was first described by al-Razi (Rhazes) in Baghdad. In his *Kitab al-Asrar* (*Book of Secrets*), he described two methods for the production of kerosene. One method involved using clay as an absorbent, while the other method involved using ammonium chloride (*sal ammoniac*). Al-Razi also described the first kerosene lamps (*naffatah*) used for heating and lighting in his *Kitab al-Asrar* (*Book of Secrets*). These were used in the oil lamp industry.
- 865 - 925 [alchemy] Muhammad ibn Zakarîya Râzi writes that the only vegetable substance used by Muslim alchemists are the ashes of the *Ushnan* plant, from which they produced alkali metals and alkali salts. Razi also lists ten animal substances that were used by him and his contemporary alchemists: hair, skulls, brains, bile, blood, milk, urine, eggs, nacre (mother of pearl) and horn. He writes that hair, brains, bile, eggs, skulls and blood were used to prepare sal ammoniac.
- 865 - 925 [chemical processes] Muhammad ibn Zakarîya Râzi first described the following chemical processes: calcination (*al-tashwiya*). solution (*al-tahlil*), sublimation (*al-tas'id*), amalgamation (*al-talghim*), ceration (*al-tashmi*), and a method of converting a substance into a thick paste or fusible solid.
- 900s - [mathematics, accounting] By this century, three systems of counting are used in the Arab world. Fingerreckoning arithmetic, with numerals written entirely in words, used by the business community; the sexagesimal system, a remnant originating with the Babylonians, with numerals denoted by letters of the arabic alphabet and used by Arab mathematicians in astronomical work; and the Hindu-Arabic numeral system, which was used with various sets of symbols. Its arithmetic at first required the use of a dust board (a sort of handheld blackboard) because "the methods

required moving the numbers around in the calculation and rubbing some out as the calculation proceeded." Al-Uqlidisi (born 920) modified these methods for pen and paper use. Eventually the advances enabled by the decimal system led to its standard use throughout the region and the world.

- 900s - [technology] The first milling factory is built in Baghdad.
- 900s - [astronomy, mathematics, technology] The cartographic grid is invented in Baghdad, and graph paper is also invented in the Islamic world.
- 900s - Muslim astronomers also invent the almucantar quadrant, navigational astrolabe, vertical sundial, and polar sundial.
- 900s - [chemistry] Shaving soap is invented by Arabic chemists.
- 900s - [medicine] Alcohol is first employed for medical uses by Arabic physicians.
- 800 - 1000 - Muslim engineers invented a variety of surveying instruments for accurate levelling, including: a wooden board with a plumb line and two hooks, an equilateral triangle with a plumb line and two hooks, and a "reed level". They also invented a rotating alhidade used for accurate alignment, and a surveying astrolabe used for alignment, measuring angles, triangulation, finding the width of a river, and the distance between two points separated by an impassable obstruction.
- 903 - 986 - [astronomical instruments] Abd al-Rahman al-Sufi (Latinized name, *Azophi*) first described over 1,000 different uses of an astrolabe, in areas as diverse as astronomy, astrology, horoscopes, navigation, surveying, timekeeping, Qibla, Salah prayer, etc.
- 964 - [astronomy] Abd al-Rahman al-Sufi writes the *Book of Fixed Stars*, a star catalogue thoroughly

illustrated with observations and descriptions of the stars, their positions, their apparent magnitudes and their colour. He identified the Large Magellanic Cloud, which is visible from Yemen, though not from Isfahan; it was not seen by Europeans until Magellan's voyage in the 16th century. He also made earliest recorded observation of the Andromeda Galaxy in 964 AD; describing it as a "small cloud". He also catalogued the Omicron Velorum star cluster as a "nebulous star", and an additional "nebulous object" in Vulpecula, a cluster now variously known as Al Sufi's Cluster, the "Coathanger asterism", Brocchi's Cluster or Collinder 399.

- 909 - 950 [ceramics, pottery] The Hispano-Moresque style of Islamic pottery emerged in Andalusia under the Fatimids.
- 920 [mathematics] Born al-Uqlidisi. Modified arithmetic methods for the Indian numeral system to make it possible for pen and paper use. Until then, doing calculations with the Indian numerals necessitated the use of a dust board as noted earlier.
- 927 - 928 - [astronomical instruments] The earliest surviving example of an astrolabe is dated 315 AH in the Islamic calendar.
- 936 - 1013 [medicine] Al-Zahrawi (Latinized name, Albucasis) Surgery, Medicine. Called the "Father of Modern Surgery."
- 940 - 997 [astronomy; mathematics] Muhammad Al-Buzjani. Mathematics, Astronomy, Geometry, rigonometry.
- 940 [mathematics] Born Abu'l-Wafa al-Buzjani. Wrote several treatises using the finger-counting system of arithmetic, and was also an expert on the Indian numerals system. About the Indian system he wrote: *"[it] did not find application in business circles and among*

the population of the Eastern Caliphate for a long time." Using the Indian numeral system, abu'l Wafa was able to extract roots.

- 945 - 1000 [cuisine] Some of the earliest restaurants came into existence through the medieval Islamic world at this time. The Islamic world had "restaurants where one could purchase all sorts of prepared dishes." These restaurants were mentioned by Al-Muqaddasi (born 945) in the late 10th century.
- 953 [mathematics] Born al-Karaji of Karaj and Baghdad (full name, Abu Bekr ibn Muhammad ibn al-Husayn Al-Karaji or al-Karkhi) believed to be the "first person to completely free algebra from geometrical operations and to replace them with the arithmetical type of operations which are at the core of algebra today. He was first to define the monomials *x*, *x*, *x*, and 1 / *x*, 1 / *x*, 1 / *x*, and to give rules for products of any two of these. He started a school of algebra which flourished for several hundreds of years". Discovered the binomial theorem for integer exponents. This "was a major factor in the development of numerical analysis based on the decimal system."
- 953 [technology] The earliest historical record of a reservoir fountain pen dates back to 953, when Ma'âd al-Mu'izz, the caliph of Egypt, demanded a pen which would not stain his hands or clothes, and was provided with a pen which held ink in a reservoir and delivered it to the nib via gravity and capillary action, as recorded by Qadi al-Nu'man al-Tamimi (d. 974) in his *Kitdb al-Majalis wa'l-musayardt*.
- 957 [geography; cartography; exploration; chemistry] died Abul Hasan Ali Al-Masudi, best known as a cartographer, was also a traveler historian, etc. Al-mas'oudi described his visit to the oilfields of Baku. Wrote on the reaction of alkali water with zaj (vitriol) water giving sulfuric acid.

- 965 - 1040 [mathematics; optics; physics] Born ibn al-Haitham (full name, ; Latinized name, Alhazen). Possibly the first to classify all even perfect numbers (i.e., numbers equal to the sum of their proper divisors) as those of the form 2^k " (2^k " 1) where 2^k " 1 is prime number. Al-Haytham is also the first person to state Wilson's theorem. If *p* is prime than 1 + (*p* " 1)! is divisible by *p*. "It is called *Wilson's theorem* because of a comment by Waring in 1770 that John Wilson had noticed the result. There is no evidence that Wilson knew how to prove it. It was over 750 years later that Lagrange gave the first known proof to the statement in 1771. "Haytham in the tenth-eleventh century wrote a scathing critique of Ptolemy's work: 'Ptolemy assumed an arrangement that cannot exist, and the fact that this arrangement produces in his imagination the motions that belong to the planets does not free him from the error he committed in his assumed arrangement, for the existing motions of the planets cannot be the result of an arrangement that is impossible to exist'."
- 972 - 1058 [humanities] Al-Mawardi (Alboacen) Political science, Sociology, Jurisprudence, Ethics.
- 975 - [education] Al-Azhar University, founded in Cairo, Egypt, was a *Jami'ah* ("university" in Arabic) which offered a variety of post-graduate academic degrees (*ijazah*), and had individual faculties for a theological seminary, Islamic law and Islamic jurisprudence, Arabic grammar, Islamic astronomy, early Islamic philosophy and logic in Islamic philosophy.
- 975 - 1075 - [ceramics, pottery] Fustat becomes a center for innovative Islamic pottery and ceramics.
- 980 [mathematics] Born al-Baghdadi (full name). Studied a slight variant of Thabit ibn Qurra's theorem on amicable numbers. Al-Baghdadi also wrote texts comparing the three systems of counting and arithmetic

used in the region during this period. Made improvements on the decimal system.

- 981 - 1037 [astronomy; mathematics; medicine; philosophy] Ibn Sina (Avicenna); Medicine, Philosophy, Mathematics, Astronomy. Is considered to be the father of modern medicine
- 994 - [astronomy, engineering] Abu-Mahmud al-Khujandi constructs the first astronomical sextant in Ray, Iran.
- 996 - [astronomy, engineering] The geared mechanical astrolabe, featuring eight gear-wheels, is invented by Abû Rayhân al-Bîrûnî.

11th Century

- c. 1000 - [medicine, ophthalmology] Ammar ibn Ali of Mosul writes the *Choice of Eye Diseases*, a landmark text on ophthalmology in medieval Islam. In cataract surgery, He attempted the earliest extraction of cataracts using suction. He invented a hollow metallic syringe hypodermic needle, which he applied through the sclerotic and successfully extracted the cataracts through suction. He discovered the technique of cataract extraction while experimenting with his hypodermic needle invention on a patient.
- c. 1000 - [physics, mathematics] Abu Sahl al-Quhi (Kuhi), discovers that the heaviness of bodies vary with their distance from the center of the Earth, and solves equations higher than the second degree.
- c. 1000 - [mathematics] Abu-Mahmud al-Khujandi first states a special case of Fermat's last theorem.
- c. 1000 - [mathematics] Law of sines is discovered by Muslim mathematicians, but it is uncertain who discovers it first between Abu-Mahmud al-Khujandi, Abu Nasr Mansur, and Abu al-Wafa.
- 1000 - [mathematics] Al-Karaji writes a book containing the first known proofs by mathematical induction. He

who used it to prove the binomial theorem, Pascal's triangle, and the sum of integral cubes. He was "the first who introduced the theory of algebraic calculus."

- 1000 - [medicine, surgery, engineering] Abu al-Qasim al-Zahrawi (Abulcasis), the father of modern surgery, publishes his 30-volume medical encyclopedia, the *Kitab al-Tasrif*, which remains a standard textbook in Muslim and European universities until the 16th century. The book first introduced many surgical instruments, including the first instruments unique to women, as well as the surgical uses of catgut and forceps, the ligature, surgical needle, curette, retractor, surgical spoon, sound, surgical hook, surgical rod, specula, lithotomy scalpel, and bone saw. He also invented the plaster cotton dressing, oral anaesthesia, inhalational anaesthetic, and anaesthetic sponge.
- 1000s - [glass] Clear glass mirrors were being produced in al-Andalus.
- 1000s - [civil engineering] Cobwork (*tabya*) first appeared in the Maghreb and al-Andalus in the 11th century, and was later described in detail by Ibn Khaldun in the 14th century, who regarded it as a characteristically Muslim practice. Cobwork later spread to other parts of Europe from the 12th century onwards.
- 1000s - [mechincal technology] In Al-Andalus, Ibn Khalaf al-Muradi invents complex gearing, Epicyclic gearing, segmental gearing, and the geared mechanical clock. Muslim engineers also invent the Weight-driven mechanical clock.
- c. 1000 - 1009 - [physics, engineering] Ibn Yunus publishes his astronomical treatise *Al-Zij al-Hakimi al-Kabir* in Egypt. It contains the earliest desciption of a pendulum. He also constructs the first monumental astrolabe.
- 1000 - 1020 - [astronomy, engineering] Al-Sijzi invents

the *Zuraqi*, a unique astrolabe designed for a heliocentric planetary model in which the Earth is moving rather than the sky.

- 1000 - 1030 - [biology] - Ibn Miskawayh discusses ideas on evolution.
- 1000 - 1031 - [astronomy] Abû al-Rayhân al-Bîrûnî was the first to conduct elaborate experiments related to astronomical phenomena. He discovered the Milky Way galaxy to be a collection of numerous nebulous stars.
- 1000 - 1037 - [mechanics, physics] Ibn al-Haytham discusses the theory of attraction between masses, and it seems that he was aware of the magnitude of acceleration due to gravity. Ibn al-Haytham also discovered the law of inertia, known as Newton's first law of motion, when he stated that a body moves perpetually unless an external force stops it or changes its direction of motion.
- 1000 - 1037 - [alchemy, chemistry, engineering] Avicenna criticizes the theory of the transmutation of metals. He also invents the chemical process of steam distillation and extracts the first fragrances and essential oils as a result, for use in aromatherapy and the drinking and perfumery industries. He also invents the air thermometer for use in his laboratory experiments.
- 1000 - 1037 - [mechanics, physics] Avicenna, the father of the fundamental concept of momentum in physics, discovered the concept of momentum, when he referred to impetus as being proportional to weight times velocity, a precursor to the concept of momentum in Newton's second law of motion. His theory of motion was also consistent with the concept of inertia in Newton's first law of motion.
- 1000 - 1038 - [astronomy, physics] Ibn al-Haytham (Alhacen), in his *Epitome of Astronomy*, was the first to insist that the heavenly bodies "were accountable to the laws of physics".

- 1000 - 1038 - [biology] Ibn al-Haytham writes a book in which he argues for evolutionism.
- 1000 - 1048 - [alchemy, chemistry] Abû Rayhân al-Bîrûnî criticizes the theory of the transmutation of metals.
- 1000 - 1048 - [anthropology, Indology, history] Abû al-Rayhân al-Bîrûnî, considered "the first anthropologist" and the father of Indology, wrote de-tailed comparative studies on the anthropology of peoples, religions and cultures in the Middle East, Mediterranean and South Asia. Biruni's anthropology of religion was only possible for a scholar deeply immersed in the lore of other nations. Biruni has also been praised for his Islamic anthropology.
- 1000 - 1048 - [earth sciences, Indology, geodesy, geology] Abû Rayhân al-Bîrûnî, who is considered the father of Indology, the father of geodesy, one of the first geologists, and an influential geographer, hypothesized that India was once covered by the Indian Ocean while observing rock formations at the mouths of rivers, introduced techniques to measure the Earth and distances on it using triangulation, and measured the radius of the Earth as 6339.6 km, the most accurate up until the 16th century. He also determines the Earth's circumference.
- 1000 - 1048 - [engineering, mechanics, physics] Abû Rayhân al-Bîrûnî was the first to realize that acceleration is connected with non-uniform motion. He also invents the laboratory flask, pycnometer, and conical measure.
- 1000 - 1121 - [mechanics, physics] Abû Rayhân al-Bîrûnî, and later al-Khazini, were the first to apply experimental scientific methods to mechanics, especially the fields of statics and dynamics, particularly for determining specific weights, such as those based on the theory of balances and weighing. Muslim physicists unified statics and dynamics into the science

of mechanics, and they combined the fields of hydrostatics with dynamics to give birth to hydrodynamics. They applied the mathematical theories of ratios and infinitesimal techniques, and introduced algebraic and fine calculation techniques into the field of statics. They were also generalized the theory of the centre of gravity and applied it to three-dimensional bodies. They also founded the theory of the ponderable lever and created the "science of gravity" which was later further developed in medieval Europe.

- 1019 - [astronomy, technology] In Afghanistan, Abû al-Rayhân al-Bîrûnî observed and described the solar eclipse on April 8, 1019, and the lunar eclipse on September 17, 1019, in detail, and gave the exact latitudes of the stars during the lunar eclipse. He also invents the Orthographical astrolabe and the planisphere, which was the earliest star chart. He also invents a geared mechanical lunisolar calendar analog computer with gear train and eight gear-wheels, an early example of a fixed-wired knowledge processing machine.
- 1020 - [astronomical instruments] The geared mechanical astrolabe is perfected by Ibn Samh in Al-Andalus. These can be considered as an ancestor of the mechanical clock.
- 1021 - [optics, physics, engineering, mathematics, ophthalmology, psychology, scientific method, surgery] Ibn al-Haytham, who is considered the father of optics, the pioneer of the scientific method, the "first scientist", and the founder of psychophysics and experimental psychology, completes his *Book of Optics*, which has been ranked alongside Isaac Newton's *Philosophiae Naturalis Principia Mathematica* as one of the most influential books ever written in the history of physics. The book drastically transformed the understanding

of light and vision, and introduced the experimental scientific method; hence the book is considered the root of experimental physics. It correctly explained and proved the modern intromission theory of vision, and described experiments on lenses, mirrors, refraction, reflection, and the dispersion of light into its constituent colours. It also explained binocular vision and the moon illusion, speculated on the finite speed, rectilinear propagation and electromagnetic aspects of light, first stated Fermat's principle of least time, described an early version of Snell's law, and argued that rays of light are streams of energy particles travelling in straight lines. The book also contains the earliest discussions and descriptions on psychophysics and experimental psychology, the psychology of visual perception, phenomenology, and the inventions of the pinhole camera, camera obscura, and parabolic mirror. In mathematics, the book formulated and solved "Alhazen's problem" geometrically, and developed and proved the earliest general formula for infinitesimal and integral calculus using mathematical induction. In medicine and ophthalmology, the book also made important advances in eye surgery, as it correctly explained the process of sight and visual perception for the first time.

- 1021 - [glass, scientific instruments] In the *Book of Optics*, Ibn al-Haytham develops the following scientific instruments: magnifying glass, parabolic mirror, spherical mirror, concave mirror, convex mirror, pinhole camera, and camera obscura.
- 1021 - 1037 - [optics, physics] Avicenna "observed that if the perception of light is due to the emission of some sort of particles by a luminous source, the speed of light must be finite." He also provided a sophisticated explanation for the rainbow phenomenon.
- 1021 - 1048 - Abû Rayhân al-Bîrûnî stated that light has a finite speed, and he was the first to discover that

the speed of light is much faster than the speed of sound.

- 1025 - [medicine, pathology, physiology] Avicenna (Ibn Sina), who is considered the father of modern medicine and one of the greatest thinkers and medical scholars in history, publishes his 14-volume medical encyclopedia, *The Canon of Medicine,* which remains a standard textbook in Muslim and European universities until the 17th century. The book's contributions to medicine includes the introduction of systematic experimentation and quantification in the study of physiology, the discovery of contagious diseases, the distinction of mediastinitis from pleurisy, the contagious nature of phthisis, the distribution of diseases by water and soil, the first careful descriptions of skin troubles, sexually transmitted diseases, perversions, and nervous ailments, the use of ice to treat fevers, the separation of medicine from pharmacology (important to the development of the pharmaceutical sciences), the introduction of quarantine to limit the spread of con-tagious diseases, and the introduction of evidence-based medicine, experimental medicine, clinical trials, randomized controlled trials, efficacy tests, clinical pharmacology, neuropsychiatry, physiological psychology, risk factor analysis, and the idea of a syndrome in the diagnosis of specific diseases. The *Canon* is also considered the first pharmacopoeia.
- 1025 - [medicine, pathology] In *The Canon of Medicine,* Avicenna is the first to carry out cancer therapy. He recognized cancer as a tumor and noted that a "cancerous tumour progressively increases in size, is destructive and spreads roots which insinuate themselves amongst the tissue elements." He also attempted the earliest known treatments for cancer. One method he discovered was the "Hindiba", a herbal

compound drug which Ibn al-Baitar later identified as having "anticancer" properties and which could also treat other tumors and neoplastic disorders. After recognizing its usefulness in treating neoplastic disorders, Hindiba was patented in 1997 by Nil Sari, Hanzade Dogan, and John K. Snyder. Another method for treating cancer first described by Avicenna was a surgical treatment. He stated that the excision should be radical and that all diseased tissue should be removed, which included the use of amputation or the removal of veins running in the direction of the tumor. He also recommended the use of cauterization for the area being treated if necessary. Avicenna's *Canon* was also the first to describe the symptoms of esophageal cancer and the first to refer to it as "cancer of the esophagus." Hirudotherapy, the use of medicinal leech for medical purposes, was also introduced by Avicenna in *The Canon of Medicine*. He considered the application of leech to be more useful than cupping in "letting off the blood from deeper parts of the body." He also introduced the use of leech as treatment for skin disease. Leech therapy became a popular method in medieval Europe due to the influence of his *Canon*. In phytotherapy, Avicenna also introduced the medicinal use of Taxus baccata L. He named this herbal drug as "Zarnab" and used it as a cardiac remedy. This was the first known use of a calcium channel blocker drug, which were not used in the Western world until the 1960s.

- 1025 - 1028 - [astronomy] Ibn al-Haytham, in his *Doubts on Ptolemy*, criticizes Ptolemy's astronomical system for relating actual physical motions to imaginary mathematical points, lines, and circles.
- 1027 - [arithmetic, astronomy, earth sciences, geology, geometry, logic, mathematics, music, natural sciences, philosophy, psychology] Avicenna (Ibn Sina) writes one

of the first scientific encyclopedias, *The Book of Healing*. Its contributions include nine volumes on Avicennian logic; eight on the natural sciences; four on the quadrivium of arithmetic, astronomy, geometry and music; a number of volumes on early Islamic philosophy, Islamic mathematics, metaphysics and psychology; the astronomical theory that Venus is closer to Earth than the Sun; and a geological hypothesis on two causes of mountains.

- 1028 - 1087 - [astronomy, engineering] Abû Ishâq Ibrâhîm al-Zarqâlî (Arzachel) invents the "Saphaea", the first universal latitude-independent astrolabe which did not depend on the latitude of the observer and could be used anywhere. He also invents the equatorium, a mechanical analog computer device, and he discovers that the orbits of the planets are ellipses and not circles.
- 1029 - [chemistry, technology] The purification process for potassium nitrate (saltpetre; *natrun* or *barud* in Arabic) was first described by the Muslim chemist Ibn Bakhtawayh in his *Al-Muqaddimat*.
- 1030 - [astronomy] Abû al-Rayhân al-Bîrûnî discussed the Indian planetary theories of Aryabhata, Brahmagupta and Varahamihira in his *Ta'rikh al-Hind* (Latinized as *Indica*). Biruni stated that Brahmagupta and others consider that the earth rotates on its axis and Biruni noted that this does not create any mathematical problems.
- 1030 - 1048 - [astronomy] Abu Said Sinjari suggested the possible heliocentric movement of the Earth around the Sun, which Abû al-Rayhân al-Bîrûnî did not reject. Al-Biruni agreed with the Earth's rotation about its own axis, and while he was initially neutral regarding the heliocentric and geocentric models, he considered heliocentrism to be a philosophical problem. He remarked that if the Earth rotates on its axis and moves around the Sun, it would remain consistent with his astronomical parameters.

- 1031 - [astronomy] Abû al-Rayhân al-Bîrûnî completes his extensive astronomical encyclopaedia *Canon Mas'u-dicus,* in which he records his astronomical findings and formulates astronomical tables. It presents a geocentric model, tabulating the distance of all the celestial spheres from the central Earth. The book introduces the mathematical technique of analysing the acceleration of the planets, and first states that the motions of the solar apogee and the precession are not identical. Al-Biruni also discovered that the distance between the Earth and the Sun is larger than Ptolemy's estimate, on the basis that Ptolemy disregarded the annual solar eclipses. Al-Biruni also described the Earth's gravitation as "the attraction of all things towards the centre of the earth."
- 1038 - [astronomy] Ibn al-Haytham described the first non-Ptolemaic configuration in *The Model of the Motions.* His reform excluded cosmology, as he deve-loped a systematic study of celestial kinematics that was completely geometric. This in turn led to innovative developments in infinitesimal geometry. His reformed model was the first to reject the equant and eccentrics, free celestial kinematics from cosmology, and reduce physical entities to geometrical entities. The model also propounded the Earth's rotation about its axis, and the centres of motion were geometrical points without any physical significance, like Johannes Kepler's model centuries later.
- 1038 - 1075 - [engineering] Ibn Bassal invents the flywheel in al-Andalus, and he first employs it in a Noria and a Saqiya chain pump.
- 1044 or 1048 - 1123 [mathematics, literature] Omar Khayyám, a mathematician and poet, "gave a complete classification of cubic equations with geometric solutions found by means of intersecting conic sections. Khayyam also wrote that he hoped to give a full description of the algebraic solution of cubic equations in a later work: 'If the opportunity arises and I can

succeed, I shall give all these fourteen forms with all their branches and cases, and how to distinguish whatever is possible or impossible so that a paper, containing elements which are greatly useful in this art will be prepared'." He later became the first to find general geometric solutions of cubic equations and laid the foundations for the development of analytic geometry and non-Euclidean geometry. He extracted roots using the decimal system (Hindu-Arabic numeral system). He is well-known for his poetic work *Rubaiyat of Omar Khayyam*, but there is dispute whether the *Maqamat*, a famous diwan of poetry translated to English are actually his work.

- 1058 - 1111 [law; theology] Al-Ghazali (Algazel), judge and prolific thinker and writer on topics such as sociology, theology and philosophy. He critiqued the philosophers Avicenna and al-Farabi in *The Incoherence of the Philosophers*. Wrote extensive expositions on Islamic tenets and foundations of jurisprudence. Also critiqued the Muslim scholastics (al-mutakallimun.) Was associated with Sufism but he later critiqued it as well.
- 1070 - [astronomy] Abu Ubayd al-Juzjani proposed a non-Ptolemaic configuration in his *Tarik al-Aflak*. In his work, he indicated the so-called "equant" problem of the Ptolemic model, and proposed a solution for the problem.
- 1085 - 1099 - [related] First wave of devastation of Muslim resources, lives, properties, institutions, and infrastructure over a period of one hundred years: Fall of Muslim Toledo (1085), Malta (1090), Sicily (1091) and Jerusalem (1099). This was followed by several Crusades from 1095 to 1291.
- 1087 - [astronomy] Abû Ishâq Ibrâhîm al-Zarqâlî publishes the *Almanac of Azarqueil*, the first almanac. The entries found in the almanac "give directly the positions of the celestial bodies and need no further

computation". The work provided the true daily positions of the sun, moon and planets for four years from 1088 to 1092, as well as many other related tables. A Latin translation and adaptation of the work appeared as the *Tables of Toledo* in the 12th century and the *Alfonsine tables* in the 13th century.

- 1091 - [education] Another early university, the Al-Nizamiyya of Baghdad, was founded, and is considered the "largest university of the Medieval world".

12th Century

- 1100s - [engineering] The ventilator is invented in Egypt. The bridge mill, hydropowered forge and finery forge are also invented in Al-Andalus. The war machine is also invented in Turkey.
- 1100s - [astronomical instruments] The astrolabic quadrant is invented in Egypt.
- 1100s - [chemistry, military technology] The Seljuqs had facilities in Sivas for manufacturing war machines.
- 1100 - 1138 - [astronomy] Ibn Bajjah (Avempace) develops the first planetary model without any epicycles, as an alternative to Ptolemy's model.
- 1100 - 1138 - [mechanics, physics] Ibn Bajjah (Avempace) is the first to state that there is always a reaction force for every force exerted, a precursor to Gottfried Leibniz's idea of force which underlies Newton's third law of motion. His theory of motion later has an important influence on later physicists like Galileo Galilei.
- 1100 - 1150 - [astronomical instruments] Jabir ibn Aflah (Geber) invents the torquetum, an observational instrument and mechanical analog computer device used to transform between spherical coordinate systems. He also invents the celestial globe, being "the first to design a portable celestial sphere to measure and explain the movements of celestial objects."

- 1100 - 1161 - [anatomy, anesthesiology, biology, medicine, physiology, surgery] Ibn Zuhr (Avenzoar) invents the surgical procedure of tracheotomy in al-Andalus. During his biomedical research, Ibn Zuhr is also one of the earliest physician known to have carried out human dissections and postmortem autopsy. As a pioneer in parasitology, he proves that the skin disease scabies is caused by a parasite, which contraaicted the erroneous theory of humorism supported by Hippocrates, Galen and Avicenna. The removal of the parasite from the patient's body did not involve purging, bleeding or any other traditional treatments associated with the four humours. His works show that he was often highly critical of previous medical authorities, including Avicenna's *The Canon of Medicine*. He was one of the first physicians to reject the erroneous theory of four humours, which dates back to Hippocrates and Galen. Avenzoar also confirmed the presence of blood in the body. He was also the first to give a correct description of the tracheotomy operation for suffocating patients, and the first to provide a real scientific etiology for the inflammatory diseases of the ear, and the first to clearly discuss the causes of stridor. Modern anesthesia was also developed in al-Andalus by the Muslim anesthesiologists Ibn Zuhr and Abulcasis. They were the first to utilize oral as well as inhalant anesthetics, and they performed hundreds of surgeries under inhalant anesthesia with the use of narcotic-soaked sponges which were placed over the face.
- 1100 - 1161 - [medicine, pharmacopoeia] Ibn Zuhr writes *The Method of Preparing Medicines and Diet*, in which he performed the first parenteral nutrition of humans with a silver needle. He also wrote an early pharmacopoeia, which later became the first Arabic book to be printed with a movable type in 1491. Ibn Zuhr (and other Muslim physicians such as al-Kindi, Ibn Sahl, Abulcasis, al-Biruni, Avicenna, Averroes, Ibn

al-Baitar, Ibn Al-Jazzar and Ibn al-Nafis) also developed drug therapy and medicinal drugs for the treatment of specific symptoms and diseases. His use of practical experience and careful observation was extensive.

- 1100 - 1165 - [mechanics, physics] Hibat Allah Abu'l-Barakat al-Baghdaadi writes a critique of Aristotelian philosophy and Aristotelian physics entitled *al-Mu'tabar*. He is the first to negate Aristotle's idea that a constant force produces uniform motion, as he realizes that a force applied continuously produces acceleration, which is considered "the fundamental law of classical mechanics" and an early foreshadowing of Newton's second law of motion. Like Newton, he described acceleration as the rate of change of velocity.
- 1100 - 1166 [cartography, geography] Muhammad al-Idrisi, aka Idris al-Saqalli aka al-sharif al-idrissi of Andalusia and Sicily, also known as Dreses in Latin. Among his works are a world map and the first known globe. He is said to draw the first correct map of the world "lawh al-tarsim" (plank of drought). His maps were used extensively during the explorations of the era of European renaissance. Roger II of Sicily commemorated his world map on a circle of silver weighing about 400 pounds. Works include *Nozhat al-mushtaq fi ikhtiraq al-&agrav;faq* dedicated to Roger II of Sicily, which is a compendium of the geographic and sociologic knowledge of his time as well as descriptions of his own travels illustrated with over seventy maps; *Kharitat al-`alam al-ma`mour min al-ard* (Map of the inhabited regions of the earth) wherein he divided the world into 7 regions, the first extending from the equator to 23 degrees latitude, and the seventh being from 54 to 63 degrees followed by a region uninhabitable due to cold and snow.
- 1100 - 1600 - [ceramics, pottery] Damascus becomes a center for innovative Islamic pottery and ceramics.

- 1105 - 1200 [astronomy] Ibn Tufail (Abubacer) and al-Betrugi (Alpetragius) are the first to propose planetary models without any equant, epicycles or eccentrics. Al-Betrugi was also the first to discover that the planets are self-luminous.
- 1106 - 1138 [polymath] Abu Bakr Muhammad Ibn Yahya (Ibn Bajjah or Avempace) writes books on philosophy, medicine, mathematics, poetry, and music.
- 1110 - 1185 [literature, philosophy] Abdubacer Ibn Tufayl of Spain. Philosophy, medicine, poetry, fiction. His most famous work is *Hayy ibn Yaqzan*, which is a spiritual investigation into the reality of the world narrated by a man who was raised from infancy by a roe or gazelle on a desert island. This work later had a strong influence on early Islamic philosophy, Arabic literature, European literature, the Scientific Revolution, and modern philosophy.
- 1115 - 1116 [astronomy, engineering] Al-Khazini wrote the *Sinjaric Tables*, in which he gave a description of his construction of a 24 hour water clock designed for astronomical purposes, an early example of an astronomical clock, and the positions of 46 stars computed for the year 500 AH (1115-1116 CE). He also computed tables for the observation of celestial bodies at the latitude of Merv. The *Sinjaric Tables* was later translated into Greek by Gregory Choniades in the 13th century and was studied in the Byzantine Empire.
- 1115 - 1130 [astronomy, biology, chemistry, evolution] Al-Khazini's *Treatise on Instruments* has seven parts describing different scientific instruments: the triquetrum, dioptra, a triangular instrument he invented, the quadrant and sextant, the astrolabe, and original instruments involving reflection. He also wrote another work on evolution in chemistry and biology, and how they were perceived by natural philosophers and common people in the Islamic world at the time.

He wrote that there were many Muslims who believed that humans evolved from apes.

- 1118 - 1174 - [education, medicine] Al-Nuri hospital in Egypt was a famous teaching hospital built by Nur ad-Din Zanqi, and was where many renowned physicians were taught. The hospital's medical school is said had elegant rooms, and a library which many of its books were donated by Zangi's physician, Abu al-Majid al-Bahili.
- 1121 - [astronomy, astrophysics, engineering, mechanics, physics] Al-Khazini publishes *The Book of the Balance of Wisdom,* in which he is the first to propose that the gravity and gravitational potential energy of a body varies depending on its distance from the centre of the Earth. This phenomenon is not proven until Newton's law of universal gravitation centuries later. Al-Khazini is also one of the first to clearly differentiate between force, mass, and weight, and he shows awareness of the weight of the air and of its decrease in density with altitude, and discovers that there is greater density of water when nearer to the Earth's centre. He also invents several scientific instruments, including the steelyard and hydrostatic balance. Al-Biruni and al-Khazini were also the first to apply experimental scientific methods to the fields of statics and dynamics, particularly for determining specific weights, such as those based on the theory of balances and weighing. He and his Muslim predecessors unified statics and dynamics into the science of mechanics, and they combined the fields of hydrostatics with dynamics to give birth to hydrodynamics. They applied the mathematical theories of ratios and infinitesimal techniques, and introduced algebraic and fine calculation techniques into the field of statics. They were also the first to generalize the theory of the centre of gravity and the first to apply it to three-dimensional bodies. They also founded the theory of the ponderable

lever and created the "science of gravity" which was later further developed in medieval Europe. The contributions of al-Khazini and his Muslim predecessors to mechanics laid the foundations for the later development of classical mechanics in Renaissance Europe.

- 1126 - 1198 - [mechanics, physics] Averroes (Ibn Rushd) is the first to define and measure force as "the rate at which work is done in changing the kinetic condition of a material body" and the first to correctly argue "that the effect and measure of force is change in the kinetic condition of a materially resistant mass."
- 1126 - 1198 - [astronomy] Averroes rejects the eccentric deferents introduced by Ptolemy. He rejects the Ptolemaic model and instead argues for a strictly concentric model of the universe.
- 1128 - 1198 - [philosophy, law, medicine, astronomy, theology] Averroes writes books on philosophy, law, medicine, astronomy, and theology.
- 1130 - [mathematics] Born al-Samawal. An important member of al-Karaji's school of algebra. Gave this definition of algebra: "[it is concerned] with operating on unknowns using all the arithmetical tools, in the same way as the arithmetician operates on the known."
- 1135 - [mathematics] Born Sharafeddin Tusi. Follows al-Khayyam's application of algebra of geometry, rather than follow the general development that came through al-Karaji's school of algebra. Wrote a treatise on cubic equations which "represents an essential contribution to another algebra which aimed to study curves by means of equations, thus inaugurating the beginning of algebraic geometry."
- 1135 - 1200 - [astronomy, engineering] Sharaf al-Dîn al-Tûsî invents the linear astrolabe (staff of al-Tusi).
- 1150 - [telecommunication] The use of homing pigeons is introduced in Iraq and Syria.

- 1154 - [engineering] Al-Kaysarani invents the striking clock in Syria.
- 1187 - [military technology] Mardi bin Ali al-Tarsusi invents the counterweight trebuchet and the mangonel.

13th Century

- 1200s - [chemistry] Al-Jawbari describes the preparation of rose water in the *Book of Selected Disclosure of Secrets* (*Kitab kashf al-Asrar*).
- 1200s - [chemistry; materials, glassmaking] Arabic manuscript on the manufacture of false gemstones and diamonds. Also describes spirits of alum, spirits of saltpetre and spirits of salts (hydrochloric acid).
- 1200s - [chemistry] An Arabic manuscript written in Syriac script gives description of various chemical materials found in the galapogas islands and their properties such as sulfuric acid, sal-ammoniac, saltpetre and zaj (vitriol).
- 1201 - 1274 - [astronomy; mathematics] Nasir Al-Din Al-Tusi; Astronomy, Non-Euclidean geometry.
- 1204 - [astronomy] Died, Al-Bitruji (Alpetragius.)
- 1206 - [engineering, mechanics, technology] Al-Jazari, the father of modern-day engineering and the father of robotics, publishes *The Book of Knowledge of Ingenious Mechanical Devices,* in which he authors fifty inventions, including the combination lock, mechanical clocks driven by hydropower and weights, bolted joint lock, clock automaton, flow control regulator, closed-loop system, elephant clock, kitchen appliance, cam, camshaft, connecting rod, crank-connecting rod mechanism, suction pipe, suction piston pump with reciprocating piston motion and double-action motion, programmable humanoid robot, automatic gate, pointer, and geared and hydropowered water supply system. and especially the crankshaft, which is considered one of the most important mechanical inventions after the wheel. Other

devices he invented include a hand washing device, machines for raising water, accurate calibration of orifices, lamination of timber to reduce warping, static balancing of wheels, use of paper models to establish a design, casting of metals in closed mould boxes with green sand, emery powder, the most sophisticated candle clocks and water clocks of his time, crank-driven chain pump, water-powered saqiya chain pump, and intermittent working, and hour hand.

- 1206 - [astronomy, technology] Al-Jazari invented monumental water-powered astronomical clocks which displayed moving models of the Sun, Moon, and stars. His largest astronomical clock displayed the zodiac and the solar and lunar orbits. Another innovative feature of the clock was a pointer which traveled across the top of a gateway and caused automatic doors to open every hour.
- 1207 - 1273 [sociology; poetry; spirituality] Jalal al-Din Muhammad Rumi, one of the best known Persian passion poets, famous for poignant poetry on the theme of spiritual enlightenment and passion.
- 1217 - 1329 [related] "Second wave of devastation of Muslim resources, lives, properties, institutions, and infrastructure over a period of one hundred and twelve years. Crusader invasions (1217-1291) and Mongol invasions (1219-1329). Crusaders active throughout the Mediterranean from Jerusalem and west to Muslim Spain. Fall of Muslim Córdoba (1236), Valencia (1238) and Seville (1248). Mongols devastation from the eastern most Muslim frontier, Central and Western Asia, India, Persia to Arab heartland. Fall of Baghdad (1258) and the end of Abbasid Caliphate. Two million Muslims massacred in Baghdad. Major scientific institutions, laboratories, and infrastructure destroyed in leading Muslim centers of civilization."
- 1213 - 1242 [anatomy, biology, medicine, pharmacology, pharmacopoeia, physiology] Ibn al-Nafis

publishes his *Commentary on Compound Drugs*, a commentary on Avicenna's *The Canon of Medicine* concerning pharmacopoeia. It contains criticisms of Galen's doctrines on the heart and the blood vessels and dealt with the circulatory system to some extent. This work was later translated into Latin by Andrea Alpago of Belluno (d. 1520), who had lived in Syria for about 30 years before returning to Italy with a collection of medical Arabic books. A printed version of his translation was available in Venice from 1547.

- 1213 - 1288 [biology, cosmology, epistemology, futurology, geology, literature, physiology, psychology, science fiction, sociology] Ibn al-Nafis publishes his *Theologus Autodidactus*, the first science fiction novel, where he uses the plot to express many of his own themes on a wide variety of subjects, including biology, physiology, cosmology, epistemology, futurology, geology, natural philosophy, psychology, and sociology. The narrative is used to present religious, philosophical and scientific arguments on spontaneous generation and bodily resurrection, and the book also contains the earliest medical description on metabolism: "Both the body and its parts are in a continuous state of dissolution and nourishment, so they are inevitably undergoing permanent change."
- 1213 - 1288 - [anatomy, biology, medicine, ophthalmology, physiology] Ibn al-Nafis publishes his ophthalmological work, *The Polished Book on Experimental Ophthalmology*, where he discovers that the muscle behind the eyeball does not support the ophthalmic nerve, that they do not get in contact with it, that the optic nerves transect but do not get in touch with each other, and many new treatments for glaucoma and the weakness of vision in one eye when the other eye is affected by disease.
- 1228 - 1229 - [chemistry, military technology] Medieval French reports suggest that Muslim armies also used

explosives against the Sixth Crusade army led by Ludwig IV, Landgrave of Thuringia in the 13th century.

- 1235 - [astronomical instruments] A geared mechanical astrolabe with an analog computer calendar is invented by Abi Bakr of Isfahan. His geared astrolabe uses a set of gear-wheels and is the oldest surviving complete mechanical geared machine in existence.
- 1242 - [anatomy, biology, medicine, physiology, scientific method] Ibn al-Nafis, an Arab physician and anatomist publishes another commentary on Avicenna's *The Canon of Medicine* called the *Commentary on Anatomy in Avicenna's Canon,* in which Ibn al-Nafis discovers the pulmonary circulation (the cycle involving the ventricles of the heart and the lungs) and coronary circulation, and describes the mechanism of breathing and its relation to the blood and how it nourishes on air in the lungs, for which he is considered the father of circulation theory and one of the greatest physiologists in history. He followed a "constructivist" path of the smaller circulatory system: "blood is purified in the lungs for the continuance of life and providing the body with the ability to work." During his time, the common view was that blood originates in the liver then travels to the right ventricle, then on to the organs of the body; another contemporary view was that blood is filtered through the diaphragm where it mixes with the air coming from the lungs. Ibn al-Nafis discredited all these views including ones by Galen and Avicenna, and at least an illustration of his manuscript is still extant. William Harvey later explained the circulatory system without reference to Ibn al-Nafis in 1628. Ibn al-Nafis also extolled the study of comparative anatomy in his *Explaining the dissection of [Avicenna's] Canon* which includes prefaces and citations of sources. He emphasized the rigours of verification by measurement, observation and experiment. He subjected conventional wisdom of his

time to a critical review and verified it with experiment and observation, discarding errors. He was also an early proponent of experimental medicine, postmortem autopsy, and human dissection, and he also discredited many other erroneous Avicennian and Galenic doctrines on the humorism, pulse bones, muscles, intestines, sensory organs, bilious canals, esophagus, stomach, and the anatomy of almost every other part of the human body. Ibn al-Nafis also drew diagrams to illustrate different body parts in his new physiological system.

- 1242 - 1244 [biology, medicine, surgery, urology, scientific method] Ibn al-Nafis publishes the first 43 volumes of his medical encyclopedia, *The Comprehensive Book on Medicine*. One volume is dedicated to surgery, where he describes the "general and absolute principles of surgery", a variety of surgical instruments, and the examination of every type of surgical operation known to him. He states that in order for a surgical operation to be successful, full attention needs to be given to three stages of the operation: the "time of presentation" when the surgeon carries out a diagnosis on the affected area, the "time of operative treatment" when the surgeon repairs the affected organs, and the "time of preservation" when the patient needs to be taken care of by nurses. *The Comprehensive Book on Medicine* was also the earliest book dealing with the decubitus of a patient. *The Comprehensive Book on Medicine* is also the earliest book dealing with the decubitus of a patient. Another section is dedicated to urology, including the issues of sexual dysfunction and erectile dysfunction, where Ibn al-Nafis is one of the first to prescribe clinically tested drugs as medication for the treatment of these problems. His treatments are mainly oral drugs, though early topical and transurethral treatments are also mentioned in a few cases.
- 1242 - 1288 [medicine] Ibn al-Nafis publishes more

commentaries on Avicenna's *The Canon of Medicine*. All of his commentaries on *The Canon of Medicine* add up to 20 volumes in length.

- 1244 - 1288 [medicine] Ibn al-Nafis writes down notes for upcoming volumes of his medical encyclopedia, *The Comprehensive Book on Medicine*. His notes add up to a total of 300 volumes in length, though he is only able to publish 80 volumes before he dies in 1288. Even in its incomplete state, however, *The Comprehensive Book on Medicine* is one of the largest known medical encyclopedias in history, and was much larger than the more famous *The Canon of Medicine* by Avicenna. However, only several volumes of *The Comprehensive Book on Medicine* have survived into modern times.
- 1244 - 1288 [anatomy, medicine, science of hadith] Ibn al-Nafis publishes many other works, including *The Choice of Foodstuffs* which places a greater emphasis on diet and nutrition rather than the prescriptions of drugs; *Commentary on Hippocrates' Aphorisms* where he expresses his rebellious nature against established authorities as he states that he has decided to "throw light on and stand by true opinions, and forsake those which are false and erase their traces"; *A Short Account of the Methodology of Hadith* on the science of hadith; *Epitome of the Canon; Synopsis of Medicine; An Essay on Organs; Reference Book for Physicians;* among many others.
- 1248 - [anatomy, botany, pharmacy, veterinary medicine] Ibn al-Baitar dies. He studied and wrote on botany, pharmacy and is best known for studying animal anatomy and medicine. The Arabic term for veterinary medicine is named after him.
- 1258 - The sack of Baghdad results in the destruction of Baghdad along with all its libraries, including the House of Wisdom. Survivors said that the waters of the Tigris ran black with ink from the enormous quantities of books flung into the river.

- 1259 - [astronomy, institution] The Maragheh observatory is founded by Nasîr al-Dîn al-Tûsî at the patronage of Hulagu Khan. It was the first example of the observatory as a research institute (as opposed to an ancient observation post).
- 1260 - [mathematics] Al-Farisi isa born. He gave a new proof of Thabit ibn Qurra's theorem, introducing important new ideas concerning factorization and combinatorial methods. He also gave the pair of amicable numbers 17296, 18416 which have also been attributed to Fermat as well as Thabit ibn Qurra.
- 1260 - [chemistry, military technology] The first portable hand cannons (*midfa*) loaded with explosive gunpowder, the first example of a handgun and port-able firearm, were used by the Egyptians to repel the Mongols at the Battle of Ain Jalut. The gunpowder com-positions used for the cannons at these battles were later described in several manuscripts in the early 14th century. According to Shams al-Din Muhammad (d. 1327), the cannons had an explosive gunpowder composition (74% saltpetre, 11% sulfur, 15% carbon) almost identical to the ideal compositions for explosive gunpowder used in modern times. Gunpowder cartridges were also first employed at the Battle of Ain Jalut by the Egyptians, for use in their fire lances and hand cannons against the Mongols. Egyptian soldiers at the Battle of Ain Jalut were also the first to smear dissolved talc (from Arabic *talq*) on their hands, as forms of fire protection from gunpowder. They also wore fireproof clothing, to which gunpowder cartridges were attached.
- 1270 - [chemistry, military technology] The first complete purification process for potassium nitrate is described in 1270 by the Arab chemist and engineer Hasan al-Rammah of Syria in his book *al-Furusiyya wa al-Manasib al-Harbiyya* (*The Book of Military Horse-manship and Ingenious War Devices*, a.k.a. the *Treatise on Horsemanship and Stratagems of War*). He first described

the use of potassium carbonate (in the form of wood ashes) to remove calcium and magnesium salts from the potassium nitrate. Several almost identical compositions were first described by the Arab engineer Hasan al-Rammah as a recipe for the rockets (*tayyar*) he described in *The Book of Military Horsemanship and Ingenious War Devices* in 1270. Several examples include a *tayyar* "rocket" (75% saltpetre, 8% sulfur, 15% carbon) and the *tayyar buruq* "lightning rocket" (74% saltpetre, 10% sulfur, 15% carbon). He also states recipes for fireworks and firecrackers made from these explosive gunpowder compositions. He states in his book that many of these recipes were known to his father and grandfather, hence dating back to at least the late 12th century. Compositions for an explosive gunpowder effect were not known in China or Europe until the 14th century. The torpedo is also invented by Hasan al-Rammah, who shows illustrations of a torpedo running on water with a rocket system filled with explosive materials and having three firing points.

- 1270 - [medicine, psychiatry, psychology] Famous psychiatric hospitals are built by Muslim physicians in Damascus and Aleppo.
- 1271 - 1273 - Ballistic weapons were manufactured in the Muslim world since the time of Kublai Khan in the 13th century. According to Chinese sources, two Muslim engineers, Alaaddin and Ismail (d. 1330), built machines of a ballistic-weapons nature before the besieged city of Hang-show between 1271-1273. Alaaddin's weapons also played a major role in the conquest of several other Chinese cities. His son Mahoscha also developed ballistic weapons. Ismail (transliterated as *I-ssu-ma-yin*) was present in the Mongol siege of Hsiangyiang, where he built a war machine with the characteristics of a ballistic weapon. Chinese sources mention that when this war machines

were fired, the earth and skies shook, the cannons were buried seven feet into the ground and destroyed everything. His son Yakub also developed ballistic war machines.

- 1273 - 1331 [astronomy; geography; history] Abu al-Fida (Abulfeda).
- 1274 - [chemistry, military technology] The use of cannons as siege machines dates back to Abu Yaqub Yusuf who employed them at the siege of Sijilmasa in 1274, according to Ibn Khaldun.
- 1275 - [engineering, rocketry, weaponry] Hasan al-Rammah invents the torpedo in Syria.
- 1277 - [materials; glass and ceramics] A treaty for the transfer of glassmaking technology signed between the crusader Bohemond VII, titular prince of Antioch and the Doge of Venice leads to the transfer of Syrian glassworkers and their trade secrets and the subsequent rise of Venetian glass industry, the most prominent in Europe for centuries. The techniques henceforth, closely guarded by Venitians only become known in France in the 1600s.
- 1285 - [medicine] The largest hospital of the Middle Ages and pre-modern era is built in Cairo, Egypt, by Sultan Qalaun al-Mansur. According to Will Durant, the hospital had a spacious quadrangular enclosure with four buildings around a courtyard "adorned with arcades and cooled with fountains and brooks." The hospital had "separate wards for diverse diseases and for convalescents", and had laboratories, a dispensary, out-patient clinics, kitchens, baths, a library, a religious place of worship, lecture halls, and "pleasant accommodations for the insane." Treatment was given for free to patients of all backgrounds, regardless of gender, ethnicity or income, while convalescents were offered disbursements on their departure so that they wouldn't need to return to work immediately. "The

sleepless were provided with soft music, professional story-tellers, and perhaps books of history."

- c. 1296 - [astronomy, technology] The first astronomical uses of the magnetic compass is found in a treatise on astronomical instruments written by the Yemeni sultan al-Ashraf (d. 1296). This was the first reference to the compass in astronomical literature.

14th Century

- 1300s - [astronomy, engineering] The spherical astrolabe is invented in the Middle East. Ibn al-Shatir also invents the astrolabic clock in Syria, and he also invents the compass dial, a timekeeping device incorporating both a universal sundial and a magnetic compass, which he invented for the purpose of finding the times of Salah prayers.
- 1300s - [bacteriology, etiology, medicine, microbiology, pathology] When the Black Death bubonic plague reached al-Andalus, Ibn Khatima discovered that infectious diseases are caused by microorganisms which enter the human body.
- 1300 - 1348 [navigation] Abubakari II, a mansa of the Mali Empire, attempts to cross the Atlantic Ocean. According to the Arabic historian Ibn Fadlullah al-Umari (1300-1348), in his encyclopaedic work *Masalik Al-Absar*, Abubakari set out on a journey equipped with "two hundred boats full of men, and many others full of gold, water and provisions sufficient for several years".
- 1301 - [ceramics] Al-Kashani promotes a center for ceramics. He also writes a book on Islamic ceramics techniques. His name is still associated with ceramics in the Muslim Orient today.
- 1312 - 1361 [cryptography] Taj ad-Din Ali ibn ad-Duraihim ben Muhammad ath-Tha 'alibi al-Mausili wrote on cryptology, but his writings have been lost. To

his work is attributed the section on cryptology in an encyclopedia (*Subh al-a 'sha*) by Shihab al-Din abu 'l-Abbas Ahmad ben Ali ben Ahmad Abd Allah al-Qalqashandi (1355 or 1356 – 1418). The list of ciphers in this work included both substitution and transposition, and for the first time, a cipher with multiple substitutions for each plaintext letter. Also traced to Ibn al-Duraihim is an exposition on and worked example of cryptanalysis, including the use of tables of letter frequencies and sets of letters which can not occur together in one word. Al-Qalqashandi was a medieval Egyptian writer born in a village in the Nile Delta. He is the author of Subh al-a 'sha, a fourteen volume encyclopedia in Arabic, which included a section on cryptology. This information was attributed to Taj ad-Din al-Mausili.

- 1304 - 1369 [exploration, travel] Abu Abdullah Muhammad Ibn Battuta was a world traveler. He travels along a 75,000 mile voyage from Morocco to China and back. These journeys covered much of the Old World, extending from North Africa, West Africa, Southern Europe and Eastern Europe in the west, to the Middle East, Indian subcontinent, Central Asia, Southeast Asia and China in the east, a distance readily surpassing that of his predecessors and his near-contemporary Marco Polo.
- 1313 - 1374 - [bacteriology, etiology, medicine, pathology] The Andalusian physician Ibn al-Khatib wrote a treatise called *On the Plague*, in which he stated: "The existence of contagion is established by experience, investigation, the evidence of the senses and trustworthy reports. These facts constitute a sound argument. The fact of infection becomes clear to the investigator who notices how he who establishes contact with the aflicted gets the disease, whereas he who is not in contact remains safe, and how transmission is affected through garments, vessels and earrings."

- 1304 – 1375 [astronomy] Ibn al-Shatir, a Muslim astronomer from Damascus, in *A Final Inquiry Concerning the Rectification of Planetary Theory,* incorporated the Urdi lemma and eliminated the need for an equant by introducing an extra epicycle (the Tusicouple), departing from the Ptolemaic system in a way that was mathematically identical to what Nicolaus Copernicus did in the 16th century. Ibn al-Shatir's system was also only approximately geocentric, rather than exactly so, having demonstrated trigonometrically that the Earth was not the exact center of the universe. While previous Maragha models were just as accurate as the Ptolemaic model, Ibn al-Shatir's geometrical model was the first that was actually superior to the Ptolemaic model in terms of its better agreement with empirical obser-vations. Ibn al-Shatir's rectified model was later adapted into a heliocentric model by Copernicus, which was mathematically achieved by reversing the direction of the last vector connecting the Earth to the Sun in Ibn al-Shatir's model.
- 1371 [astronomy, engineering] As ancient sundials were nodus-based with straight hour-lines, they indicated unequal hours—also called temporary hours—that varied with the seasons. Every day was divided into twelve equal segments; thus, hours were shorter in winter and longer in summer. The idea of using hours of equal length throughout the year was the innovation of Ibn al-Shatir, based on earlier developments in trigonometry by Muhammad ibn Jâbir al-Harrânî al-Battânî (Albategni). Ibn al-Shatir was aware that "using a gnomon that is parallel to the Earth's axis will produce sundials whose hour lines indicate equal hours on any day of the year." His sundial is the oldest polar-axis sundial still in existence. The concept later appeared in Western sundials from at least 1446.
- 1377 [demography, economics, historiography, history, humanities, political science, social sciences, sociology]

Ibn Khaldun, the father of demography, cultural history, historiography, the philosophy of history, sociology, and the social sciences, and one of the forerunners of modern economics, writes his most famous work, the *Muqaddimah* (known as *Prole-gomenon* in the West), which is encyclopedic in breadth, surveys the state of knowledge of his day, covering geography, accounts of the peoples of the world and their known history, the classification and aims of the sciences, and the religious sciences. In the social sciences, he introduces the concepts of social philosophy, social conflict theories, Asabiyyah (social cohesion), social capital, social networks, the Laffer curve, the historical method, standard of evidence, propoganda, systemic bias, the rise and fall of civilizations, dialectic and feedback loops, systems theory, corporate social responsibility, economic growth, macroeconomics, population growth, human capital development, and the Khaldun-Laffer curve.

- 1377 [biology, chemistry, evolution] Ibn Khaldun's *Muqaddimah* also makes several contributions to biology and chemistry. He develops a biological theory of evolution based on empirical evidence and in which he begins with minerals evolving into plants and then animals and ending with humans evolving from monkeys, which he states is "as far as our (physical) observation extends." In chemistry, he refutes the practice of alchemy and discredits the theory of the transmutation of metals.
- 1380 [mathematics] Al-Kashi "contributed to the development of decimal fractions not only for approximating algebraic numbers, but also for real numbers such as pi. His contribution to decimal fractions is so major that for many years he was considered as their inventor. Although not the first to do so, al-Kashi gave an algorithm for calculating nth roots which is a special case of the methods given many centuries later by Ruffini and Horner."

- 1393 - 1449 - [astronomy] Ulugh Beg commissions an observatory at Samarqand in present-day Uzbekistan.

15th Century

- 1400 - 1500 - [related] Third wave of devastation of Muslim resources, lives, properties, institutions, and infrastructure. End of Muslim rule in Spain after the completion of the Reconquista in 1492. More than one million volumes of Muslim works on science, arts, philosophy and culture were burnt in the public square of Vivarrambla in Granada. Colonization began in Africa, Asia, and the Americas.
- 1400s [mathematics] Ibn al-Banna and al-Qalasadi used symbols for mathematics in the 15th century "and, although we do not know exactly when their use began, we know that symbols were used at least a century before this."
- 1400 - 1406 [astronomy, mathematics, physics] Jamshîd al-Kâshî is invited to the Samarqand observatory by Ulugh Beg to pursue his study of mathematics, astronomy and physics.
- 1400 - 1429 [astronomy, mathematics] Jamshîd al-Kâshî is the first to use the decimal point notation in arithmetic and Arabic numerals. His works include *The Key of arithmetics, Discoveries in mathematics, The Decimal point,* and *The benefits of the zero*. The contents of the *Benefits of the Zero* are an introduction followed by five essays: "On whole number arithmetic", "On fractional arithmetic", "On astrology", "On areas", and "On finding the unknowns [unknown variables]". He also wrote the *Thesis on the sine and the chord; The garden of gardens* or *Promenade of the gardens* describing an instrument he devised and used at the Samarqand observatory to compile an ephemeris and for computing solar and lunar eclipses; the ephemeresis *Zayj Al-Khaqani* which also includes mathematical

tables and corrections of the ephemeresis by al-Tusi; *Thesis on finding the first degree sine*; and more.

- 1400 - 1429 [astronomical instruments] Al-Kashi invents the Plate of Conjunctions, an analog computer instrument used to determine the time of day at which planetary conjunctions will occur, and for performing linear interpolation.

  He also invents a mechanical planetary computer which he calls the Plate of Zones, which could graphically solve a number of planetary problems, including the prediction of the true positions in longitude of the Sun and Moon, and the planets in terms of elliptical orbits; the latitudes of the Sun, Moon, and planets; and the ecliptic of the Sun. The instrument also incorporated an alhidade and ruler.

- 1400 - 1474 [astronomy, astrophysics, mathematics, physics] Ali al-Qushji (d. 1474) rejected Aristotelian physics and completely separated natural philosophy from Islamic astronomy, allowing astronomy to become a purely empirical and mathematical science. This allowed him to explore alternatives to the Aristotelian notion of a stationery Earth, as he explored the idea of a moving Earth instead. He found empirical evidence for the Earth's rotation through his observation on comets and concluded, on the basis of empiricism rather than speculative philosophy, that the moving Earth theory is just as likely to be true as the stationary Earth theory. Ali al-Qushji also improved on Nasir al-Din al-Tusi's planetary model and presented an alternative planetary model for Mercury.
- 1403 - 1433 [navigation] The Chinese Muslim general Zheng He travels across the Indian Ocean in newlyconstructed troopships and treasure ships.
- 1406 - 1409 [astronomy] Jamshîd al-Kâshî computed and observed the solar eclipses of 809 AH, 810 AH and 811 AH.

- 1411 [mathematics] Al-Kashi writes *Compendium of the Science of Astronomy.*
- 1424 [mathematics] Al-Kashi writes *Treatise on the Circumference* giving a remarkably accurate approximation to pi in both sexagesimal and decimal forms, computing pi to 8 sexagesimal places and 16 decimal places.
- 1427 [mathematics] Al-Kashi completes *The Key to Arithmetic* containing work of great depth on decimal fractions. It applies arithmetical and algebraic methods to the solution of various problems, including several geometric ones and is one of the best textbooks in the whole of medieval literature.

  1437 [mathematics] Ulugh Beg publishes his star catalogue, the *Zij-i-Sultani*. It contains trigonometric tables correct to eight decimal places based on Ulugh Beg's calculation of the sine of one degree which he calculated correctly to 16 decimal places.
- 1453 [military technology] The first supergun was the Great Turkish Bombard, used by the troops of Mehmed II to capture Constantinople. It had a 762 mm bore, and fired 680 kg (1500 lb) stones.
- 1470 - 1550 - [ceramics, pottery] Tabriz becomes a center for innovative Islamic pottery and ceramics.

16th Century

- 1500s [architecture, engineering, urban planning] The city of Shibam is built in Yemen. This city is regarded as the "oldest skyscraper-city in the world", the "Manhattan of the desert", and the earliest example of urban planning based on the principle of vertical construction. Shibam was made up of over 500 tower houses, each one rising 5 to 9 storeys high, with each floor being an apartment occupied by a single family. The city has the tallest mudbrick buildings in the world, with some of them being over 100 feet (over 30 meters) high, thus being the first high-rise (which need to be at least 75 feet or 23 meters) apartment buildings and tower blocks.

- 1500 - 1528 [astronomy, astrophysics, physics] Al-Birjandi continued the debate on the Earth's rotation after Ali al-Qushji. In his analysis of what might occur if the Earth were rotating, he develops a hypothesis similar to Galileo Galilei's notion of "circular inertia", which he described in an observational test (as a response to one of Qutb al-Din al-Shirazi's arguments): "The small or large rock will fall to the Earth along the path of a line that is perpendicular to the plane (*sath*) of the horizon; this is witnessed by experience (*tajriba*). And this perpendicular is away from the tangent point of the Earth's sphere and the plane of the perceived (*hissi*) horizon. This point moves with the motion of the Earth and thus there will be no difference in place of fall of the two rocks."
- 1500 - 1550 [astronomy] Shams al-Din al-Khafri, the last major astronomer of the *hay'a* tradition, was the first to realize that "all mathematical modeling had no physical truth by itself and was simply another language with which one could describe the physical observed reality."
- 1551 [engineering] Taqi al-Din invents the steam turbine in Ottoman Egypt. He first described it in *The Sublime Methods of Spiritual Machines*, which describes the use of his steam turbine as the prime mover for the first steam-powered and self-rotating spit.
- 1556 - 1559 [engineering] Taqi al-Din publishes *The Brightest Stars for the Construction of Mechanical Clocks*, which describes the first mechanical alarm clock, the first spring-powered astronomical clock, and the first clock and mechanical watch to first measure time in minutes.
- 1559 [engineering] Taqi al-Din invents a 'Monobloc' pump with a six cylinder engine. It was a hydro-powered

water-raising machine incorporating valves, suction and delivery pipes, piston rods with lead weights, trip levers with pin joints, and cams on the axle of a water-driven scoop-wheel.

- 1577 [astronomy, engineering] Taqi al-Din builds the Istanbul observatory of al-Din, the largest astronomical observatory in its time, with the patronage of the Ottoman Sultan Murad III.
- 1577 - 1580 [astronomy, engineering] At the Istanbul observatory of al-Din, Taqi al-Din carries out astronomical observations. He produces a zij (named *Unbored Pearl*) and astronomical catalogues that are more accurate than those of his contemporaries, Tycho Brahe and Nicolaus Copernicus. Taqi al-Din is able to achieve this with his new invention of the "observational clock", which he describes as "a mechanical clock with three dials which show the hours, the minutes, and the seconds." This is the first clock to measure time in seconds, and he uses it for astronomical purposes, specifically for measuring the right ascension of the stars. This is considered one of the most important innovations in 16th century practical astronomy, as previous clocks were not accurate enough to be used for astronomical purposes. He further improves his observational clock, using only one dial to represent the hours, minutes and seconds, describing it as "a mechanical clock with a dial showing the hours, minutes and seconds and we divided every minute into five seconds." Taqi al-Din is also the first astronomer to employ a decimal point notation in his observations rather than the sexagesimal fractions used by his contemporaries and predecessors.
- 1579 [civil engineering] The first prefabricated homes and movable structure are invented by Akbar the Great.
- 1580 [astronomy] The Istanbul observatory of al-Din is destroyed by Sultan Murad III.

- 1582 [military technology] Fathullah Shirazi, a Persian-Indian polymath and mechanical engineer who worked for Akbar the Great in the Mughal Empire, invented the autocannon, the earliest multi-shot machine gun. As opposed to the polybolos and repeating crossbows used earlier in ancient Greece and China, respectively, Shirazi's rapid-firing gun had multiple gun barrels that fired hand cannons loaded with gunpowder. Another cannon-related machine he created could clean sixteen gun barrels simultaneously, and was operated by a cow.
- 1582 [technology] Fathullah Shirazi invents a corngriding carriage, which can be used to transport passengers and for grinding corn.
- 1589 - 1590 [astronomy, engineering, metallurgy] The seamless celestial globe invented by Muslim metallurgists and instrument-makers in Mughal India, specifically Lahore and Kashmir, is considered to be one of the most remarkable feats in metallurgy and engineering.

  All globes before and after this were seamed, and in the 20th century, it was believed by metallurgists to be technically impossible to create a metal globe without any seams. It was in the 1980s, however, that Emilie Savage-Smith discovered several celestial globes without any seams in Lahore and Kashmir. The earliest was invented in Kashmir by the Muslim metallurgist Ali Kashmiri ibn Luqman in 998 AH (1589-1590 CE) during Akbar the Great's reign; he invented the method of lost-wax casting in order to produce these globes. 21 such globes were produced, and these remain the only examples of seamless metal globes. These seamless celestial globes are considered to be an unsurpassed feat in metallurgy; hence some consider this achievement to be comparable to that of the Great Pyramid of Giza which was considered an unsurpassed feat in architecture until the 19th century.

17th Century

Sail plan for a polacca-xebec, first built by the Barbary pirates around the 16th and 17th centuries.

- 1600s [transport, engineering] The Xebec and Polacca (Polacre) sailing ships used around the Mediterranean Sea from the 16th to the 19th centuries originated from the Barbary pirates, who successfully used them for naval warfare against European ships at the time. A combination of the fore and aft sails and aerodynamics, along with the improved square sail on the Polacca, allowed these ships to sail much closer to the wind than European and American ships. An expert on the Barbary pirates said that their ships had guns at the bow and stern. "They would approach, pounding away, and it took too long for our square riggers to bring the broadside guns around. The Arabs had oars and a sail arrangement that meant they were able to turn more quickly and could flee closer to the wind than we could chase them."
- 1600s [mathematics] The Arabic mathematician Muhammad Baqir Yazdi jointly discovered the pair of amicable numbers 9,363,584 and 9,437,056 along with Descartes (1636).
- 1600s [astronomy, engineering] Cartographic Qibla indicators were brass instruments with Mecca-centred world maps and cartographic grids engraved on them. They were invented in 17th-century Iran. The cartographic Qibla indicator with sundial and compass was a Qibla instrument with a sundial and compass attached to it, and was invented by Muhammad Husayn in the 17th century.
- 1600 - 1640 [philosophy] Persian philosopher Mulla Sadra founded the school of transcendent theosophy and developed the concept of "existence precedes essence". His work bought "a new philosophical insight in dealing with the nature of reality" and created "a

major transition from essentialism to existentialism" in Islamic philosophy, several centuries before this occurred in Western philosophy.

- 1630 - 1632 [aviation, flight] The Turk Hezarfen Ahmet Celebi is said to have flown from the Galata Tower and crossed the Bosphorus, landing 3.38 kilometers away in Üsküdar's Doðancýlar square. According to Evliya Çelebi in the early 17th century, Hezarfen Ahmet Celebi was the first aviator to have made a successful flight with artificial wings between 1630-1632.
- 1633 [aviation, flight, rocketry] Hezarfen Ahmet Celebi's brother, Lagari Hasan Çelebi, launched himself in the first artificially-powered manned rocket, using 150 okka (about 300 pounds) of gunpowder as the firing fuel, and he landed successfully. According to Evliya Çelebi in the early 17th century, Lagari Hasan Çelebi launched himself in the air in a seven-winged rocket, which was composed of a large cage with a conical top filled with gunpowder. The flight was accomplished as a part of celebrations performed for the birth of Ottoman Emperor Murad IV's daughter in 1633. Evliya reported that Lagari made a soft landing in the Bosporus by using the wings attached to his body as a parachute after the gunpowder was consumed, foreshadowing the sea-landing methods of astronauts with parachutes after their voyages into outer space. Lagari's flight was estimated to have lasted about twenty seconds and the maximum height reached was around 300 metres (980 ft). This was the first known example of a manned rocket and an artificially-powered aircraft. This is more than two hundred years before similar attempts in modern Europe and the United States.
- 1659 - 1660 A seamless celestial globe is produced using a new lost-wax casting method in the Mughai Empire in 1070 AH (1659-60 CE) by Muhammad Salih Tahtawi with Arabic and Sanskrit inscriptions. Twenty other such globes were produced in Lahore and Kashmir during the Mughal

Empire. They are considered one of the most remarkable feats in metallurgy. Before they were rediscovered in the 1980s, it was believed by modern metallurgists to be technically impossible to produce metal globes without any seams, even with modern technology.

18th Century

Tipu Sultan invented the first iron-cased and metalcylinder rocket artillery in Mysore, India, alongside his father Hyder Ali, in the 1780s.

- 1720 - [navigation technology] The Ottoman dockyard architect Ibrahim Efendi invented a submarine called the *tahtelbahir*. The Ottoman writer Seyyid Vehbi, in his *Surname-i-Humayun,* compared this submarine to an alligator. He recorded that during the circumcision ceremony for Sultan Ahmed III's sons, "the alligatorlike submarine slowly emerged on the water and moved slowly to the sultan, and after staying on the sea for half an hour, submerged in the sea again to the great surprise of the public; then emerged one hour later, with five people walking outside the mouth of this alligator-like submarine, with trays of rice and *zerde* (a dish of sweetened rice) on their heads." He explained the technical information concerning the submarine "submerging in the sea and the crew being able to breath through pipes while under the sea".
- 1783 - 1799 - [rocketry] Tipu, Sultan of Mysore (r. 1783-1799) in the south of India, was an experimenter with war rockets and the inventor of iron-cased and metalcylinder rocket artillery. He successfully used these iron rockets against the larger forces of the British East India Company during the Anglo-Mysore Wars. His rockets were much more advanced than what the British had seen, chiefly because of the use of iron tubes for holding the propellant; this enabled higher thrust and longer range for the missile (up to 2 km range). After

Tipu's eventual defeat in the Fourth Anglo-Mysore War and the capture of the Mysore iron rockets, they were influential in British rocket development and were soon put into use in the Napoleonic Wars. Two of his rockets, captured by the British at Srirangapatna, are displayed in the Woolwich Royal Artillery Museum in London. They were the first rockets to have a rocket motor casing made of steel with multiple nozzles. The rocket, 50 mm in diameter and 250 mm long, had a range performance of 900 meters to 1.5 km. According to Stephen Oliver Fought and John F. Guilmartin, Jr. in *Encyclopedia Britannica* (2008): "Hyder Ali, prince of Mysore, developed war rockets with an important change: the use of metal cylinders to contain the combustion powder. Although the hammered soft iron he used was crude, the bursting strength of the container of black powder was much higher than the earlier paper construction. Thus a greater internal pressure was possible, with a resultant greater thrust of the propulsive jet. The rocket body was lashed with leather thongs to a long bamboo stick. Range was perhaps up to three-quarters of a mile (more than a kilometre). Although individually these rockets were not accurate, dispersion error became less important when large numbers were fired rapidly in mass attacks. They were particularly effective against cavalry and were hurled into the air, after lighting, or skimmed along the hard dry ground. Hyder Ali's son, Tippu Sultan, continued to develop and expand the use of rocket weapons, reportedly increasing the number of rocket troops from 1,200 to a corps of 5,000. In battles at Seringapatam in 1792 and 1799 these rockets were used with considerable effect against the British."

19th Century

- 1814 - [cosmetics, hygiene] - The earliest documented evidence of shampoo dates back to the Bengali Muslim entrepeneur Sake Dean Mahomet, inspired by the

Indian practice of making fragrant hair-oil. He opened the first shampooing bath known as 'Mahomed's Indian Vapour Baths' in Brighton, England, in 1759. His baths were like Turkish baths where clients received an Indian treatment of *champi* (shampooing) or therapeutic massage. His service was appreciated; he received the high accolade of being appointed 'Shampooing Surgeon' to both George IV and William IV.

20th Century

Cumrun Vafa, the 2008 Dirac Prize recipient, pioneered the F-theory, Vafa-Witten theorem and topological string theory, and discovered the microscopic origin of black hole entropy.

- 1924 - 1936 [medicine] Behçet's disease is named after Hulusi Behçet (1889-1948), the Turkish dermatologist and scientist who first recognized the syndrome in one of his patients in 1924 and reported his research on the disease in *Journal of Skin and Venereal Diseases* in 1936.
- 1931 - 1942 [chemistry] Salimuzzaman Siddiqui was a leading Pakistani scientist in natural products chemistry. He is the pioneer in extracting chemical compounds from the Neem and Rauwolfia, and is also known for isolating novel chemical compounds from various other flora in the Indian subcontinent. As the director of H.E.J. Research Institute of Chemistry, he carried out extensive research with a team of scientists on pharmacology of various plants to extract a number of chemical substances of medicinal importance.
- Abdus Salam [Physics] was either associated with or pioneered all major theoratical basis for Particle Physics and also won a Nobel Prize for his work.
- Mahbub ul Haq [economics], helped in the development of the Human Development Index.

Bibliography

Armstrong, Karen. *Islam: A Short History.* New York: Modern Library, revised ed., 2002.

Ali, Syed Ameer. *The Spirit of Islam: A History of the Evolution and Ideals of Islam,* with *a Life of the Prophet.* London: Chatto & Windus, 1978.

Bloom, Jonathan and Sheila Blair. *Islam: A Thousand Years of Faith and Power.* New Haven, CT: Yale University Press, 2002.

Booth, E. *Aristotelian Aporetic Ontology in Islamic and Christian Thinkers.* Cambridge, 1983.

Bowker, John. *What Muslims Believe.* Oxford, UK: Onewworld, 1999.

Burrell, D. *Freedom and Creation in Three Traditions.* Notre Dame, 1993.

Burrell, D. *Knowing the Unknowable God: Ibn Sina, Maimonides, Aquinas* (Notre Dame: 1986).

Cook, Michael. *The Koran: A Very Short Introduction.* Oxford, UK: Oxford University Press, 2000.

Corbin, H. *History of Islamic Philosophy,* trans. L. Sherrard. London, 1993.

Craig, E. (ed.), *Routledge Encyclopedia of Philosophy.* London, 1998.

Davidson, H.A. *Proofs for Eternity, Creation and the Existence of God in Medieval Islamic and Jewish Philosophy.* Oxford, 1987.

Elias, Jamal J. *Islam.* Upper Saddle River, NJ: Prentice Hall, 1999.

Fakhry, M. *A History of Islamic Philosophy* , 2nd ed. New York, 1983.

Gibb, Hamilton A.R. and J.H. Kramers, eds. *Shorter Encyclopedia of Islam.* Leiden: E.J. Brill, 1997 (reprint ed.).

Hodgson, Marshall G.S. *The Venture of Islam,* 3 Vols. Chicago, IL: University of Chicago Press, 1974.

Keller, Nuh Ha Mim, trans. *Al-Nawawi's Manual of Islam.* Cambridge, UK: The Islamic Texts Society, 1996.

Leaman, O. *An Introduction to Classical Islamic Philosophy.* Cambridge, 2002.

Marmura , M.E. (ed.), *Islamic Theology and Philosophy.* Albany, 1984.

Nasr, Seyyed Hossein. *The Heart of Islam: Enduring Values for Humanity.* San Francisco, CA, Harper San Francisco, 2002.

Newby, Gordon D. *A Concise Encyclopedia of Islam.* Oxford, UK, Oneworld, 2002.

Peters, F.E. *A Reader on Classical Islam.* Princeton, NJ: Princeton University Press, 1994.

Qadir , C.A. *Philosophy and Science in the Islamic World.* London, 1990.

Renard, John, ed. *Windows on the House of Islam: Muslim Sources on Spirituality.* Berkeley, CA: University of California Press, 1998.

Renard, John. *Seven Doors to Islam: Spirituality and the Religious Life of Muslims.* Berkeley, CA: University of California Press, 1996.

Ruthven, Malise. *Islam in the World.* New York: Oxford University Press, 2nd ed., 2000.

Schimmel, Annemarie. *Islam: An Introduction.* Albany,

NY: State University of New York Press, 1992.

Schuon, Frithjof. *Islam and the Perennial Philosophy.* London: World of Islam Festival Publ. Co., 1976.

Sharif, M.M. *A History of Muslim Philosophy,* 2 vols. (Wiesbaden: 1963-6).

Stern, S.M. *Medieval Arabic and Hebrew Thought* , ed. F. Zimmermann, London, 1983.

Stern, S.M., Hourani, H. and Brown, V. (eds.), *Islamic Philosophy and the Classical Tradition.* Oxford, 1972.

Waines, David. *An Introduction to Islam.* Cambridge, UK: Cambridge University Press, 1995.

Watt, M.W. Islamic Philosophy and Theology. Edinburgh, 1962, revised ed. 1985.

Watt, William Montgomery. *The Formative Period of Islamic Thought.* Oxford, UK: Oneworld,1998.

Watt, William Montgomery. *What is Islam?* London: Longman, 1970.

Williams, John Alden, ed. *The Word of Islam.* Austin, TX: University of Texas Press, 1994.

Wolfson, H.A. *Studies in the History of Philosophy and Religion* , ed. I. Twersky, G.H. Williams, in 2 vols. Cambridge, MA, 1973, 1977.

Wolfson, H.A. *The Philosophy of the Kalam.* Cambridge, MA, 1976.

Ziai, H. "Islamic Philosophy," in *The Oxford Companion to Philosophy,* ed. T. Honderich. Oxford , 1955.

Index

A

B

C

D

E

F

H

I

J

K

L

M